DATE DUE

MR 17 '95			
MY 30 '96			
AG 1 05			
OC 2 2 08			
NO - 6 '08			

DEMCO 38-296

Global Biodiversity Strategy

*Guidelines for Action to Save, Study, and Use
Earth's Biotic Wealth Sustainably and Equitably*

WORLD RESOURCES INSTITUTE (WRI)

THE WORLD CONSERVATION UNION (IUCN)

UNITED NATIONS ENVIRONMENT PROGRAMME (UNEP)

In consultation with

FOOD AND AGRICULTURE ORGANIZATION (FAO)

UNITED NATIONS EDUCATION, SCIENTIFIC AND CULTURAL ORGANIZATION (UNESCO)

1992

This report represents a timely, scientific treatment of a subject of public concern. Its sponsors take responsibility fo choosing and focusing the study topics and guaranteeing its authors and researchers freedom of inquiry. The report's author have also solicited and responded to the guidance of advisory panels and expert reviewers. Unless otherwise stated, howevei all the interpretations and findings set forth here are those of the authors.

Contents

Foreword		v
I	The Nature and Value of Biodiversity	1
II	Losses of Biodiversity and Their Causes	7
III	The Strategy For Biodiversity Conservation	19
IV	Establishing a National Policy Framework For Biodiversity Conservation	37
V	Creating An International Policy Environment That Supports National Biodiversity Conservation	55
VI	Creating Conditions and Incentives For Local Biodiversity Conservation	79
VII	Managing Biodiversity Throughout the Human Environment	97
VIII	Strengthening Protected Areas	117
IX	Conserving Species, Populations, and Genetic Diversity	133
X	Expanding Human Capacity to Conserve Biodiversity	147
Notes		169
Bibliography		173
User's Guide to the Global Biodiversity Strategy		183
Contributors to the Global Biodiversity Strategy		199
Glossary		227
List of Acronyms		231
Index		233

The Global Biodiversity Strategy was developed through a process of research and consultation beginning in 1989 and involving six consultations, six workshops, and more than 500 individuals. This report would not have been possible without the dedication and contributions of these many people.

Sponsors of the Biodiversity Strategy Program
British Overseas Development Administration
Dutch Ministry of Foreign Affairs
Government of Switzerland
Norwegian Royal Ministry of Foreign Affairs
Swedish International Development Authority
The Surdna Foundation
United Nations Development Programme
United States Agency for International Development
W. Alton Jones Foundation

Organizing Committee of the Biodiversity Strategy Program
Kenton Miller, *World Resources Institute, USA*
Jeffrey McNeely, *World Conservation Union (IUCN), Switzerland*
Reuben Olembo, *United Nations Environment Programme, Kenya*

Biodiversity Strategy Program Coordinator
Kenton Miller, *World Resources Institute, USA*

International Coordinating Group
Suraya Afiff, *Indonesian Environmental Forum (WALHI), Indonesia*
JoAnne DiSano, *Department of the Arts, Sport, Environment, Tourism, and Territories, Australia*
Rodrigo Gamez, *National Biodiversity Institute, Costa Rica*
Vernon Heywood, *IUCN Plants Office, U.K.*
Calestous Juma, *African Centre for Technology Studies, Kenya*
Michael Lesnick, *The Keystone Center, USA*
Jeffrey McNeely, *World Conservation Union (IUCN), Switzerland*
Kenton Miller, *World Resources Institute, USA*
Reuben Olembo, *United Nations Environment Programme, Kenya*
Maria Tereza Jorge Padua, *Fundacão Pro-natureza (FUNATURA), Brazil*

Robin Pellew, *World Conservation Monitoring Centre, U.K.*
Samar Singh, *Ministry of Environment and Forests, India*

Principal Writers
Walter Reid, *World Resources Institute, USA*
Charles Barber, *World Resources Institute, USA*
Kenton Miller, *World Resources Institute, USA*

Editor
Kathleen Courrier

Editorial Consultant
Raisa Scriabine

Production Manager
Hyacinth Billings

Graphics
Allyn Massey, Gary Ridley

Cover Design
Pamela Reznick

Book Design
Gary Ridley

Project Staff
Donna Dwiggins, Lori Scarpa, Janet Abramovitz, Joanna Erfani, Lea Borkenhagen, Vinay Gidwani, Bruce Goldstein, Kathy Quick, Patrice Kent

Photography
Ron Jautz/FOLIO
Marvin Ickow/FOLIO
PHOTRI/Jeffrey Rotman
PHOTRI/John McCauley
PHOTRI/Lisa Sardan
Andrew Young/Conservation International
Andrew Young/Conservation International
Mark Plotkin/Conservation International

Foreword

All life on Earth is part of one great, interdependent system. It interacts with, and depends on, the non-living components of the planet: atmosphere, oceans, freshwaters, rocks, and soils. Humanity depends totally on this community of life—this biosphere—of which we are an integral part.

In the remote past, human actions were trivial when set against the dominant processes of nature. No longer. The human species now influences the fundamental processes of the planet. Ozone depletion, worldwide pollution, and climate change are testimonies to our power.

Economic development is essential if the millions of people who live in poverty and endure hunger and hopelessness are to achieve a quality of life commensurate with the most basic of human rights. Economic progress is urgent if we are not only to meet the needs of the people alive today but also to give hope to the billions born into the world over the next century. Better health care, education, employment, and other opportunities for a creative life are also essential components of a strategy for keeping human numbers within the planet's "carrying capacity."

Development has to be both people-centered and conservation-based. Unless we protect the structure, functions, and diversity of the world's natural systems—on which our species and all others depend—development will undermine itself and fail. Unless we use Earth's resources sustainably and prudently, we deny people their future.

Development must not come at the expense of other groups or later generations, nor threaten other species' survival.

The conservation of biodiversity is fundamental to the success of the development process. As this *Global Biodiversity Strategy* explains, conserving biodiversity is not just a matter of protecting wildlife in nature reserves. It is also about safeguarding the natural systems of the Earth that are our life-support systems; purifying the waters; recycling oxygen, carbon and other essential elements; maintaining the fertility of the soil; providing food from the land, freshwaters, and seas; yielding medicines; and safeguarding the genetic richness on which we depend in the ceaseless struggle to improve our crops and livestock.

Recent years have seen many major reviews of the world situation and of human needs. A decade ago, the *World Conservation Strategy* drew attention to the inseparable link between conservation and development and emphasized the need for sustainability. The report of the World Commission on Environment and Development—*Our Common Future*—brought this necessity home to a worldwide audience, whose governments examined the need for action in their *Environmental Perspective to the Year 2000 and Beyond*. Biennial *World Resources* and *Environmental Data* reports and annual *UNEP State of the Environment* reports have provided authoritative—and often disturbing—overviews of the state of the planet. Most recently, the successor and complement to the *World Con-*

servation Strategy, entitled *Caring for the Earth: A Strategy for Sustainable Living* has once more emphasized the need for the world community to change policies, reduce excessive consumption, conserve the life of the planet, and live within the Earth's carrying capacity.

The three organizations that jointly produced this *Global Biodiversity Strategy* have also been involved with these other major reports and reviews. In that process, we have become more and more aware that a report is useful only if it leads to action—more action and better action than would have been taken otherwise. That is precisely why this new *Strategy* is built around 85 specific proposals for action and why it spells out what should be done in sufficient detail for governments and non-governmental organizations to take up these proposals and develop them further.

This *Strategy* appears at a time when representatives of many of the world's governments are negotiating a Convention on Biological Diversity. We offer this *Strategy* as a complementary initiative. We see it as a basis for the practical action that should be taken while the Convention is being ratified and entering into force. And we see it as an outline for the diverse actions that will need to be taken by governments and non-governmental organizations alongside and in support of the Convention.

Our own organizations are already deeply involved in action to conserve biodiversity. This *Strategy* is as much for us as for other organizations and governments. We shall be further developing our own programs in its light. We will be monitoring its implementation and all our own work will reflect the assumption that successful action to conserve the diversity of life on earth is essential for a sustainable human future.

James Gustave Speth
President, World Resources Institute

Martin W. Holdgate
Director General, The World Conservation Union

Mostafa K. Tolba
Executive Director, United Nations
Environment Programme

I

The Nature and Value
of Biodiversity

*We cannot even estimate the number of species of organisms on Earth
to an order of magnitude, an appalling situation in terms of knowledge and our ability
to affect the human prospect positively. There are clearly few areas of science
about which so little is known, and none of such direct relevance to human beings.*

PETER RAVEN, MISSOURI BOTANICAL GARDENS, UNITED STATES

Earth's plants, animals, and microorganisms—interacting with one another and with the physical environment in ecosystems—form the foundation of sustainable development. Biotic resources from this wealth of life support human livelihoods and aspirations and make it possible to adapt to changing needs and environments. The steady erosion of the diversity of genes, species, and ecosystems taking place today will undermine progress toward a sustainable society. Indeed, the continuing loss of biodiversity is a telling measure of the imbalance between human needs and wants and nature's capacity. *(See Box 1.)*

The human race had 850 million members when it entered the industrial age, sharing Earth with life forms nearly as diverse as the planet has ever possessed. Today, with population nearly six times as large and resource consumption proportionally far greater, both the limits of nature and the price of overstepping them are becoming clear. A turning point is upon us. We can continue to simplify the environment to meet immediate needs, at the cost of long-term benefits, or we can conserve life's precious diversity and use it sustainably. We can deliver to the next generation (and the next) a world rich in possibilities or one impoverished of life; but social and economic development will succeed only if we do the first.

BOX 1

The Diversity of Life

Biodiversity is the totality of genes, species, and ecosystems in a region. The wealth of life on Earth today is the product of hundreds of millions of years of evolutionary history. Over the course of time, human cultures have emerged and adapted to the local environment, discovering, using, and altering local biotic resources. Many areas that now seem "natural" bear the marks of millennia of human habitation, crop cultivation, and resource harvesting. The domestication and breeding of local varieties of crops and livestock have further shaped biodiversity.

Biodiversity can be divided into three hierarchical categories—genes, species, and ecosystems—that describe quite different aspects of living systems and that scientists measure in different ways:

Genetic diversity refers to the variation of genes within species. This covers distinct populations of the same species (such as the thousands of traditional rice varieties in India) or genetic variation within a population (which is very high among Indian rhinos, for example, and very low among cheetahs). Until recently, measurements of genetic diversity were applied mainly to domesticated species and populations held in zoos or botanic gardens, but increasingly the techniques are being applied to wild species.

Species diversity refers to the variety of species within a region. Such diversity can be measured in many ways, and scientists have not settled on a single best method. The number of species in a region—its species "richness"—is one often-used measure, but a more precise measurement, "taxonomic diversity," also considers the relationship of species to each other. For example, an island with two species of birds and one species of lizard has greater taxonomic diversity than an island with three species of birds but no lizards. Thus, even though there may be more species of beetles on earth than all other species combined, they do not account for the greater part of species diversity because they are so closely related. Similarly, many more species live on land than in the sea, but terrestrial species are more closely related to each other than ocean species are, so diversity is higher in marine ecosystems than a strict count of species would suggest.

Ecosystem diversity is harder to measure than species or genetic diversity because the "boundaries" of communities—associations of species—and ecosystems are elusive. Nevertheless, as long as a consistent set of criteria is used to define communities and ecosystems, their number and distribution can be measured. Until now, such schemes have been applied mainly at national and sub-national levels, though some coarse global classifications have been made.

Besides ecosystem diversity, many other expressions of biodiversity can be important. These include the relative abundance of species, the age structure of populations, the pattern of communities in a region, changes in community composition and structure over time, and even such ecological processes as predation, parasitism, and mutualism. More generally, to meet specific management or policy goals, it is often important to examine not only compositional diversity—genes, species, and ecosystems—

The Value of Biodiversity's Components

From both wild and domesticated components of biodiversity humanity derives all of its food and many medicines and industrial products. Economic benefits from wild species alone make up an estimated 4.5 percent of the Gross Domestic Product of the United States—worth $87 billion annually in the late 1970s.[1] Fisheries, largely based on wild species, contributed about 100 million tons of food worldwide in 1989.[2] Indeed, wild species are dietary

but also diversity in ecosystem structure and function.

Human *cultural diversity* could also be considered part of biodiversity. Like genetic or species diversity, some attributes of human cultures (say, nomadism or shifting cultivation) represent "solutions" to the problems of survival in particular environments. And, like other aspects of biodiversity, cultural diversity helps people adapt to changing conditions. Cultural diversity is manifested by diversity in language, religious beliefs, land-management practices, art, music, social structure, crop selection, diet, and any number of other attributes of human society.

FIGURE 1

Relative Number of Described Species in Major Taxa
(Size of Organisms Represents Number of Described Species)

Size of individual organisms represents number of described species in major taxon.
Unit Area: ☐ = approximately 1,000 described species.

	Taxon	No. of Described Species		Taxon	No. of Described Species
1	Monera (Bacteria, Blue-green Algae)	4,760	11	Mollusca (Mollusks)	50,000
2	Fungi	46,983	12	Echinodermata (Starfish etc.)	6,100
3	Algae	26,900	13	Insecta	751,000
4	Plantae (Multicellular Plants)	248,428	14	Non-insect Arthropoda	
5	Protozoa	30,800		(Mites, Spiders, Crustaceans etc.)	123,161
6	Porifera (Sponges)	5,000	15	Pisces (Fish)	19,056
7	Coelenterata		16	Amphibia (Amphibians)	4,184
	(Jellyfish, Corals, Comb Jellies)	9,000	17	Reptilia (Reptiles)	6,300
8	Platyhelminthes (Flatworms)	12,200	18	Aves (Birds)	9,040
9	Nematoda (Roundworms)	12,000	19	Mammalia (Mammals)	4,000
10	Annelida (Earthworms etc.)	12,000			

Illustration by Frances L. Fawcett.   From Q.D. Wheeler.   1990.   Ann. Entomol. Soc. Am. 83:1031-1047.

Source: "Species-scape" illustration in which size of organisms are proportionate to the number of species in group it represents. Drawing by Frances Fawcett. From: Wheeler, Quentin D. 1990. Insect diversity and cladistic constraints. Annals of the Entomological Society of America, *vol. 83, pp. 1031-1047*

mainstays in much of the world. In Ghana, three out of four people look to wildlife for most of their protein. Timber, ornamental plants, oils, gums, and many fibers also come from the wild.

The current economic value of domesticated species is even greater. Agriculture accounts for 32 percent of GDP in low-income developing countries and 12 percent in middle-income countries.[3] Trade in agricultural products amounted to $3 trillion in 1989.[4]

The components of biodiversity are also important to human health. Once, nearly all medicines came from plants and animals, and even today they remain vital. Traditional medicine forms the basis of primary health care for about 80 percent of people in developing countries, more than 3 billion people in all.[5] More than 5,100 species are used in Chinese traditional medicine alone, and people in northwestern Amazonia have tapped some 2,000 species.[6] Traditional medicine is now encouraged by the World Health Organization, and in many countries—including industrialized countries—its use is expanding rapidly. Nearly 2,500 plant species in the Soviet Union have been used for medicinal purposes and the demand for drug plant material has tripled in the last decade.[7]

As for modern pharmaceuticals, one-fourth of all prescriptions dispensed in the United States contain active ingredients extracted from plants, and over 3000 antibiotics—including penicillin and tetracycline—are derived from microorganisms. Cyclosporin, developed from a soil fungus, revolutionized heart and kidney transplant surgery by suppressing the immune reaction. Aspirin and many other drugs that are now synthesized were first discovered in the wild. Compounds extracted from plants, microbes, and animals were involved in developing all of the twenty best-selling drugs in the United States, drugs whose combined sales approached $6 billion in 1988.[8]

Biotic resources also serve recreation and tourism. Fully 84 percent of all Canadians fish, photograph wildlife, or base other recreational activities on nature—a national passion and pastime worth $800 million annually.[9] Worldwide, nature tourism generates as much as $12 billion in revenues each year.[10] In Namibia, the national constitution itself includes a call to protect the "beauty and character" of the environment.[11] And for many, simply knowing that a particular species or ecosystem exists is inspiring or comforting.

The Value of Diversity

The sheer *variety* of life has enormous value.

The variety of distinctive species, ecosystems, and habitats influence the productivity and services provided by ecosystems. As the variety of species in an ecosystem changes—a legacy of extinction or species introduction—the ecosystem's ability to absorb pollution, maintain soil fertility and micro-climates, cleanse water, and provide other invaluable services changes too. When the elephant—a voracious vegetarian—disappeared from large areas of its traditional range in Africa, the ecosystem was altered as grasslands reverted to woodlands and woodland wildlife returned. When the sea otter was all but exterminated from the Aleutian Islands by fur traders, sea urchin populations swelled and overwhelmed kelp production.

The value of variety is particularly apparent in agriculture. For generations, people have raised a wide range of crops and livestock to stabilize and enhance productivity. The wisdom of these techniques—including their contributions to watershed protection, soil fertility maintenance, and receptivity to integrated pest-management strategies—is being reaffirmed today as farmers around the world turn to alternative low-input production systems.

The genetic diversity found within individual crops is also of tremendous value. Genetic diversity provides an edge in the constant evolutionary battle between crops and livestock and the pests and diseases that prey on them. In age-old systems, several genetically distinct varieties of crops are planted together as a hedge against crop failure. The Ifugao of the Philippine island of Luzon can name more than 200 varieties of sweet potato, and Andean farmers cultivate thousands of varieties of potatoes.

Breeders and farmers also draw on the genetic diversity of crops and livestock to increase yields and to respond to changing environmental conditions. The opportunities provided by genetic engineering—which allows the transfer of genes among species—will further increase the opportunities genetic diversity provides for enhancing agricultural productivity. A wild tomato, found only in the Galápagos Islands, can grow in seawater and possesses jointless fruitstalks—a trait that has been bred into domesticated tomatoes to make them easy to harvest mechanically.[12] A wild relative of rice collected in India provided a "resistance gene" that now protects high-yielding rice varieties in South and Southeast Asia from their nemesis, the brown plant-hopper. Plant breeding is to thank for fully half of the gains in agricultural yields in the United States from 1930 to 1980: an estimated $1 billion annually has been added to the value of U.S. agricultural output by the widened genetic base.[13]

Over time, the greatest value of the variety of life may be found in the opportunities it provides humanity for adapting to local and global change. The unknown potential of genes, species, and ecosystems represents a never-ending biological frontier of inestimable but certainly high value. Genetic diversity will enable breeders to tailor crops to new climatic conditions. Earth's biota—a biochemical laboratory unmatched for size and innovation—hold the still-secret cures for emerging diseases. A diverse array of genes, species, and ecosystems is a resource that can be tapped as human needs and demands change.

Because biodiversity is so closely intertwined with human needs, its conservation should rightfully be considered an element of national security. It has become increasingly apparent that national security means much more than military might. Ecological dimensions of national security cannot be ignored when countries fight over access to water or when environmental refugees strain national budgets and public infrastructure. A secure nation means not only a strong nation, but also one with a healthy and educated populace, and a healthy and productive environment as well. National security will be strongest in countries that care for their biodiversity and the services it provides.

For many, these technical definitions and economic calculations may be eclipsed by still more basic reasons for conservation. Attitudes toward biodiversity and the respect that people show for other species are strongly influenced by moral, cultural, and religious values. The reason is not surprising.

Biodiversity is closely linked to cultural diversity—human cultures are shaped in part by the living environment that they in turn influence—and this linkage has profoundly helped determine cultural values. Most of the world's religions teach respect for the diversity of life and concern for its conservation. Indeed, the variety of life is the backdrop against which culture itself languishes or flourishes.

Even so, some reduction in biodiversity has been an inevitable consequence of human development, as species-rich forests and wetlands have been converted to relatively species-poor farmlands and plantations. Such conversions are themselves an aspect of the use and management of biodiversity, and there can be no doubt that they are beneficial. But many ecosystems have been converted to impoverished systems that are less productive—economically as well as biologically. Such misuse not only disrupts ecosystem function, it also imposes a cost. In the United States, the destruction of estuarine ecosystems between 1954 and 1978 cost over $200 million annually in revenues lost from commercial and sport fisheries alone. Expensive engineering was needed to defend against storms as substitutes for the natural defenses provided by coastal wetlands.

The many values of biodiversity and its importance for development suggest why biodiversity conservation differs from traditional nature conservation.[14] Biodiversity conservation entails a shift from a defensive posture—protecting nature from the impacts of development—to an offensive effort seeking to meet peoples' needs from biological resources while ensuring the long-term sustainability of Earth's biotic wealth. It thus involves not only the protection of wild species but also the safeguarding of the genetic diversity of cultivated and domesticated species and their wild relatives. This goal speaks to modified and intensively managed ecosystems as well as natural ones, and it is pursued in the human interest and for human benefit. In sum, biodiversity conservation seeks to maintain the human life support system provided by nature, and the living resources essential for development.

II

Losses of Biodiversity and Their Causes

We aren't quite sure who is cutting our forests and who is going to flood our land,

but we know they live in towns, where rich people are getting richer,

and we poor people are losing what little we have.

STATEMENT OF THE IBAN PEOPLE, SARAWAK, MALAYSIA

Biological diversity is being eroded as fast today as at any time since the dinosaurs died out some 65 million years ago. The crucible of extinction is believed to be in tropical forests. Around 10 million species live on earth, according to the best estimates *(See Box 2)*, and tropical forests house between 50 and 90 percent of this total. About 17 million hectares of tropical forests—an area four times the size of Switzerland—are now being cleared annually,[15] and scientists estimate that at these rates roughly 5 to 10 percent of tropical forest species may face extinction within the next 30 years.[16] *(See Figure 2.)* This estimate may prove conservative, however. Rates of tropical forest loss are accelerating, and some particularly species-rich forests are likely to be largely destroyed in our lifetime. Some scientists believe that about 60,000 of the world's 240,000 plant species, and perhaps even higher proportions of vertebrate and insect species, could lose their lease on life over the next three decades unless deforestation is slowed immediately.[17]

Tropical forests are by no means the only sites with endangered biodiversity. Worldwide, nearly as much temperate rain forest—once covering an area nearly the size of Malaysia—has also been lost.[18] Although the total extent of forest in the northern temperate and boreal regions has not changed much in recent years, in many areas the species-rich, old-growth forests have been steadily replaced by second-growth forests and plantations. Evidence of accelerating clearance of temperate forests is also appearing: between 1977 and 1987, 1.6 million hectares of forest was lost in the United States alone.[19]

In several spots in Europe, fungal species diversity has dropped by 50 percent or more over the past 60 years.[20]

In such "Mediterranean" climes as California, South Africa, central Chile, and Southwest Australia, at least 10 percent of all plant and animal species are imperilled. The largest number of recent extinctions have been on oceanic islands: some 60 percent of plant species endemic to the Galápagos Islands are endangered, as are 42 percent of the Azores' endemic species and 75 percent of the endemic plant species of the Canary Islands.

The biodiversity of marine and freshwater systems faces serious loss and degradation. Perhaps hardest hit of all are freshwater ecosystems, battling long-term pollution and the introduction of many alien species. *(See Box 3.)* Marine ecosystems too are suffering from the loss of unique populations of many species and are undergoing major ecological changes. *(See Box 4.)*

The number of documented species extinctions over the past century is small compared to those predicted for the coming decades. This difference is due, in part, to the acceleration of rates of habitat loss over recent decades but also to the difficulty of documenting extinctions. The vast majority of species has not yet even been described, and many may disappear before they are even known to science. Moreover, species are generally not declared to be extinct until years after they have last been seen— so figures for documented extinctions are highly conservative. Finally, some species whose populations are reduced by habitat loss below the level necessary for long-term survival may hang on for several decades without hope of recovery as their population dwindles—these are the "living dead."

Still, evidence of extinction, especially of distinct populations of species, is only too plentiful. In 1990, the otter died out in the Netherlands, and in 1991 Britain declared the mouse-eared bat extinct.[21] In the eastern Pacific, elevated sea temperatures in the 1980s caused the extinction of a hydrocoral.[22] In the past decade, at least 34 species or unique populations of plants and vertebrates have become extinct in the United States while awaiting federal

FIGURE 2

Percent of Tropical Forest Species Likely to be Sentenced to Extinction in Coming Decades

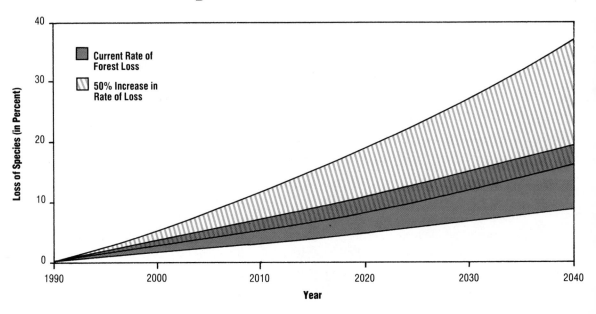

Source: Ehrlich and Wilson, 1991; Reid, 1992

protection.[23] Worldwide, over 700 extinctions of vertebrates, invertebrates, and vascular plants have been recorded since 1600.[24] How many species went extinct elsewhere, unnoticed?

Habitat loss not only precipitates species extinctions, it also represents a loss of biodiversity in its own right. In many countries, relatively little natural vegetation remains untouched by human hands. In Bangladesh, only 6 percent of the original vegetation remains. Forests around the Mediterranean Sea probably once covered 10 times their current area, and in the Netherlands and Britain, less than 4 percent of lowland raised bogs remain undamaged.

The dramatic losses of species and ecosystems obscure equally large and important threats to *genetic* diversity. Worldwide, some 492 genetically distinct populations of tree species (including some full species) are endangered.[25] In the northwestern United States, 159 genetically distinct populations of ocean-migrating fish are at high or moderate risk of extinction, if they have not already slipped into oblivion.[26]

Loss of genetic diversity could imperil agriculture. How much the genetic base has already eroded is hard to say, but since the 1950s, the spread of modern "Green Revolution" varieties of corn, wheat, rice, and other crops has rapidly squeezed out native landraces. Modern varieties were adopted on 40 percent of Asia's rice farms within 15 years of their release, and in the Philippines, Indonesia, and some other countries, more than 80 percent of all farmers now plant the new varieties. In Indonesia, 1500 local rice varieties have become extinct in the last 15 years.[27] A recent survey of sites in Kenya with wild coffee relatives found that the coffee plants in two of the sites had disappeared, three sites were highly threatened, and six were possibly threatened. Only two were secure.

The impact of such losses of genetic diversity often registers swiftly. In 1991, the genetic similarity of Brazil's orange trees opened the way for the worst outbreak of citrus canker recorded in the country.[28] In 1970, U.S. farmers lost $1 billion to a disease that swept through uniformly susceptible

---

BOX 2

How Many Species Are There?

Surprisingly, scientists have a better understanding of how many stars there are in the galaxy than how many species there are on Earth. Estimates of global species diversity have varied from 2 million to 100 million species, with a best estimate of somewhere near 10 million, and only 1.4 million have actually been named. The problems stemming from the limits of current knowledge of species diversity are compounded by the lack of a central database or list of the world's species.

New species are still being discovered—even new birds and mammals. On average, about three new species of birds are found each year, and as recently as 1990 a new species of monkey was discovered. Other vertebrate groups are still far from being completely described: an estimated 40 percent of freshwater fishes in South America have not yet been classified.

Scientists were startled in 1980 by the discovery of a tremendous diversity of insects in tropical forests. In one study of just 19 trees in Panama, fully 80 percent of the 1,200 beetle species discovered were previously unknown to science. At least 6 million to 9 million species of arthropods—and possibly more than 30 million—are now thought to dwell in the tropics with only a small fraction currently described.

As scientists begin investigating other little-known ecosystems, like the soil and the deep sea, "surprising" discoveries of species become commonplace. Small wonder. A single square meter of temperate forest can hold 200,000 mites and tens of thousands of other invertebrates. A similar-sized plot from tropical grasslands can hold 32 million nematodes, and one gram of the same soil might hold 90 million bacteria and other microbes. How many species these communities contain is still anyone's guess.

Marine systems too are revealing an unsuspected diversity. Scientists believe that the deep sea floor may contain as many as a million undescribed species. Entirely new communities of organisms—hydrothermal vent communities—were found less than two decades ago. More than 20 new families or subfamilies, 50 new genera, and 100 new species from these vents have been identified.

Source: Thomas, 1990; Grassle, 1989; Grassle et al., 1990

BOX 3

Biodiversity in Freshwater Ecosystems

Both Old World and New World cultures have been centered on freshwater habitats—Babylon between the Tigris and Euphrates Rivers, Egypt on the Nile, Rome on the Tiber, the Aztec capital built on man-made islands in Lake Tenochtitlan, Paris on the Seine, Kinshasa on the Zaire River. The world's rivers, lakes, streams, and wetlands provide most of the world's water for drinking, agriculture, sanitation, and industry, as well as huge quantities of fish and shellfish.

Freshwaters are also home to a tremendous diversity of fish, amphibians, aquatic plants, invertebrates, and microorganisms. The Amazon River alone contains an estimated 3000 species of fish— only 25 percent less than the total number of mammals worldwide. And freshwater biodiversity is among the most poorly known on Earth. Scientists believe that Thailand may have as many as 1000 species of freshwater fish, but only some 475 have actually been recorded.

Freshwater biodiversity is seriously threatened today—a telling indicator of the status of the world's freshwater ecosystems. All native fishes in the Valley of Mexico are extinct. A recent survey in Malaysia found fewer than half of the 266 fish species previously known from the country. On the island of Singapore, 18 out of 53 species of freshwater fish collected in 1934 could not be located in exhaustive searches only 30 years later. In the southeastern United States, 40 to 50 percent of freshwater snail species are now extinct or endangered due to the impoundment and channelization of rivers. Even on a continental scale, species loss can be very high. In North America, one-third of the native freshwater fish species are extinct or endangered to some degree.

Biodiversity in freshwater systems is distributed in a fundamentally different pattern from that in marine or terrestrial systems. Organisms on land or in the sea live in media that are more or less continuous over extensive regions, and species adjust their ranges to some degree as climate or ecological conditions change. But freshwater habitats are relatively discontinuous, and many freshwater species do not disperse easily across the land barriers that separate river drainages into discrete units. This has three important consequences: a) freshwater species must survive climatic and ecological changes in place; b) freshwater biodiversity is usually highly localized, and even small lake or stream systems often harbor unique, locally evolved forms of life; and c) freshwater species diversity is high even in regions where the number of species at any given site is low, since species differ between one site and the next.

Freshwater lakes are classical examples of "habitat islands" (in this case, bodies of water surrounded by expanses of land). Like islands in general, the larger, more ancient lakes tend to have high levels of endemism, and in the rift lakes of Africa or Lake Baikal of Central Asia, species diversity can be spectacular. With hundreds of species each—90 percent of them in some cases found nowhere else—the East African lakes harbor some of the world's greatest concentrations of locally endemic species.

Unfortunately, lakes are like islands in another way too: they suffer high rates of extinction when habitat modification begins or when exotic species are introduced. The introduction of non-native species— regrettably still often sanctioned or promoted by governments—is associated with the depletion of biodiversity and the collapse of major fisheries in such lakes as Lake Chapala of Mexico, Lake Gatun of Panama, and the Great Lakes of North America.

Other factors contributing to the decline of freshwater ecosystems and their native biota are chemical and thermal pollution, over-harvesting, and habitat modifications (such as dam construction). These factors have affected biodiversity to different degrees in both industrialized and developing regions. In Europe and North America, pollution, acidification, and the physical modification of streams have had the greatest impact. In much of South America and Africa, over-harvesting and introduction of non-native species are relatively more important as agents of biodiversity loss.

Programs to protect freshwater biodiversity in industrialized countries have lagged far behind the programs for saving terrestrial biota. Many protected areas include lakes or small portions of watersheds, but rivers and streams are often too linear to incorporate adequately into protected areas. Moreover, rivers and streams frequently pass through more than one political jurisdiction or may themselves constitute political boundaries. (The Danube crosses or borders upon seven European nations.) Consequently, effective management of riverine biodiversity is often a casualty of politics.

The primary method of protecting freshwater biodiversity has been to designate particular species as threatened or endangered, making them subject to national recovery programs or international protection. Unfortunately, this approach is failing. In the United States, for example, no aquatic species has ever graduated from the government's endangered species list, but 10 species of fish have been removed due to extinction.

Source: Usher, 1991; Diamond, 1989; Miller, et. al., 1989; Reid and Miller, 1989; Williams et. al., 1989; Prance, 1987; IUCN, 1983; Mohsin and Ambak, 1983

corn varieties. Similarly, the Irish potato famine in 1846, the loss of a large portion of the Soviet wheat crop in 1972, and the citrus canker outbreak in Florida in 1984 all stemmed from reductions in genetic diversity.[29] In such countries as Bangladesh, where some 62 percent of rice varieties come from a single maternal plant, Indonesia (74 percent), and Sri Lanka (75 percent), such outbreaks could occur at any time.

Gene banks have slowed the loss of genetic diversity, but the high costs of periodically regenerating the seeds and the risk of mechanical failures make seedbanks less than fail-safe. In 1980, experts estimated that even in developed countries between one-half and two-thirds of the seeds collected in past decades had been lost.[30] In 1991, representatives of 13 national germplasm banks in Latin America reported that between 5 and 100 percent of the maize seed collected between 1940 and 1980 is no longer viable.[31]

The loss of genetic, species, and ecosystem diversity both stems from and invites the loss of cultural diversity. Diverse cultures have bred and sustained numerous varieties of crops, livestock, and habitats. By the same token, the loss of certain crops, the replacement of traditional crops with export crops, the extinction of species embedded in religion, mythology, or folklore, and the degradation or conversion of homelands are cultural as well as biological losses. Since 1900, experts say, about one Indian tribe has disappeared from Brazil each year.[32] Almost one half of the world's 6000 languages may die out in the next 100 years. Of the 3000 languages expected to survive for a century, nearly half will probably not last much longer.[33]

Causes and Mechanisms of Biodiversity Impoverishment

The current losses of biodiversity have both direct and indirect causes. The direct mechanisms include habitat loss and fragmentation, invasion by introduced species, the over-exploitation of living resources, pollution, global climate change, and industrial agriculture and forestry. *(See Box 5.)* But these are not the root of the problem. Biotic impoverishment is an almost inevitable consequence of the ways in which the human species has used and misused the environment in the course of its rise to dominance.

As people awaken to the damage unsustainable development is increasingly inflicting on the web of life and the human prospect, the search for solutions must turn inward. The roots of the biodiversity crisis are not "out there" in the forest or on the savannah, but embedded in the way we live. They lie in burgeoning human numbers, the way in which the human species has progressively broadened its ecological niche and appropriated ever more of the earth's biological productivity, the excessive and unsustainable consumption of natural resources, a continuing reduction in the number of traded products from agriculture and fisheries, economic systems that fail to set a proper value on the environment, inappropriate social structures, and weaknesses in legal and institutional systems. Just as biodiversity is an essential resource for sustainable development, finding sustainable ways to live is essential if biological diversity is to be conserved.

Six fundamental causes of biodiversity loss

■ *the unsustainably high rate of human population growth and natural resource consumption*

In most countries with high fertility rates, about half the population is under the age of 16. The resulting demographic momentum—that is, high birth rates in coming years due to the large number of people who will be reaching their reproductive years—means that global population will continue to grow for at least the next half century and probably longer, barring catastrophe. *(See Figure 3.)* Another billion people are likely to be added to the world population for each of the next three decades. The rates and magnitude of this growth and the eventual size at which the global population stabilizes—critical considerations for biodiversity—depend on social and economic measures, especially on the rate of economic development in the developing countries.

BOX 4

Biodiversity in Marine Ecosystems

In 1768, only 27 years after its discovery in the Bering Sea, the last Steller's sea cow was killed—a fate shared by the great auk in the 1840s, the Caribbean monk seal in the 1950s, and unknown numbers of other marine species. Far less publicized than loss of biological diversity on land, the loss of marine genetic, species, and ecosystem diversity is a global crisis in its own right.

Although fewer marine than land species have been described, in some respects the marine realm is more diverse. It hosts 31 of the world's 32 extant animal phyla, 14 of them exclusively marine. Coral reefs, like tropical forests, are renowned for their dazzling species diversity, though recent evidence suggests that the deep sea might also have a remarkably high species diversity. Because many marine species defend themselves chemically, marine biochemical diversity is an exciting source of new medicines. The diversity of life in marine systems also affords recreational and aesthetic pleasures.

The oceans' biotic wealth extends beyond numbers of species; the highest measured productivity on Earth is in North Pacific kelp beds. Seafoods provide much of humankind's protein supply. Marine photosynthesizing and shell-forming organisms tie up carbon dioxide that would otherwise intensify global warming. The diversity of marine ecosystems, from structurally complex mangrove forests to seemingly featureless oceanic midwaters, is at least comparable to the land's.

Marine scientists are continually reminded of how little is known about the seas. Not until 1938 was it learned that coelacanth fish, until then known only as fossils, still survive in the Indian Ocean. And it was as recently as 1977 that hydrothermal vents, with diverse and unique associated ecosystems, were discovered in the East Pacific.

As technology and international trade have intensified, their impact has extended even to the remote oceans, which bear the "fingerprints" of humanity. Even in Antarctica, penguins far from any agriculture contain DDT, shorelines have been fouled by oil spills, and blue whales are critically endangered. The species and ecosystems suffering most, however, are in the coastal waters closest to humankind.

Several distinctive aspects of the sea complicate the task of conservation. First, marine ecosystems are at the receiving end of drainage from the land, and most wastes eventually wind up there. Second, reproduction of marine organisms can be very uneven in space and time. In widespread species, such as the tropical West Atlantic Nassau grouper, spawning may occur in just a few places. Long-lived species, such as the geoduck clam of Northeast Pacific coastal bays, may recruit successfully only once in many years.

Many marine organisms release their eggs into the surface waters of the sea. Planktonic larvae can disperse hundreds, even thousands, of kilometers, and because of this widespread dispersal marine fishes, invertebrates, and plants might seem to be at low risk of extinction. Not so. The endangered totoaba fish of the Sea of Cortez, the extinct (1930s) West Atlantic eelgrass limpet, and an extinct (1980s) hydrocoral of the East Pacific's Gulf of Chiriqui all had wide-dispersing planktonic larvae.

Several categories of marine species are particularly vulnerable. Surface-dwellers (including larvae of many commercial fishes) are vulnerable to oil and other floating pollutants and increased ultraviolet radiation. Species requiring more than one habitat during development (such as Pacific salmon populations) are threatened by activities in any one of them. Species that mature slowly and produce few young (such as sea turtles, seabirds, and sharks) are vulnerable to over-exploitation. So are the exceptionally large species favored by people for food and other products, who have decimated once-sizable populations of giant clams, king crabs, bluefin tunas, and the great whales.

Preventing extinctions is essential but not sufficient. Maintaining the integrity of the sea and, hence, its sustained production of resources and services requires attention to whole ecosystems as well as to their component species. Estuaries and salt marshes, mangrove forests, and seagrass beds near cities and towns are severely degraded worldwide. And, because ships carry millions of larvae in their ballast tanks, alien species are common in the busiest harbors, where more than half of the species can be interlopers. Many estuaries draining rural watersheds are contaminated with agricultural chemicals and choked with silt eroded from farming and forestry. And the increasingly observed worldwide bleaching of corals could portend massive ecological changes for coral reefs and other marine ecosystems. Global atmospheric change will touch even the remotest areas.

Marine conservation has only become an issue of global concern within the last 20 years. There are three main reasons for this delay. First, because the sea is not their element, people seldom notice damages that would be readily observed on land. Wastes, for example, simply seem to disappear. So widespread is the notion that the seas are infinite and inexhaustible that few become alarmed even when fisheries crash and ecosystems become sewers. Second, there is no tradition of managing marine areas for conservation, whereas protected areas have existed on land for over a century. Strategies and plans for marine protected areas are a product of the last 15 years and have still to gain general acceptance. Integrated resource management in the coastal zone, though the key to conservation and sustainable use, is hardly being applied anywhere. Third, most of the seas and oceans lie outside the jurisdiction of states, and even territorial waters and those within Exclusive Economic Zones are communal property. Because the ocean has been an "open access resource," competitive exploitation has been the norm. Even though fisheries conventions and international agreements on the management of whales and seals have existed for some time, only within the past 20 years have regional seas conventions, conventions to prevent marine pollution, and the UN Convention on the Law of the Sea (still lacking enough ratifications to bring it into force) begun to impose a framework of international law on the 70 percent of the Earth's surface that is ocean.

BOX 5

Mechanisms for the Loss of Biodiversity

Habitat Loss and Fragmentation

Relatively undisturbed ecosystems have shrunk dramatically in area over past decades as the human population and resource consumption have grown. Ninety-eight percent of the tropical dry forest along Central America's Pacific coast has disappeared. Thailand lost 22 percent of its mangroves between 1961 and 1985, and virtually none of the remainder is undisturbed. In freshwater ecosystems, dams have destroyed large sections of river and stream habitat. In marine ecosystems, coastal development has wiped out reef and near-shore communities. In tropical forests, a major cause of forest loss is the expansion of marginal agriculture, though in specific regions commercial timber harvest may pose an even greater problem.

Introduced species

Introduced species are responsible for many recorded species extinctions, especially on islands. In these isolated ecosystems, a new predator, competitor, or pathogen can rapidly imperil species that did not co-evolve with the newcomer. In Hawaii, some 86 introduced plant species seriously threaten native biodiversity; one introduced tree species has now displaced more than 30,000 acres of native forest.

Over-exploitation of plant and animal species

Numerous forest, fisheries, and wildlife resources have been over-exploited, sometimes to the point of extinction. Historically, both the great auk and the passenger pigeon succumbed to such pressure, and the Lebanon cedar that once blanketed 500,000 hectares now is found in only a few scattered remnants of forest. Over-exploitation of the Peruvian anchovy between 1958 and 1970 dramatically reduced the population size and the catch. Today, the Sumatran and Javan rhinos have been hunted to the verge of extinction, along with numerous other vertebrates. Many extinctions attend the human harvest of food, but the search for precious commodities—notably, ivory—and for pets, curiosities, and collector's items has also impinged on some populations and obliterated others.

Pollution of soil, water, and atmosphere

Pollutants strain ecosystems and may reduce or eliminate populations of sensitive species. Contamination may reverberate along the food chain: barn owl populations in the United Kingdom have fallen by 10 percent since new rodenticides were introduced, and illegal pesticides used to control crayfish along the boundaries of Spain's Cota Donana National Park in 1985 killed 30,000 birds. Some 43 species have been lost in Poland's Ojcow National Park, due in part to severe air pollution. Soil microbes have also suffered from pollution as industry sheds heavy metals and irrigated agriculture brings on salinization. Acid rain has made thousands of Scandinavian and North American lakes and pools virtually lifeless, and, in combination with other kinds of air pollution, has damaged forests throughout Europe. Marine pollution, particularly from non-point sources, has defiled the Mediterranean and many estuaries and coastal seas throughout the world.

Global climate change

In coming decades, a massive "side-effect" of air pollution—global warming—could play havoc with the world's living organisms. Human-caused increases in "greenhouse gases" in the atmosphere are likely to commit the planet to a global temperature rise of some 1° to 3°C (2° to 5° F) during the next century, with an associated rise in sea level of 1 to 2 meters. Each 1°C rise in temperature will displace the limits of tolerance of land species some 125 km towards the poles, or 150 m vertically on the mountains. Many species will not be able to redistribute themselves fast enough to keep up with the projected changes, and considerable alterations in ecosystem structure and function are likely. In the United States rising seas in the next century may cover the entire habitat of at least 80 species already at risk of extinction. Many of the world's islands would be completely submerged by the more extreme projections of sea level rise—wiping out their fauna and flora. And protected areas themselves will be placed under stress as environmental conditions deteriorate within and suitable habitat for their species cannot be found in the disturbed land surrounding them.

Industrial agriculture and forestry

Until this century, farmers and pastoralists bred and maintained a tremendous diversity of crop and livestock varieties around the world. But on-farm diversity is shrinking fast thanks to modern plant-breeding programs and the resulting productivity gains achieved by planting comparatively fewer varieties of crops that respond better to water, fertilizers, and pesticides. Similar trends are transforming diverse forest ecosystems into high-yielding monocultural tree plantations—some of which now resemble a field of maize as much as a natural forest—and even fewer tree genes than crop genes have been preserved off-site as an insurance policy against disease and pests.

Source: Reid and Trexler, 1991; IPCC, 1990; Thorsell, 1990; Reid and Miller, 1989; Schneider, 1989; Janzen, 1988; Vitousek et al., 1987; MacKenzie, 1986; Chaney and Basbous, 1978

As numbers have increased and new technologies have developed, humanity has appropriated an ever-increasing share of the earth's resources. People consume, divert, or destroy an estimated 39 percent of the terrestrial productivity of photosynthetic plants, algae, and bacteria, the fundamental source of the energy available for virtually all living systems.[34] This trend is unsustainable. The world's biotic systems simply cannot accommodate an ever-growing claim on primary productivity to meet further growth in human population and consumption. The inherent limits of the natural resource base will impose a corresponding limit on the number of people who rely on it. Of course, an ecosystem's (or, for that matter, a planet's) "ecological carrying capacity" can be increased by technology (as the history of agriculture demonstrates), but ultimate constraints on consumption are nevertheless real.

Critical environmental resources are now under stress. Emissions of pollutants, including greenhouse gases, are already overtaxing the tolerance of ecosystems and the dispersal capacity of the atmosphere. Ozone layer depletion, acid rain, and air pollution are all taking a toll on biodiversity today and may threaten it even more severely in the future, particularly if climate change accelerates. Excessive consumption of minerals and other nonrenewable resources and a gross over-use and waste of energy, especially by the industrialized nations, aggravates these problems. The developed countries bear the principal responsibility for these impacts, and they need to move swiftly toward a more sustainable way of life. New patterns of development are essential if projected population growth is to be accommodated without straining the planet's carrying capacity.

■ *the steadily narrowing spectrum of traded products from agriculture, forestry, and fisheries*

For millennia, the world was a patchwork of relatively autonomous regions. Knowledge, subsistence strategies, and social structures evolved in each region more or less independently, and people's demands on the environment rarely exceeded nature's capacity. In forest areas, traditional agriculture did not appreciably erode diversity where population densities remained low, market pressure was slack, and the combination of shifting cultivation, hunting, fishing, and the gathering of forest products that formed the backbone of most traditional subsistence strategies was well-balanced. No one group could undermine biodiversity overall, and some even enhanced it. But the global exchange economy that has emerged over the past century, based on principles of comparative advantage and specialization, has increased both uniformity and interdependence.

In agriculture, producers now specialize in

FIGURE 3

Human Population Growth

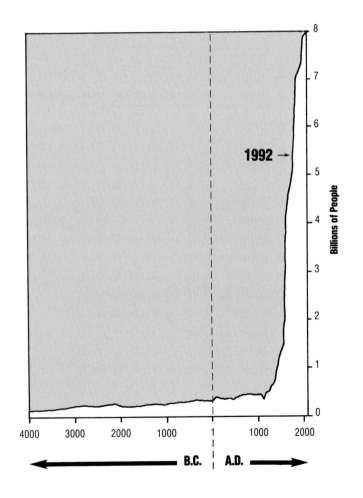

the relatively few crops that provide an edge in the world economy. As the number of crop species declines, local nitrogen-fixing bacteria, mycorrhizae, predators, pollinators, seed dispersers, and other species that co-evolved over centuries with traditional agricultural systems die out. The use of fertilizers, pesticides, and high-yielding varieties to maximize production and profits over the short-term exacerbates this loss. In forest areas, the rapid and total conversion of forests (often to monocultural cash crops) is widespread. When the price of coffee or palm oil drops, the plantation cannot quickly revert to the biologically diverse forest that preceded it, even if left alone. Similarly, large global markets have fostered the development of what might be called blanket fishing. Monofilament drift nets, for instance, catch enormous quantities of target species—and enormous numbers of "incidental" marine mammals, birds, and so-called non-target fish.

■ *economic systems and policies that fail to value the environment and its resources*

Many conversions of natural systems—such as forests or wetlands to farmlands and rangelands—are economically and biologically inefficient. They happen partly because of the urgent need for land to cultivate, regardless of how sustainable cultivation is, and partly because natural habitats are commonly under-valued economically.

There are several reasons for the misvaluation of biological resources. First, many biological resources are consumed directly and never enter markets. Among forest products, sawn timber, pulpwood, rattan, and gums are likely to be marketed while much of the food, fuelwood, and medicinal plants harvested by local people and the clean water supplied by the forest to the rivers will not. Accordingly, the economic values of logging and other potentially exhaustive uses are overestimated while sustainable uses (and aesthetic and spiritual benefits) are underestimated, creating incentives to impoverish the forest.

Second, biodiversity's benefits are in large part

"public goods" that no single owner can claim. Wetland protection, for example, benefits the public tangibly and quantifiably, but the benefits are so diffuse that no market incentives for wetland conservation ever develop. This undervaluation then justifies government policies—such as tax incentives—that further encourage wetland conversion to use with greater "market" value.

Third, property rights are more likely to be granted to those who clear and settle forests and other lands covered with natural vegetation than to forest dwellers living by the sustainable harvest of natural products. Formal property rights are also often easier to obtain by people living in cities and working in the formal sector of the economy—which itself favors the extraction and marketing of products such as timber over the sustainable harvest of products with limited market value. Any uncertainty over property rights weakens incentives for stewardship and encourages over-exploitation. Few farmers will plant woodlots that they might not own five years later. People who do not benefit from a tourist industry, but need food, are more likely to kill than to protect wild animals. People who have no stake in a resource are the least likely to care for it and the most likely to alter it if doing so establishes ownership.

Correctly valued, biologically diverse natural systems are major economic assets. But because such systems are commonly undervalued, biodiversity conservation is seen as a cost rather than an investment. Correcting this error is essential to conserving global and national biodiversity.

■ *inequity in the ownership, management and flow of benefits from both the use and conservation of biological resources*

In most countries, ownership and control of land and biotic resources, and all the benefits they confer, are distributed in ways that work against biodiversity conservation and sustainable living. The rapid depletion of species and the destruction of habitats are the norm in many countries where a minority of the population owns or controls most of the land. Quick profits from excessive logging or overfishing flow to the few, while the local communities dependent on the continued production of the resources pay the price.

A second problem arises from the concentration of resource control and responsibility for environmental policy decisions primarily in the hands of urban men. In many societies women manage the environment and possess far greater knowledge of biodiversity's value to farming and health.

A third issue is the way international trade, debt and technology transfer policies and practices foster inequities that resemble—and often reinforce—those found within nations. By 1988, developing countries were transferring $32.5 billion net to industrialized countries, excluding other implicit resource transfers not involving direct financial flows. (At the beginning of the decade, $42.6 billion had been flowing to developing countries.)[35] To conserve biodiversity, industrialized countries must reverse this flow. If the developing countries continue to be shut out of markets, deprived of access to technology, and burdened with debt, they will have neither the means nor the incentive to conserve their resources for the future.

■ *deficiencies in knowledge and its application*

Scientists still do not have adequate knowledge of natural ecosystems and their innumerable components. This ignorance is compounded by the destruction of cultures that possess a traditional understanding of nature. Even where knowledge exists, it does not flow efficiently to decision-makers, who have in consequence often failed to develop policies that reflect the scientific, economic, social and ethical values of biodiversity. Information also fails to flow properly between central decision-makers and the local communities who depend directly on biological resources, and who may have their livelihood jeopardized by inappropriate development projects and other actions. A final difficulty stems from public reluctance to accept policies that reduce excessive resource consumption, no matter how logical or necessary such policies may be.

■ *legal and institutional systems that promote unsustainable exploitation*

Ecological and economic realities clearly call for a cross-sectoral approach to biodiversity conservation and management. Yet, many national and international institutions operate along rigidly sectoral lines, and many environmental institutions are small and short of resources. Cross-sectoral coordinating machinery is being introduced, both at international level and within countries, but it has yet to prove its effectiveness.

A second problem is the overcentralization of government and corporate planning, which hinders local implementation, discourages local participation, and closes the process to citizen's groups and non-governmental organizations.

A third problem is the weakness of most agencies and organizations charged with nature conservation. Few have the personnel or financial resources needed even to support minimal programs. Their efforts are commonly fragmented and overlapping; what conservation planning they do is neither comprehensive nor strategic, and they do not integrate *in situ* and *ex situ* conservation tools and technologies.

Adding to these difficulties, many countries lack an adequate system of environmental laws and other instruments to ensure the protection of the environment and the sustainable use of its resources. In many developing countries, customary laws that conserved biological resources well have been replaced by less effective legal systems; national policy-making and planning processes are ineffective, the use of economic instruments to promote environmental protection is insufficient, and basic scientific knowledge is inadequate.

Largely because of these legal and institutional constraints, biodiversity conservation has typically been piecemeal and concentrated on traditional wildlife protection techniques—a protected area here, a regime for managing an endangered or threatened species there. Even multiplied many times, such efforts seldom fulfill species' habitat requirements, particularly those of migratory animals, since land-use practices outside protected areas can alter water supplies, introduce pollutants, and change micro-climates. And such efforts do nothing to ensure that policies for sustainable resource use are integrated, which is at the heart of biodiversity conservation.

Region-wide management approaches are needed to address the habitat needs of whole biotic communities and to integrate conservation with regional development. In most situations, managing entire regions as national parks, forest reserves, or marine reserves is inappropriate. But lack of the integrated expertise and authority needed to manage a mix of developed and wild ecosystems impedes sound regional management. Regions big enough for effective development and resource management incorporating biodiversity conservation typically come under various local, state, or provincial government jurisdictions, and some involve two or more nations—an administrative nightmare.

III

The Strategy for Biodiversity Conservation

*The one process ongoing in the 1990s that will take millions of years
to correct is the loss of genetic and species diversity by the destruction of natural habitats.
This is the folly that our descendants are least likely to forgive us.*

E.O. WILSON, HARVARD UNIVERSITY, UNITED STATES

The Goal of Biodiversity Conservation

Successful action to conserve biodiversity must address the full range of causes of its current loss and embrace the opportunities that genes, species, and ecosystems provide for sustainable development. Because the goal of biodiversity conservation—supporting sustainable development by protecting and using biological resources in ways that do not diminish the world's variety of genes and species or destroy important habitats and ecosystems—is so broad, any biodiversity conservation strategy must also have a broad scope. But the campaign can be broken down into three basic elements: saving biodiversity, studying it, and using it sustainably and equitably.

Saving biodiversity means taking steps to protect genes, species, habitats, and ecosystems. The best way to maintain species is to maintain their habitats. Saving bio-

diversity therefore often involves efforts to prevent the degradation of key natural ecosystems and to manage and protect them effectively. But since many of the world's habitats have been modified for such human uses as agriculture, the program must include measures to maintain diversity on lands and in waters that have already been disturbed. A third component is restoring lost species to their former habitats and preserving species in genebanks, zoos, botanic gardens, and other off-site *(ex situ)* facilities.

Studying biodiversity means documenting its composition, distribution, structure, and function; understanding the roles and functions of genes, species, and ecosystems; grasping the complex links between modified and natural systems; and using this understanding to support sustainable development. It also means building awareness of biodiversity's values, providing opportunities for people to appreciate nature's variety, integrating biodiversity issues into educational curricula, and ensuring that the public has access to information on biodiversity, especially on developments that will influence it locally.

Using biodiversity sustainably and equitably means husbanding biological resources so that they last indefinitely, making sure that biodiversity is used to improve the human condition, and seeing that these resources are shared equitably. "Use" does not, however, automatically imply consumption. Often,

FIGURE 4

Elements of Biodiversity Conservation

A. Slowing the loss of biodiversity requires greater understanding of its role in ecosystems and its importance for human life. Conversely, to increase understanding of biodiversity, representative and viable samples of ecosystems, species, and populations must be maintained.

B. Greater incentives will exist to slow the loss of biodiversity if its immediate value to humanity is increased. Conversely, the many current and potential benefits that biodiversity can provide to humanity cannot be sustained unless the biological resource base is maintained.

C. Developing sustainable uses of biodiversity requires the application of both traditional and modern knowledge of biodiversity and biological resources. Conversely, users needs should help set biodiversity research priorities.

the best economic use of biodiversity may be to maintain it in its natural state for its ecological or cultural values, as in the cases of forested watersheds or sacred groves.

The biodiversity conservation agenda must encompass much more than concern for protected areas, threatened species, zoos or seedbanks, and its constituency must be broad-based. It has to take place within the wider context of the move toward sustainable living discussed in *Our Common Future*—the report of the World Commission on Environment and Development—and detailed in *Caring for the Earth*, the successor and complement to the *World Conservation Strategy*. *(See Box 6, a summary of the central proposals in Caring for the Earth.)*

How can biodiversity conservation be addressed within the context of sustainable development, as it must to succeed? There must be new contacts and partnerships within communities, bringing biologists and resource managers together with social scientists, political leaders, businessmen, religious leaders, farmers, journalists, artists, planners, teachers, and lawyers. There must be dialogue between central and local governments, industry, and citizen's groups, including non-governmental environment and development organizations, and women's and indigenous peoples organizations. New mechanisms for discussion, negotiation, and common action are all essential.

Biodiversity conservation must take place at the individual level, the global level, and in between. Effective conservation efforts begin in the fields, forests, watersheds, grasslands, coastal zones, and settlements where people live and work. But complementary governmental efforts are needed to address the many facets of biodiversity conservation beyond the capacity of local communities, or involving resources that are of national importance. By the same token, international cooperation is essential, given the global nature of the biodiversity crisis and the lack of national resources in many countries.

Many essential elements of biodiversity conservation require sustained commitment, but will not show immediate results. Policies, institutions,

BOX 6

Building a Sustainable Society:
The Context for Conserving Biodiversity

Steps to conserve biodiversity can ultimately succeed and endure only in the larger context of a worldwide transition to sustainable living. *Caring for the Earth: A Strategy for Sustainable Living,* published in 1991 by IUCN, UNEP, and WWF, identified the following principles for building a sustainable society:

Respect and care for the community of life— An ethic based on respect and care for each other is the foundation of sustainable living. This means that the costs and benefits of resource use, development, and environmental protection should be shared fairly among communities and nations and between our generation and those who will come after us.

Improve the quality of human life—Development should enable people to realize their potential and lead dignified, fulfilled lives. Economic growth is part of development, but it cannot be a goal in itself; it cannot go on indefinitely.

Conserve Earth's vitality and diversity— Development must be conservation-based: It must protect the structure, functions, and diversity of the world's natural systems, on which our species depends.

Minimize the depletion of non-renewable resources— While resources such as minerals, oil, gas and coal cannot be used sustainably, their "life" can be extended by recycling, using them more efficiently, or switching to renewable substitutes where possible.

Keep within the Earth's carrying capacity—There are limits to the carrying capacity of the Earth's ecosystems—and to the impacts that they can withstand

without deteriorating dangerously. Policies that bring human numbers and lifestyles into balance with the Earth's carrying capacity must be complemented by technologies that enhance that capacity by careful management.

Change personal attitudes and practices—To adopt an ethic for living sustainably, people must reexamine their values and alter their behavior. Society must promote values that support such an ethic and discourage those that are incompatible with a sustainable way of life.

Enable communities to care for their own environments—For this to happen, communities need the authority, power, and knowledge to act.

Provide a national framework for integrating development and conservation—A national program for achieving sustainability should involve all interests and seek to identify and prevent problems before they arise. It must be adaptive, continually redirecting its course in response to experience and new needs.

Forge a global alliance—Global sustainability will depend upon a firm alliance among all countries. But lower-income countries must be helped to develop sustainably and protect their environments. Global and shared resources—especially the atmosphere, oceans, and shared ecosystems—can be managed only if there is a strong sense of common purpose and resolve. The ethic of care applies at the international as well as the national, community, and individual levels.

FIGURE 5

The Scope of Biodiversity Conservation

Levels For Action

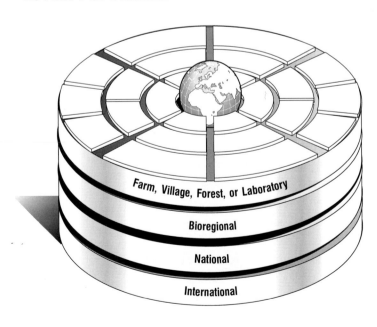

laws, and attitudes do not change overnight; expanding human capacity, carrying out first-rate research, and conducting biodiversity inventories take time and money and may have no immediate pay-off. But they create the larger context in which enduring change can take hold and emergency measures have at least a hope of succeeding.

Still, immediate action *is* needed. Irreplaceable genes, species, and ecosystems are disappearing at a rate unprecedented in human history, and essential development is at risk as a result. Immediate action is needed to defend these threatened living resources; to reform the policies that invite such losses; to conduct inventory and study of resource use in key ecosystems and countries; to monitor changes and impending threats; to better manage threatened protected areas; to mobilize funding; and to support national and grassroots conservation initiatives.

The Approach of the Strategy

The limited conservation resources available must be focussed strategically on opportunities likely to yield the greatest conservation benefits, and five key strategic objectives offer significant possibilities for effective action.

The first objective of a strategy for conserving biodiversity must be the development of national and international policy frameworks that foster the sustainable use of biological resources and the maintenance of biodiversity. The economic policies and legal frameworks established by national governments create the incentives and obstacles that influence decisions about how to utilize and manage biological resources, and these policies—ranging from those covering natural resource exploitation to incentives for technological innovation—need to be revised. To support such changes, better techniques must be developed for determining the value of biological resources and incorporating those values into local and national accounting and cost-benefit analyses.

Nations must also take steps to ensure that benefits from the use of genetic resources are gained

---

BOX 7

Ten Principles for Conserving Biodiversity

These ten principles have guided the individuals and institutions involved in development of the Global Biodiversity Strategy.

1. Every form of life is unique, and warrants respect from humanity.

2. Biodiversity conservation is an investment that yields substantial local, national, and global benefits.

3. The costs and benefits of biodiversity conservation should be shared more equitably among nations and among people within nations.

4. As part of the larger effort to achieve sustainable development, conserving biodiversity requires fundamental changes in patterns and practices of economic development worldwide.

5. Increased funding for biodiversity conservation will not, by itself, slow biodiversity loss. Policy and institutional reforms are needed to create the conditions under which increased funding can be effective.

6. Priorities for biodiversity conservation differ when viewed from local, national, and global perspectives; all are legitimate, and should be taken into account. All countries and communities also have a vested interest in conserving their biodiversity; the focus should not be exclusively on a few species-rich ecosystems or countries.

7. Biodiversity conservation can be sustained only if public awareness and concern are substantially heightened, and if policy-makers have access to reliable information upon which to base policy choices.

8. Action to conserve biodiversity must be planned and implemented at a scale determined by ecological and social criteria. The focus of activity must be where people live and work, as well as in protected wildland areas.

9. Cultural diversity is closely linked to biodiversity. Humanity's collective knowledge of biodiversity and its use and management rests in cultural diversity; conversely, conserving biodiversity often helps strengthen cultural integrity and values.

10. Increased public participation, respect for basic human rights, improved popular access to education and information, and greater institutional accountability are essential elements of biodiversity conservation.

---

nationally and locally. Biotechnology is radically altering the market value of genetic resources. If the right policies are established, countries rich in species and genetic resources stand to benefit substantially from these assets. Aided by the international community, all countries should establish policies that foster the development, acquisition, and adaptation of biotechnologies and the development of in-country technical expertise.

Internationally, the increasingly interconnected global economy conditions what nations and communities can do to conserve and benefit from biodiversity. Trade patterns and practices greatly influence what individuals and nations grow, harvest, buy, and sell. The crushing debt burden shouldered by many developing countries absorbs public resources and makes producing cash commodities to generate foreign exchange irresistible. Development assistance neglects biodiversity conservation, and some contributes to projects that hasten biodiversity loss. Many transnational investment practices drain resources from developing countries, and do nothing to help host communities and countries develop their own technological, professional, and institutional capacities significantly.

The second strategic need is to create conditions and incentives for effective conservation by local communities. Action to conserve biodiversity must ultimately be carried out where people live and work. Unless local communities have the incentives, the capacities, and the latitude to manage biodiversity sustainably, national and international actions are unlikely to produce results. Thus, the policy reforms likely to have the greatest short-term impact on biodiversity conservation will be steps taken to create conditions for conservation locally.

Local biodiversity conservation cannot succeed unless communities receive a fair share of the benefits, and assume a greater role in managing their biotic resources—be they protected areas, coastal fisheries, or forests. In particular, countries should ensure that people who possess local knowledge of genetic resources are rewarded financially when that knowledge is used. Local communities should play a fundamental role in the management of wildlands, as well as in stewardship of their natural resources as a whole. In the many countries where land-tenure systems and the skewed distribution of land ownership pose almost insuperable barriers to conservation, they should be changed. These conditions cannot be met without community empowerment and organization, the development of new resource-management skills, the adaptation of traditional practices to current pressures and conditions, and respect for cultural differences and basic human rights.

Third, the tools for conserving biodiversity must be strengthened and applied more broadly. The world's protected areas are vital tools for conserving biodiversity. Combined with such off-site facilities as zoos, botanic gardens, and seedbanks, they can protect a substantial fraction of the world's biodiversity and help to mobilize its benefits. But these conservation tools cannot serve this role if they remain underfunded and understaffed.

But more funding and personnel are not all that is needed. Biodiversity conservation efforts must be planned and implemented "bioregionally" to reflect both ecological and social realities. The division of government responsibilities among such specialized "sectors" as forestry, agriculture, and fisheries reflects neither. Under a bioregional approach, cooperation among sectors, and sometimes across national boundaries, would be built in. This approach is also characterized by some degree of decentralization, receptiveness to variations in local conditions, and the integration of social and ecological objectives. Changes in the organization of government agencies are needed to carry it out, as is broad participation in decision-making.

Protected areas would retain their central importance if planning were done bioregionally, though their role would be increasingly complemented by forestry, agricultural, and fisheries-management techniques that adopt biodiversity conservation among their management objectives. Additionally, national networks of protected areas must be strengthened and expanded to cover all key biomes and ecosystems, and the management objectives of protected areas must be harmonized with those for the surrounding ecosystems and human communities. By employing management techniques ranging from strict protection to extractive reserves and conservation easements on private lands, a nation's network of protected areas can both conserve diversity and meet short-term economic needs.

In many parts of the world, the best means of strengthening protected areas is to better integrate them with local social and economic needs. This *Strategy* emphasizes mechanisms for increasing benefits to local communities through ecotourism and sustainable use of non-timber forest products, the establishment of effective buffer zones between protected areas and surrounding communities, compensation to local communities for lost resources, and the use of integrated conservation/development strategies in establishing protected areas.

Often, the protection of ecosystems must be supplemented by the conservation of extremely vulnerable or valuable species either in the wild, or off-site in zoos, botanic gardens, aquaria, or seedbanks. In many cases, off-site options represent the last resort for the rescue of threatened species and populations, but they are indispensable tools for increasing public awareness, and for discovering and developing new or improved products and services from biodiversity. Unfortunately, many gaps in the off-site conservation of species remain to be filled, and the integration of off-site conservation with conservation in the wild is embryonic at best.

Fourth, the human capacity for conserving and using biodiversity sustainably must be greatly strengthened, particularly in developing countries. Conservation can succeed only if people understand the distribution and value of biodiversity, see how it influences their own lives and aspirations, and learn to manage areas to meet human needs without diminishing biodiversity. But this capacity is woefully inadequate today: resource managers are not trained to conserve biodiversity; the number of taxonomists specializing in tropical species is grossly inadequate; no country has a complete listing of its species; and for most ecosystems little information exists on indicator and keystone species.

Chronic underinvestment in human capacity-building accounts for these gaps. Indeed, many governments have considered actions to save and study biodiversity wasteful expenditures, mainly because they have not grasped biodiversity's current and potential contribution to national development and human needs. But if taxonomic research for its own sake seems like an extravagance, taxonomy as a tool for managing biodiversity and mobilizing its benefits is a necessity.

Committed, skilled people are needed in all countries to work on biodiversity conservation. Experts in the biological and social sciences, economics, law, policy analysis, ethics, and community organizations are all required. Needs are most acute in many developing countries, where biodiversity losses are high.

The key to conserving genes, species, and ecosystems is increasing our knowledge of biodiver-sity and its role in human society. Research must be explicitly linked to national and local resource and development needs. Findings, in turn, must be accessible and understandable to decision-makers. The capacities for undertaking research and disseminating data should be developed close to those who need the information—at the national or sub-national level—though the support of international networks is vital. Similarly, the priorities for research and information systems should grow out of consultation with those who need and will use new data and analyses. For many countries, the best option is establishing institutions such as "national biodiversity institutes" to catalogue and explore a nation's biotic wealth, thus helping to mobilize biodiversity to meet national needs.

Finally, conservation action must be catalyzed through international cooperation and national planning. The international cooperation needed to slow biodiversity loss requires more effective international mechanisms than those we have now. International law and institutions must be able to establish widely accepted international norms of conduct, elicit firm commitments to action from governments, mobilize financial resources, develop accurate and timely information, and invite broad participation from scientific and non-governmental sectors. Existing mechanisms simply cannot perform these functions.

As important as international cooperation is, national or regional planning processes are also key mechanisms for catalyzing and focusing policy reform to ensure sustainable resource use and support biodiversity conservation. During planning, biodiversity concerns can be injected into mainstream economic development policy provided that planning mechanisms are more broadly cross-sectoral and participatory than is usually the case. Of course, the changes needed to slow biodiversity loss will involve policy adjustments, some of which will not be easy. If disputes are anticipated and mechanisms for resolving them established now, any hardships born of change can be minimized.

The Strategy:
Contents and Catalysts

The *Global Biodiversity Strategy* calls on all nations and peoples to initiate and sustain a Decade of Action to conserve the world's biodiversity for the benefit of present and future generations.

During this period, a new and broader policy context must be created—one that addresses the fundamental need for sustainable development and tackles such international issues as world trading patterns and economic policy, debt and technology transfer, and such national issues as population growth, resource consumption and waste, land tenure, education, health care, and poverty. *(See Chapters 4-6.)* Supported by this policy context, biodiversity must be managed and conserved on the entire landscape, and throughout the full spectrum of human interactions with the environment. *(See Chapter 7.)* Traditional approaches to conservation must be at once strengthened and modified to fit into a more comprehensive approach. *(See Chapters 8-9.)* At the same time, the human capacity to live sustainably and advance conservation must be expanded through education, information and training. *(See Chapter 10.)*

The 85 actions proposed in the following chapters supports these broad goals and involve a diverse array of individuals and institutions, including international institutions, national governments, non-governmental organizations, scientists, and the private sector. They cannot and should not be undertaken or controlled by a single institution or program. Nevertheless, the *Strategy* will not work without a mechanism to stimulate the actions proposed here. For this reason, five of the 85 actions called for here have been identified as catalytic actions that can be undertaken quickly and at low cost to set off a cascade of subsequent actions by various sectors and institutions.

First, a key catalyst for conservation action will be the adoption, in 1992, of the international Convention on Biological Diversity currently being negotiated under the auspices of UNEP. Until this international legal framework is adopted, an international response to the current crisis will be hindered.

Second, to implement the actions detailed in the Global Biodiversity Strategy, a minimum of a decade of concerted work at local, national, and international levels is required. Accordingly, the General Assembly of the United Nations, should consider designating 1994-2003 the International Biodiversity Decade to ensure that this issue does not fade from governments' attention—or the public's—once the first actions are taken.

Third, a mechanism such as an International Panel on Biodiversity Conservation, composed of governmental representatives, scientists, citizen groups, industry, UN organizations, and non-governmental organizations should be created immediately to ensure broad participation in international decisions concerning biodiversity. This panel would be linked to the Convention on Biological Diversity and provide a forum for continuing dialogue on conservation needs and focus sustained attention on the threats created by biodiversity loss. The panel would immediately begin to develop priority lists of endangered species, sites, and ecosystems; and to advise on international priorities for research, funding, and action. Once the Biodiversity Convention comes into force, this same panel can help implement it.

Fourth, timely information on immediate threats to biodiversity must be provided to individuals and organizations that can act directly or indirectly to avert those threats: an Early Warning Network—which will again need to be appropriately linked to the Convention on Biological Diversity—should be established to monitor urgent threats to biodiversity and mobilize action against them. This Network would strengthen the global Earthwatch System, as called for by the U.N. General Assembly.

BOX 8

The Strategy in Brief

Catalyzing action through international cooperation and national planning

Establishing a national policy framework for biodiversity conservation -
■ Reform existing public policies that invite the waste or misuse of biodiversity.
■ Adopt new public policies and accounting methods that promote conservation and the equitable use of biodiversity.
■ Reduce demand for biological resources.

Creating an international policy environment that supports national biodiversity conservation -
■ Integrate biodiversity conservation into international economic policy.
■ Strengthen the international legal framework for conservation to complement the Convention on Biological Diversity.
■ Make the development assistance process a force for biodiversity conservation.
■ Increase funding for biodiversity conservation, and develop innovative, decentralized, and accountable ways to raise funds and spend them effectively.

Creating conditions and incentives for local biodiversity conservation -
■ Correct imbalances in the control of land and resources that cause biodiversity loss, and develop new resource management partnerships between government and local communities.
■ Expand and encourage the sustainable use of products and services from the wild for local benefits.
■ Ensure that those who possess local knowledge of genetic resources benefit appropriately when it is used.

Managing biodiversity throughout the human environment -
■ Create the institutional conditions for bioregional conservation and development
■ Support biodiversity conservation initiatives in the private sector.
■ Incorporate biodiversity conservation into the management of biological resources.

Strengthening protected areas -
■ Identify national and international priorities for strengthening protected areas and enhancing their role in biodiversity conservation.
■ Ensure the sustainability of protected areas and their contribution to biodiversity conservation.

Conserving species, populations, and genetic diversity -
■ Strengthen capacity to conserve species, populations, and genetic diversity in natural habitats.
■ Strengthen the capacity of off-site conservation facilities to conserve biodiversity, educate the public, and contribute to sustainable development.

Expanding human capacity to conserve biodiversity -
■ Increase appreciation and awareness of biodiversity's values and importance.
■ Help institutions disseminate the information needed to conserve biodiversity and mobilize its benefits.
■ Promote basic and applied research on biodiversity conservation.
■ Develop human capacity for biodiversity conservation.

FIGURE 6

Five Catalysts for Action

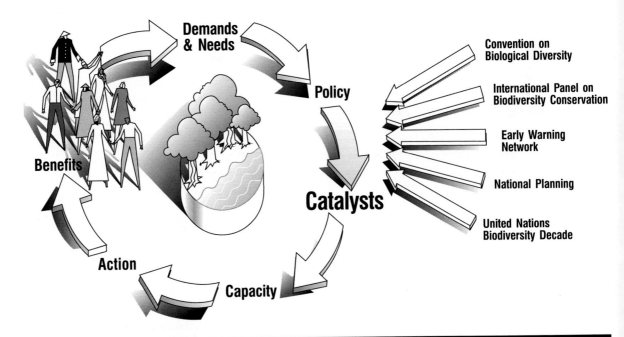

Since most of the actions needed to conserve biodiversity must be taken at the national level, the fifth critical catalytic action is the integration of biodiversity conservation into national planning processes. When governments incorporate biodiversity conservation into planning processes—a move that will probably take place only if public pressure mounts—the stimulus to build capacity, strengthen conservation tools, and mobilize biodiversity's benefits will be institutionalized and self-perpetuating.

Although these five catalytic actions, explained in detail below, can trigger action, mobilize funding, build awareness, and ensure broader dialogue and participation, they are not a substitute for action in the field. Nor are they the only catalytic elements of the action agenda. Many other measures that will stimulate governments, non-governmental organizations, and local communities to act are not featured here because their purpose is clearer in the context of other actions proposed in later chapters.

Financial support is urgent and could be considered another catalytic action. New international funding for biodiversity conservation is urgently required. *(See Action 27.)* Wide and balanced participation of countries in the North and South in the decisions over how those resources will be allocated is vital, as are equitable mechanisms for raising and spending funds. So is *national* commitment, since it is in each nations' interest to spend substantially more on conserving their own biodiversity.

Similarly, the identification of specific national priorities for protected areas and *ex situ* conservation will also help catalyze action. Both national and international assessments of present and future protected area needs are proposed in Chapter 8, and Chapter 9 calls for steps to strengthen genetic resources conservation capacity, building on the recently concluded Keystone International Dialogue on Plant Genetic Resources.

Catalysts for Action

Adopt, in 1992, the international Convention on Biological Diversity.

The Convention on Biological Diversity, currently being negotiated under the auspices of the United Nations Environment Programme (UNEP), should serve as a key coordinating, catalyzing, and monitoring mechanism for international biodiversity conservation. It will also be the primary means of establishing accepted international norms for biodiversity conservation. Although current international agreements cover some elements of biodiversity conservation, taken together they do not cover all of the world's threatened biodiversity, and they do not adequately address the closely related issues of use, ownership, funding, and technology transfer.

Equally important, most current agreements are aimed at saving biodiversity, not at using it sustainably and equitably. An international agreement is needed to set guidelines for how genetic resources will be used and to identify who will benefit from their use, particularly as biotechnology's importance grows.

Another key function for the Convention on Biological Diversity will be to establish a mechanism to provide substantial new funding for biodiversity conservation in developing countries. Experience with the Interim Multilateral Fund for the Montreal Protocol (on stratospheric ozone depletion) and the pilot Global Environment Facility (GEF) during its three years of operation (1991-1993) may provide guidance on how to set up and operate the Convention's funding mechanism. The Convention will also need to establish some way to develop funding priorities, perhaps building on the proposed International Panel on Biodiversity Conservation *(Action 3)* and the UNEP-led Biodiversity Country Studies. Finally, the Convention could incorporate various functions of the proposed Biodiversity Early Warning Network *(Action 4)*.

For developing countries, the attraction of the Convention is that it solidifies commitments of international financial and technical support for conservation, affords these nations greater say than they now have over how that support is allocated, strengthens their technical capacity for benefiting from biodiversity, and recognizes their sovereignty over biological resources within their territories. For industrialized countries, the convention will help ensure their continued access to genetic resources—albeit at a higher cost than before. The convention will also help all countries meet their shared commitment to conserve and rationally use biodiversity, and assure equitable sharing of benefits.

The Convention on Biological Diversity itself will include concrete commitments to deal with specific subjects. The process of negotiating all of the required protocols is expected to continue beyond 1992. The Convention or the protocols will have to cover such issues as technology transfer, additional funding, property rights, and access to genetic material.

Implementation of the actions called for in this *Strategy* need not be delayed until the Convention and its protocols are in place. To the contrary, taking action on the agenda proposed here will speed the convention process and increase its effectiveness.

BOX 9

Essential Elements of a Convention on Biodiversity

■ A commitment by governments to survey their natural living resources—both domesticated and wild—and to conserve sites noted for their rich biological diversity, as well as threatened species and domesticated varieties;

■ Recognition that both *in situ* conservation and *ex situ* preservation of biodiversity are key tools in any effective biodiversity conservation strategy.

■ A commitment by governments to ensure that any use of biodiversity is sustainable and equitable.

■ Recognition that conservation of biodiversity is a common concern of all humankind and that states have the sovereign right to use their biological resources.

■ Recognition that access to biodiversity is contingent upon prior informed consent of the country concerned and that those who possess traditional knowledge about genetic resources and farmers who have contributed to and maintained diversity in crops and livestock deserve just compensation for the use of their knowledge or their varieties.

■ The establishment of a financial mechanism that would provide both technical and financial assistance to developing countries in need of support for surveying, characterizing, and conserving their biodiversity.

■ The establishment of an administrative structure giving equal control to developed and developing countries that are Parties to the Convention in the distribution of funds under the Convention, and ensuring participation of scientists, governments, and non-governmental organizations to advise on funding priorities.

■ Arrangements by which the commercial exploiters of biodiversity help finance much of its conservation in the countries that give it refuge.

■ Mechanisms to ensure access for developing countries to technologies for conserving and using biodiversity.

■ The establishment of a monitoring and early-warning system to alert governments and the public to potential threats to biodiversity.

Action 2

Adopt, in the General Assembly of the United Nations, a resolution designating 1994-2003 the International Biodiversity Decade.

Declaration by the U.N. General Assembly of an International Biodiversity Decade would greatly increase awareness about biodiversity and the need to conserve it. A declaration would also signal the intent of governments to act to slow biodiversity loss, and would provide a tool for citizens to use in encouraging their governments to take action. It would help to coordinate and intensify the work of the U.N specialized agencies on biodiversity conservation. Finally, a U.N. Biodiversity Decade would provide impetus for many of the international actions called for in this *Strategy*, including establishment of the International Panel on Biodiversity Conservation, ratification and implementation of the Convention on Biological Diversity, and the establishment of a Biodiversity Early Warning Network.

Action 3

Establish a mechanism such as an International Panel on Biodiversity Conservation (preferably within the Convention on Biological Diversity), including scientists, non-governmental organizations, and policy-makers to provide guidance on priorities for the protection, understanding, and sustainable and equitable use of biodiversity.

Growing international awareness of the threats to biodiversity and increased funding for international conservation alike make it imperative that priorities are set through a process fully representative of local and national interests, and that global cooperation respects national sovereignty. The currently incomplete scientific understanding of biodiversity and lack of agreement on principles for action create a risk that poor choices will be made. Moreover, no framework exists to help guide action to promote and generate knowledge about biodiversity which can in turn guide actions and policies.

To remedy this situation, a mechanism—perhaps temporary—is needed to ensure the participation of all groups with an interest in biodiversity conservation and knowledge to contribute. Accordingly, a mechanism such as an International Panel on Biodiversity Conservation (IPBC) should be

established. Members should include representatives of governments, inter-governmental agencies, the scientific community, non-governmental organizations, and private business, from every part of the globe. The panel would commission studies and contributions by inter-governmental, national, and non-governmental technical and scientific centers, to provide background materials, and would publish guidelines and criteria to orient and assist governments, non-governmental groups, business and communities in their conservation activities.

This panel, which might eventually be replaced by a permanent body established under

FIGURE 7

International Panel on Biodiversity Conservation

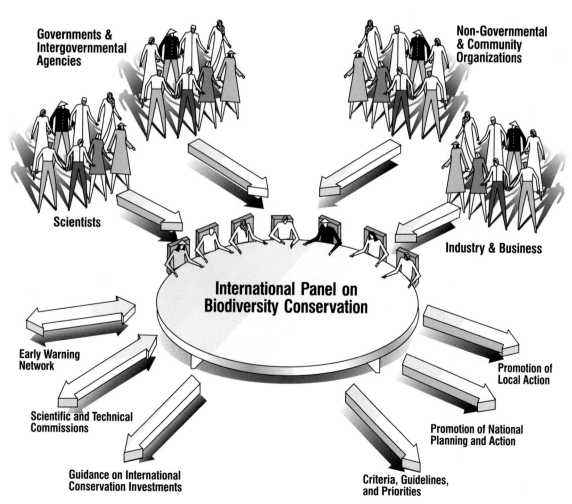

Governments & Intergovernmental Agencies

Non-Governmental & Community Organizations

Scientists

Industry & Business

International Panel on Biodiversity Conservation

Early Warning Network

Promotion of Local Action

Scientific and Technical Commissions

Promotion of National Planning and Action

Guidance on International Conservation Investments

Criteria, Guidelines, and Priorities

the Convention on Biological Diversity, would address five key needs. First, it would provide an international forum for continuing dialogue and debate among interested parties on the options for action to save, study and use biodiversity sustainably and equitably. This dialogue process, initiated under the auspices of this *Strategy*, the Keystone Center, FAO, IBPGR, UNEP's multidisciplinary advisory team for Biodiversity, Global Environment Facility/Scientific and Technical Advisory Panel (GEF/STAP) working group on Biodiversity, and other groups, is currently far from complete. Second, the Panel would summarize knowledge of the current status of biodiversity, rates of loss, and their implications for sustainable development. Third, it would provide advice on priorities for research, funding, and action. Fourth, anticipating the needs of the Biodiversity Convention, it would begin to make priority lists of endangered species, sites, and ecosystems. Finally, it would develop the terms of reference for an Early Warning Network for Biodiversity.

Specifically, the Panel's charge would be to:

■ produce within two years a comprehensive summary of current knowledge on the level of threats to biodiversity and the potential impacts of biodiversity's loss on sustainable development;

■ develop technical and scientific guidelines for setting priorities for ecosystem, species, and genetic conservation, based on such factors as endemism, species richness and interrelations, and ecological value, and upon the potential for sustainable management;

■ work with U.N. Agencies, IBPGR, The World Conservation Union (IUCN), governments, indigenous communities, and environmental NGOs to develop priority lists of wild, domesticated, or *ex situ* genetic resources threatened with extinction or genetic erosion; species or distinct populations threatened with extinction; regions and sites threatened with grave loss of biological diversity;

■ identify priority needs for building human capacity to protect, study, and use biodiversity; and,

■ develop terms of reference for an Early Warning Network for Biodiversity to monitor potentially urgent threats to biodiversity and to disseminate information about those threats. *(See Action 4.)*

Several mechanisms could be used for setting up the IPBC. For example, governments could establish the Panel through the U.N. General Assembly, the UNEP Governing Council, or the "Earth Summit" process (UNCED). Alternatively, the Panel could be formed under auspices of joint governmental/non-governmental organizations through UNEP, The World Conservation Union (IUCN), and WRI. Either way, the IPBC must *not* be restricted to government and international agency participation. Instead, it must function as a truly new kind of partnership among a broad set of actors if it is to be useful.

For example, the Panel could consist of approximately 60 members, with one-quarter of the membership drawn from governments, one quarter from international agencies, one-quarter from non-governmental conservation and development organizations, and one-quarter from the scientific community. To the extent possible, each of these groups should be free to choose their representatives, although the Ecosystems Conservation Group (composed of UNEP, UNESCO, FAO, IUCN, WWF and UNDP) might usefully serve as an *ad hoc* steering committee.

To function effectively, the Panel will require a full-time secretariat to coordinate its work, commission studies requested by the Panel, and carry out day-to-day administration. But to avoid excessive centralization, the Panel should convene regional consultations in all parts of the world—an approach that worked well during the development of this *Strategy*.

Funding for the Panel's work should be sought from governments, intergovernmental organizations, international conservation organizations, and private foundations. If the IPBC or its functions are institutionalized by the Convention on Biological Diversity, funding should be provided through the Convention's financial mechanism.

Action 4

Establish an Early Warning Network, linked to the Convention on Biological Diversity, to monitor potential threats to biodiversity and mobilize action against them.

Much can be done to avert loss of biodiversity in specific regions *if* adequate information on potential threats is available. If a development project is planned for a remote valley, non-governmental organizations or government institutions can arrange to collect traditional varieties of crops or wild relatives before the ecosystem is disturbed, or collaborate with local farmers to better conserve their traditional varieties. The environment ministry and national or international non-governmental organizations can speed up biodiversity assessments to determine if certain areas deserve protected status. And, in some cases, advance notice of project plans may bring to light new data that triggers a change in those plans.

A Biodiversity Early Warning Network should be set up to monitor urgent threats to biodiversity, disseminate information about those threats, and mobilize action against them. Within countries, the network would make use of governmental and non-governmental data sources, channeling information either formally through institutions and data collection networks or informally to the Early Warning Network secretariat. The IPBC could help set criteria for evaluating the urgency of threats, and disseminate information.

An Early Warning Network should monitor:

- traditional crop or livestock varieties threatened by planned or ongoing development projects or the introductions of new varieties;
- genebank facilities with germplasm at risk due to lack of funding for recurring costs;
- protected areas in urgent need of financial, technical, or other support;

- communities that lost access to resources when protected areas were established;
- increasing genetic uniformity of crops;
- climatic threats to biodiversity—including desertification, floods, drought, and global warming;
- introductions of exotic species;
- pollutant discharges presenting immediate threats to biodiversity or chronic pollution that might pose longer-term threats;
- rapid habitat loss; and,
- evidence of the over-exploitation of species.

Non-governmental organizations and scientists working in the field are the best sources of early warning information; the challenge is to make this information widely available to enforcement authorities, advocacy groups, and the general public, so that appropriate actions are swiftly mobilized. A number of existing environmental data reports and evaluations, notably *Global Biodiversity: Status of the Earth's Living Resources* (WCMC), *World Resources* reports (WRI), the *Environmental Data Report* (UNEP), and the UNEP Biodiversity Country Studies can provide valuable baseline information, as well as a vehicle for monitoring longer-term trends. Some of the organizations that produce these reports might also serve as focal points for data collection and dissemination in the Early Warning Network.

These institutions do not, however, provide a mechanism for "real time" alerts to impending threats to biodiversity. The Early Warning Network should be constructed to meet this need. It should be able to verify reports of threats rapidly, and communicate its findings in a fashion that is most likely to help avert the threat. The Secretariat of the Network could release "Action Alerts" to governments, conservation agencies, conservation organizations, the media, or individuals who have volunteered to serve as members of the Network. Such individual members could then press action on those responsible. Funding for the Network could come from individual memberships and donations as well as corporate and institutional sources: what is important is that the Network would not be constrained in its operations by its funding sources.

Action 5

Integrate biodiversity conservation into national planning processes.

Virtually all countries have various explicit or *de facto* planning processes for setting policy priorities, allocating resources, and dividing authority and responsibility among government agencies, between national and local governments, and between government and the private sector. In most, however, biodiversity concerns are neglected. Until biodiversity conservation becomes a stated national goal, investments will not be targeted to developing the national human, technological, and institutional capacity required to save, study, and use biodiversity comprehensively. Nor will the appropriate policy environment be established.

Incorporating biodiversity conservation into national policies and planning can help countries define and articulate their international interests. In addition, developing a "foreign policy on biodiversity" is increasingly important in the context of proposed conventions or agreements on biodiversity, forests, and climate change, the renegotiation of the General Agreement on Tariffs and Trade (GATT) and the International Tropical Timber Agreement (ITTA), and the increasing importance of biodiversity conservation as a criterion for development assistance. Countries that have not set biodiversity priorities, assessed their own biological resources, and determined both what they have to offer and what they want in return are at a distinct disadvantage at the international bargaining table.

Various planning mechanisms can be used to promote and integrate biodiversity conservation in development. Many countries may find national conservation strategies, tropical forest action plans, or environmental action plans useful. Others may be ready for an explicit National Biodiversity Action Plan that integrates disparate initiatives, covers the full range of biodiversity conservation issues, helps set priorities, and catalyzes action. Australia, for example, has established a Biological Diversity Advisory Committee to develop a National Strategy for the Conservation of Biodiversity for adoption in 1992, and Indonesia developed a National Biodiversity Action Plan in 1991.[36] Several other countries established National Biodiversity Units to oversee and coordinate the preparation of country studies to develop biodiversity conservation strategies. While each country's path will reflect its own goals, history, opportunities, and constraints, the principles and prerequisites listed in Box 10 should be considered by every country.

Implementing the Strategy

This *Strategy* calls for urgent action at all levels, from the international through the national, to local communities. These actions must be cross-sectoral and decentralized. Experience shows that the work of governments is hampered when sectoral divisions are rigid, and that grand "top-down" plans developed and decreed by central institutions cannot accommodate multiple interests or ensure fairness and accountability in the distribution of costs and benefits; they do not work very well either.

National governments must take the lead to set the normative policy framework, allocating resources and integrating biodiversity into their planning processes. Regional biodiversity plans are needed too, especially among countries that share important ecosystems. Community-level organizations and activities represent the front lines in making biodiversity conservation equitable and effective. International agreements, conventions, and institutions will make regional and global progress possible. Other key players include non-governmental organizations, indigenous communities, private business, education and training bodies, researchers, and information disseminators.

The partners and collaborators that compiled this *Strategy* will themselves incorporate the actions it calls for in their continuing programs, and they will monitor its implementation. They call upon other international agencies, governments and non-governmental organizations to join this campaign.

BOX 10

Principles and Guidelines for Planning Biodiversity Conservation

All sectors that influence biodiversity should help plan its conservation.

If biodiversity conservation is to expand beyond the traditional agenda—protected areas, programs to protect individual species, and *ex situ* conservation—then this broader mandate must be reflected in national biodiversity planning. All affected sectors and groups should get to present their views and priorities, and they should be held accountable for how their activities and investments affect the country's biodiversity.

Biodiversity planning must involve bottom-up and participatory negotiations, and priorities must be set at a bioregional level.

Although coordination among national government agencies is essential for effective biodiversity planning, many other actors and interests depend on biodiversity, influence it, possess valuable knowledge about it, and possess perspectives different from those of central government agencies. Because hard choices must be made in biodiversity planning, negotiation and compromise are essential. Effective negotiation and compromise among all stakeholders take time and cost money, and the process of coming to terms is likely to be initially contentious. But there is no other way to develop a plan that is truly national and that has a hope of being implemented. Moreover, the interests and viewpoints of particular "bioregions" within the country need to be directly represented in all national planning for biodiversity conservation. As a practical matter, once broad national goals are set, state or provincial planning meetings are needed to flesh out the actions to achieve those goals.

The ultimate planning authority for biodiversity conservation should rest within agencies with real power.

Where the locus of biodiversity planning is a relatively weak agency, plans rarely work. Conversely, effective planning requires leadership by one or more agencies with real power to allocate resources and set national priorities. For this reason, agencies charged with managing protected areas, forestry, or wildlife may not be the most suitable political center of biodiversity planning, even though they will certainly be important participants. Rather, ministries or departments of planning or finance—or those with equivalent power—should catalyze biodiversity planning, capitalizing on their proven ability to elicit cross-sectoral cooperation.

Biodiversity planners must set clear objectives and priorities.

Part of effective biodiversity planning is deciding what *not* to do. Financial, human, and institutional resources for biodiversity conservation are limited, and a lengthy "wish list" of everything that might be done with unlimited resources is no plan at all. Effective biodiversity planning begins with the elaboration of national objectives derived from broad-based participation and consultation. Once a consensus forms on objectives, practical priorities can be set along with corollary priorities for policy reform, legal change, institutional fortification, human resources development, and investments in the field.

continued on page 36

Policy reform and institutional change must be the central elements of biodiversity planning.

Most national environmental planning exercises focus excessively on developing projects for investment and getting them into the national plan. However, no biodiversity conservation investment or project should be approved until the policies and institutions that influence it are scrutinized. Indeed, concrete plans for eliminating or reducing policy weaknesses and institutional problems must be *part* of the plan. Since planning is too often equated with haggling over how to spend money, a focus on policy and institutional reform must be explicitly written into the legal terms of reference for biodiversity planning and championed by the agencies and individuals leading the planning.

The full range of conservation techniques and technologies must be considered in developing biodiversity conservation plans.

No single tool—be it national parks, zoos, agroforestry, or seed banks—can meet all the objectives of biodiversity conservation. Quite the contrary, the full range of options must be systematically considered in developing national biodiversity action plans. Traditionally, however, *in-situ* and *ex-situ* conservation techniques have been developed, deployed, and managed piecemeal by separate agencies and private institutions. As a result, there is little shared understanding of the advantages and limitations of each approach, and the various approaches are not used to support each other's objectives.

Biodiversity conservation planning exercises must include systematic attention to implementation.

Environmental planning and "national plans" of any sort have earned a bad name among those eager for swift, effective action. All too frequently, elaborate plans languish forgotten on the shelf. Lack of political sponsorship and broad participation may be to blame,

or lack of attention to implementation capacity, or both. Implementation issues get overlooked partly because institutions' formal mandates are often confused with their true operating capacities. Ministries of forestry in many countries, for example, are legally responsible for managing vast portions of public forest estate, but do not actually plant or harvest many trees. Similarly, many non-governmental organizations may have a deeply held commitment to, say, fostering community empowerment or conserving habitats but lack the wherewithal needed to do the job properly. Institutions involved in biodiversity planning must honestly evaluate their strengths and weaknesses. They must be prepared to shoulder more—or less—authority and responsibility where circumstances dictate and decide how to strengthen their roles in implementing the biodiversity conservation plan.

Mechanisms for monitoring implementation must be built into the planning process.

Monitoring implementation is essential. A program for evaluation must be clearly defined and the plan must include milestones and criteria for measuring success. Ongoing evaluation not only ensures implementation, it also provides the feedback needed to improve the plan in response to changing circumstances and new data. Implementation depends not only on the commitment of real programs and funds by governments, but also on citizen participation. Just as keen public interest is necessary at the front end of a planning exercise, citizens are also needed as "watchdogs" as the plan is implemented.

IV

Establishing a National Policy Framework for Biodiversity Conservation

Biodiversity is such an important national concern that the developing countries need to formulate policies that recognize its economic importance. The parallel is to do for biodiversity what Japan has done for microelectronics. Biodiversity in this respect would become a lead sector around which other developments would revolve. This is also a renewable resource, if treated as such, and is thus more reliable than oil or diamonds. We recently stated to a senior Kenyan government official that biodiversity was more important to Kenya than diamonds were to South Africa. We got an appointment to see him the same afternoon!

CALESTOUS JUMA, AFRICAN CENTER FOR TECHNOLOGY STUDIES, KENYA

Biodiversity is ultimately lost or conserved at the local level. Government policies, however, create the incentives that facilitate or constrain local action. Governments regularly intervene in markets to increase agricultural production, spur industrial growth, provide a "safety net" for the poor, protect the environment, and support other public goods that the market allocates poorly. Unfortunately, many industrial, transportation, natural resource, and urban development policies fail to value environmental resources correctly and may even hasten resource depletion and biodiversity loss. Indeed, some policies explicitly invite the over-exploitation of species, conversion of valuable natural habitats, and over-simplification of agricultural ecosystems.

Reforming such policies makes economic as well as ecological sense. Inappropriate subsidies for resource use drain national economies and impede development. Agricultural support policies in industrialized countries cost consumers and taxpayers an estimated $150 billion annually, yet lead to environmental impoverishment.[37] Some

57 percent of the budget of the European Community went to agricultural price supports in 1990, compared to only 1 percent spent on environmental protection.[38] Indonesia's forest policies cost the country $2 billion between 1979 and 1982.[39] Given the magnitude of these expenditures and losses, investments in biodiversity conservation may be more than offset by savings from policy reforms.

The resource and trade policies of most countries do not take biodiversity's potential benefits into account. Enhanced food security, economic development, and improved medical care are all based on biological productivity and the diversity of genes and species. But to reap these benefits, governments must first develop a sound policy framework. Many nations fail to provide incentives for either the development or acquisition of the technical skills needed to conserve biodiversity, or to explore its capacity to yield new products.

Objective:

Reform existing public policies that invite the waste or misuse of biodiversity

The aim of environmental management policies should be the optimal and sustainable use of natural resources. Policies that provide incentives for the wasteful and unsustainable exploitation of such resources, and the unnecessary reduction of biodiversity should be primary candidates for overhaul. Such policies include those that promote over-exploitation of forests, damaging extension of urbanization and agriculture onto diverse natural habitats, over-use of freshwater and marine fisheries, or the excessive use of monocultures and agrochemicals.

Action 6

Abandon forestry policies that encourage resource degradation and the conversion of forest ecosystems to other less valuable uses.

Public policies governing logging, the development of timber-processing industries, and reforestation catalyze deforestation in many countries. *(See Figure 8.)* Timber revenues capture only a small portion of the economic rent available from forest production, and governments sell timber at far below market rates. Throughout the world, many private contractors who obtain timber concessions extract only the best specimens of the most valuable species, disturbing extensive forest areas in the process. The short duration of most concessions also reinforces a "cut and run" mentality, and few incentives for forest regeneration are on the books. Even where laws provide for reforestation, they are seldom backed up by effective regulation and enforcement.

In the past decade, many timber-producing countries have also provided subsidies and adopted other policies to give domestic wood-processing industries a boost. Because it generates additional revenues from the same amount of raw material, value-added domestic processing is in theory an efficient way to reduce pressure on standing forests. However, such policies are often impeded by the imposition by developed countries of import tariffs that weigh much more heavily on manufactured products like furniture than on raw materials like logs. The result is that disproportionate volumes of unsawn timber have to be exported to sustain national income. It is important that such obstacles are removed, but it also is important that economic policies in exporting countries do not promote the establishment of more processing facilities than market demand indicates and sustainably managed forests can supply.

Many governments are also developing policies to promote timber plantations to meet growing demand for industrial wood and fiber and to reforest degraded lands. Rapid plantation development, especially in the tropics, is also receiving attention as a way to respond to global warming. Such plantations can, of course, reduce pressure on natural forests and provide vegetative cover for degraded lands. But policies in some countries, especially in Southeast Asia, are turning timber plantations into an *agent* of deforestation rather than a solution to it. Such is the case where plantations on marginal agricultural lands force former residents to move into natural forest areas, or where natural forest stands are converted to plantations.

Sound timber plantation policy must avoid three particular traps. First, no policy should promote the conversion of diverse natural forests to plantations. Plantations should be sited on already deforested and unproductive lands. Second, no policy should condone or support the displacement of rural communities through the privatization of their *de facto* common lands. Many lands categorized legally as "degraded public land" are, in fact, much more valuable in their present form to rural communities than if they were converted into a commercial plantation. Third, no policy should promote the establishment of uninterrupted monocultural stands over large areas. Although such stands are cheap to establish and easy to harvest, they are also vulnerable to disease, market fluctuations, and changes in technology. Accordingly, plantations should be employed only within a patchwork of land use that includes native tree species and wildlife and that provides products, livelihoods, and living space to local communities.

Action 7

Reform policies that result in the degradation and loss of biodiversity in coastal and marine ecosystems.

There are many causes of the loss during recent decades of marine biodiversity, especially in the

---

BOX 11

Biodiversity and Industry

Industry, already burdened with environmental regulations, is far from enthusiastic about biodiversity conservation, but it should be. The corporate interests that stand to lose from biodiversity conservation are those that base their profits on unsustainable resource use. But for industries that do seek to manage resources sustainably, biodiversity conservation provides significant opportunities.

One of industry's greatest needs is *predictability*. Today, a firm might invest substantial sums in a development project, only to find its plans halted when an environmental review turns up an endangered species or a rare plant community. Biodiversity conservation, in contrast, involves up-stream planning that can prevent such financial fiascos. The time and work spent inventorying and protecting species and ecosystems means that the distribution of threatened fauna and flora will be known *before* the first dollar is invested in a project. Granted, some sites will be closed to development as a result, but certainty about the rest will more than offset those losses.

Moreover, biodiversity conservation provides greater *options* for industry and development planning. Current regulatory practices come into effect only when a crisis is already at hand—when a species is on the brink of extinction. No options are left: either the species goes or the development project goes. In contrast, the upstream planning entailed in biodiversity conservation reveals new opportunities for planners and helps them keep potential conflicts from erupting.

Despite these opportunities, industry cannot be expected to support biodiversity conservation until criteria and guidelines are developed that will clarify the actions it must take. Currently, industry is being taken to task for not conserving biodiversity, but it has no widely accepted indicators of biodiversity's status to use in planning.

---

coastal waters of industrialized countries. Among the most important are direct habitat destruction through the erection of engineering and drainage works that disturb the physical integrity of coastal and marine systems; poor fisheries management; the uncontrolled exploitation of corals and mollusks; the "by-catch" of large numbers of non-target species in fisheries; the introduction of alien species; and the overall lack of an integrated approach to coastal zone management. As a consequence, the productivity of fisheries and such important ecosystems as mangroves and coral reefs has been depressed, and local communities have suffered.

Four basic kinds of policy change are needed to put marine resource management on a sustainable footing. First, governments should review all the activities within their jurisdiction that affect the coastal zones and oceans, including activities on land and within river catchments. They should then develop integrated policies that coordinate the allo-

cation of uses in the coastal zone, especially to safeguard the rights and interests of local communities. They should also regulate activities—like the overcutting of mangroves or inappropriate extension of mariculture—that have destroyed coastal ecosystems or increased the vulnerability of coasts to erosion and storm surges.

Second, pollutant discharge into coastal seas and via inflowing rivers should be strictly controlled. About 70 to 80 percent of marine pollution comes from land-based sources.[40] Governments should adopt the "precautionary principle" to minimize inputs of potentially damaging substances and draw up plans for rehabilitating degraded coastal ecosystems.

Third, fishery policies should be reviewed. Small-scale, community-based fisheries account for almost half the world food catch, employ more than 95 percent of the people engaged in fishing, and use only 10 percent of the energy of large-scale corporate fisheries.[41] They are also vital to the livelihood of local communities. Governments should reverse policies that discriminate against such fisheries, especially policies that invalidate local common property systems for managing fisheries. Governments should also adopt an ecosystem approach to the management of fishery resources in both coastal and nearshore seas and ensure that catches are kept within maximum sustainable yields. *(See Figure 9.)* They should also ban the use of unselective and destructive fishing systems (such as monofilament drift nets) by their nationals and in their coastal waters and Exclusive Economic Zones. Governments should base fisheries policy primarily on ecological assessments of sustainable harvest levels, rather than on political and economic considerations.

Fourth, governments should support international legal instruments for protecting the seas against pollution and misuse. The United Nations Convention on the Law of the Sea should be brought into force immediately. International cooperation, especially within UNEP's Regional Seas Programme, should be extended. Research collabora-

FIGURE 8

Forest Clearing in Central America, 1940 to 1982

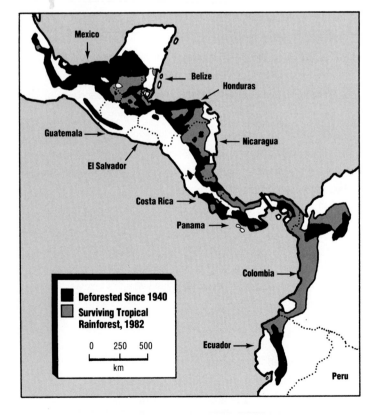

Deforested Since 1940
Surviving Tropical Rainforest, 1982

0   250   500
km

Source: Nations and Comer 1982

tion under international agreements should also be strengthened. All states that have not done so should ratify the conventions controlling pollution from ships and from the dumping of wastes.

Action 8

Reform policies that hasten loss of biodiversity in freshwater ecosystems.

Freshwater ecosystems are damaged primarily because the potential impacts of industrial, urban, energy, and agricultural policies on these ecosystems are disregarded. Around the world, hydropower and irrigation development has destroyed freshwater habitat, and pollutants from farms, cities, and factories have been discharged into rivers, killing off species and dramatically altering riverine ecosystems.

To promote local agriculture and urban and industrial development, governments have often subsidized water, thereby encouraging waste. Some legal regimes make matters worse by recognizing water rights only if they are continually exercised; thus, farmers who conserve water may lose their rights to the water saved. Governments should fully evaluate the environmental impacts of water development projects and strictly control pollutant discharges into freshwater systems. They should also end inappropriate freshwater subsidies and reform the legal regimes governing water rights and allocations so as to encourage better maintenance of fresh water quality and supply. The full environmental impact of water impoundments should be assessed and the effects on biodiversity minimized. Finally, governments should regulate groundwater extraction carefully to ensure that aquifers are not being depleted faster than they can recharge naturally and that locally endemic species of fish, amphibians, and invertebrates do not fall victim to groundwater depletion.

FIGURE 9

Level of Exploitation and Maximum Sustainable Yield of Marine Fishery Resources in the Gulf of Thailand and the West Coast of Peninsular Thailand, 1983

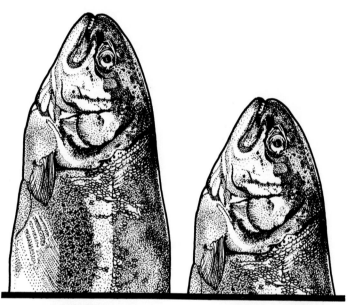

2,055,255 Tons
1983 Level of Exploitation

1,450,000 Tons
Estimated Maximum Sustainable Yield

Source: Arbhabhirama et. al. 1987

Action 9

Eliminate agricultural policies that promote excessive uniformity of crops and crop varieties or that encourage the overuse of chemical fertilizers and pesticides.

Despite astounding gains in agricultural productivity in past decades, many national agricultural policies are economically inefficient and environmentally unsound. By enriching mainly farmers with large land holdings, they have also penalized

FIGURE 10

Growing World Market in Pesticides and Growing Resistance of Species to Pesticides

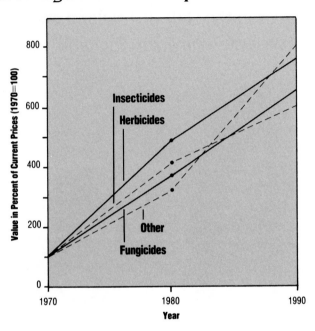

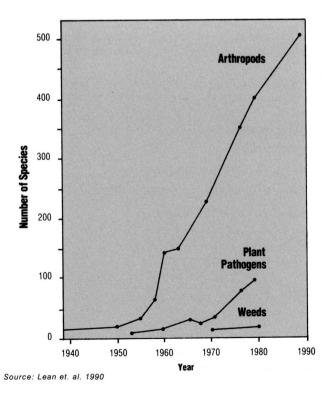

Source: Lean et. al. 1990

farmers cultivating smaller parcels. In developing countries, food-price controls and subsidies for agricultural inputs have combined to meet short-term consumer demands but have removed incentives to step up agricultural production and have undermined food security. These policies have also decreased the diversity of species used by farmers, increased crop and livestock uniformity, and made farmers dependent on expensive and often unreliable sources of agricultural inputs.

Up to a point, uniformity in agricultural practices and varieties can improve crops' productivity. But many current policies, especially the following, exceed that point:

■ *agricultural input subsidies.* By reducing the cost of such inputs as water, pesticides, and chemical fertilizers, subsidies promote "industrial" agriculture based on a small number of highly uniform crops at the expense of farming systems based on a wider crop variety. Cheap inputs sometimes also replace natural processes—based on biodiversity—that are equally effective at lower cost to people and to the environment. Pesticides, for instance, have displaced such natural enemies of agricultural pests as microorganisms and invertebrates. *(See Figure 10.)*

■ *food price subsidies.* Government actions to reduce food prices for urban consumers cut into farm profits. Combined with subsidies for inputs, such food-price controls can greatly reduce agricultural diversity. For farmers using modern crop varieties requiring irrigation and heavy doses of agrochemicals, input subsidies help neutralize the impact of food-price controls. But farmers using low-input systems and traditional varieties receive no such offsetting benefit. This policy combination also discourages low-input farmers from developing new varieties of their own and it indirectly erodes knowledge of traditional varieties.

■ *overvalued exchange rates.* Many governments in developing countries have overvalued their currencies to subsidize imported capital goods for industry, lower the costs of imported food, and lower the prices of exported food. These policies basically "tax" all agriculture, but farmers who use fewer manufactured imports are taxed more than those who use more. Like the combination of input subsidies and food price controls discussed above, this combination favors industrial agriculture, with its attendant reduction in diversity.

■ *research biased toward high-input agriculture.* The driving force in national agricultural research has always been to increase production of a few major crops through technology change. This research model, exported from the industrialized to the developing world through the international agricultural research system, may have provided much-needed "breathing room" in the race between production and population. But to meet future production needs, national governments must support agricultural systems that meet food needs while maintaining important components of diversity.

■ *credit policies that discriminate against "minor" crops and traditional varieties.* All too often, governments fail to extend agricultural credit to farmers planting traditional crop varieties or growing crops consumed locally. Particularly in developing countries, where the benefits of "improved" varieties may be negligible in marginal agriculture, reduced productivity and accelerated loss of crop diversity are the results.

Objective:

Adopt new public policies and accounting methods that promote conservation and the equitable use of biodiversity

Action 10

Assert national sovereignty over genetic resources and regulate their collection.

Genetic resources have traditionally been treated as though they were a common heritage of humankind—free to all who could use them. In practice, some restrictions on access have existed for decades—notably, the limited monopoly rights to germplasm granted to plant breeders in many countries. But until now most nations have supported free access to the "unimproved" germplasm in wild species or traditional varieties of crops or livestock.

The growing importance of biotechnology has forced a reassessment of the ownership issue. Simply put, biotechnology has made genetic resources much more valuable and called into question the wisdom of treating them as free goods. The emergence of new chemical screening technologies has prompted many large pharmaceutical corporations to reestablish programs to screen wild plant and animal species for potential drugs. And new genetic engineering techniques have increased plant breeders' interest in genes from wild plant relatives, unrelated plants, animals, or microorganisms. Since biotechnology depends on biodiversity for its raw material, the value of genetic resources will grow with the industry.

As the value of genetic resources grows, so do incentives to conserve biodiversity. Countries should not necessarily begin to charge for access to these resources, recognize private rights to the country's genetic wealth, or restrict flows of genetic resources. But national governments should assert their right to control the genetic resources that they hold, consider establishing property rights regimes, and carefully regulate the collection of plants, animals, and microorganisms, particularly those collected for commercial purposes. This will lay the groundwork should the market dictate significant changes in laws governing ownership and access.

The ownership question has two distinct but related dimensions: property rights over genetic resources (physical property) and rights over intellectual contributions to the resource's development (intellectual property). In the past, intellectual property rights for genetic resources covered only innovations made by plant breeders, pharmaceutical firms, and chemical companies. Practical constraints aside, however, such protection should not be denied to medicinal healers, small farmers who have developed new local varieties of crops, or other informal innovators. To keep this possibility open, countries should require collectors of genetic resources to negotiate contracts with those who possess extraordinary knowledge of these resources. (See Chapter 6.)

Still further removed from physical property are property interests in the development of information about a genetic resource or the provision of services related to the resource. Since either can command a financial return, whether or not the genetic resource itself is private property, public institutions or private firms within a country could increase the share of economic benefits from the commercial use of genetic resources that remains within the country. For example, even if a local firm screening plants for potential therapeutic activity could not patent any knowledge gained, it could use knowledge of the extracts to command a higher royalty with a pharmaceutical company than it otherwise would have obtained. Similarly, a genebank could charge for the value it added to germplasm when it evaluates and characterizes the material. Such a scheme would make available more information about the resource and provide

financial incentives for its conservation, thereby facilitating the flow of the material (not impeding it, as some fear). Genebanks must ensure, however, that they take no steps that violate their obligation to hold germplasm in trust for the world's people. Genebanks may have the right to control access to information that they develop about genetic material but not to regulate access to the genetic material itself.

Both public and private institutions that sample and screen genetic resources could easily make their efforts pay. Some businesses now broker deals between biotechnology and pharmaceutical firms and the companies that collect or screen genetic resources in developing countries. The firm developing the product pays an up-front sum to the collecting institution and agrees to pay a royalty if a product is marketed. A related model is being used by the National Biodiversity Institute (INBio) in Costa Rica. INBio screens biological materials for useful products and enters into royalty agreements with companies interested in developing a product. Funds generated this way will go into a conservation fund for Costa Rica, managed by a national board. (See Box 34, Chapter 10.) In both cases, by working through brokering and collecting institutions in return for a share of the royalties, the biotechnology or pharmaceutical company receives reliable quantities of clearly identified species for less than they could collect the material themselves, and the contract minimizes the room for patent disputes.

Even more important than the financial benefits of such agreements is their potential to foster technology exchange and help local institutions develop. New agreements could require that further screening take place in the materials' country of origin, that the buying institution train local laboratory workers, or that workers from recipient institutions spend time at the local facility.

Even without claiming ownership of the genes themselves, intellectual property rights and "value added" enterprises could yield handsome profits for the nation. But what about the physical property itself? Suppose a foreign biotechnology company randomly collects plants and animals on public and private lands. Should the company negotiate contracts with the state? With the private landowners? Who should get the royalty if a botanical garden collects a specimen, and a decade later a pharmaceutical company isolates a valuable compound in the material? Should countries claim ownership of the germplasm they have donated to international seedbanks? If private landowners are granted ownership rights to the genetic resources on their land, what prevents a collector from playing one landowner against another to reduce the royalty, since most species span relatively large areas? If the state assumes ownership, what prevents a collector from trying to strike a deal with the adjacent state?

Because these questions still lack answers, there is no reason yet to establish regimes governing physical ownership of genetic resources. Moreover, huge amounts of money are not yet involved. By one estimate, the total return to developing countries of imposing royalties or fees on traditional crop varieties probably would not exceed $100 million per year.[42] (Up-front payments for randomly collected material are on the order of $30 for each one-half to one-kilogram sample, and royalties are typically only 1 or 2 percent of profits.) Similarly, the likelihood of a randomly collected plant yielding a patentable chemical is roughly one chance in ten thousand.

Short of establishing strict ownership regimes over the physical property of genetic resources, states could also tax commercial collecting or plant-screening operations, seed companies, biotechnology firms, and pharmaceutical houses that use genetic resources. This way, some of the practical difficulties of establishing property rights regimes could be skirted while still capturing some resource value, thereby providing a conservation incentive.

Action 11

Strictly regulate the transfer of species and genetic resources and their release into the wild.

Although reforming policies governing the exploitation of biological resources can greatly reduce threats to biodiversity from habitat loss, pollution, over-exploitation, and industrialized agriculture, they do nothing to curb the introduction of exotic species and genetic resources. But such controls are essential to the safe exchange of biodiversity. *(See Box 12.)*

Some countries have no such regulatory policies, but in most countries, the need is for stronger policies and better enforcement. The stakes are high. Between 1967 and 1972, an African cichlid fish introduced into Gatun Lake in Panama wiped out six of the eight previously common fish species,

---

BOX 12

Guidelines for Translocations of Living Organisms

■ Introduction of an alien species should be considered only if clear and well-defined benefits to man or natural communities can be expected.

■ Introduction of an alien species should be considered only if no native species seems suitable for the same purpose.

■ No alien species should be deliberately introduced into any natural habitat (one not perceptibly altered by man), island, lake, or ocean, whether within or beyond the limits of national jurisdiction.

■ Introductions should not be made into semi-natural habitats except for exceptional reasons and only when the operation has been comprehensively investigated and carefully planned in advance.

■ Introductions into highly modified habitats should take place only after the effects on surrounding natural and semi-natural habitats are assessed.

Source: IUCN, 1987

drastically reduced populations of a seventh, and took a toll up and down the food chain among aquatic invertebrates, algae, and fish-eating birds.[43] A species of snail introduced on the South Pacific island of Moorea in 1977 (to control another introduced species) wiped out six native species of snails (one of which became extinct, while six were preserved in captivity).[44] Zebra mussels, native to the Black and Caspian seas and introduced into North

American inland waters in 1986 when a ship emptied its ballast water near Detroit, have clogged water supply systems which will cost $5 billion over the next decade.[45] The screwworm arrived in Libya in 1988, probably with a shipment of livestock from Central America, and the potentially lethal parasite spread through 40,000 square miles before a $40-million eradication program apparently succeeded in 1991. The screwworm threatened some 70 million head of livestock in North Africa and could have spread to Sub-Saharan Africa, the Middle East, southern Europe and Asia.[46] *(See Figure 11.)*

Even introducing the *same* species can present hazards through the mixing of genetic stocks. In many fish hatcheries, the wild population has been genetically "contaminated" by interbreeding with the introduced varieties. Furthermore, largely homozygous fish under culture in ponds or in cages at sea can reduce the heterozygosity of the same species in the wild should they escape and interbreed.

In many cases, introducing new crops or livestock or new varieties can be extremely beneficial. All countries grow some crops imported from other regions. In Australia, the Mediterranean, northern Europe, northern Asia, the United States, and Canada, more than 90 percent of agricultural production derives from introduced species; in many countries in tropical Africa (such as Kenya), most of the major crops are derived from foreign species.[47] But agricultural introductions (especially of genetically modified organisms) can also be risky, and countries need strong regulatory policies governing domesticated species introductions.

Regulations need to consider the potential *social* impacts of introductions too. Introducing high-yielding crop varieties that are dependent on expensive inputs can significantly influence local employment, land costs, and local business; communities should have a say about the types of varieties introduced, and regulations should stress the need for public information on proposed releases. Even where an introduction is judged beneficial, the potential impacts cannot be minimized unless the

FIGURE 11

Spread of the Screwworm in Libya Prior to 1991 Control Program and Potential Range of Screwworm

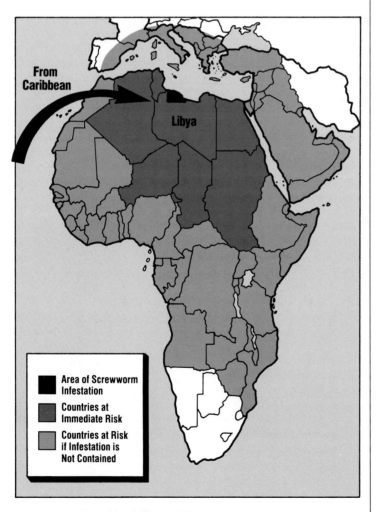

From Caribbean

Libya

Area of Screwworm Infestation

Countries at Immediate Risk

Countries at Risk if Infestation is Not Contained

Source: FAO/SENCA, 1991 (unpublished data)

local communities and institutions responsible for conserving biodiversity are alerted to upcoming releases. Fundamentally, regulations must ensure that no organism can be released without first getting the host country government's consent.

Introducing genetically engineered organisms presents unique risks since laboratory results alone make a poor guide to their behavior, ecological impacts, and potential socio-economic effects. Accordingly, strict codes of conduct related to the release of such organisms are urgently needed in all countries and at the international level. *(See Box 13.)*

A draft "International Code of Conduct for Plant Germplasm Collecting and Transfer" is currently under review by the FAO Commission on Plant Genetic Resources. Chances are that the commission will accept this code when it meets in April, 1993. Governments should expand their own regulations even beyond the proposed FAO code to explicitly include other living organisms.

Action 12

Establish incentives for effective and equitable private-sector plant breeding and research.

Agricultural advances come most efficiently through a combination of both public and private research. In industrialized countries, considerable emphasis has been placed on strengthening incentives for private-sector innovation by creating intellectual property rights (IPR) regimes, including plant breeders' rights, plant patents for asexually reproducing plant varieties, and utility patents. This suite of IPR regimes has had mixed success and for several reasons is now changing. Four factors in particular are forcing these changes: the emergence of new biotechnologies, the continuing erosion of genetic diversity, the recognition of inequities in current regimes, and the acceptance of IPRs' importance in technology transfer.

BOX 13

Guidelines for Minimizing the Potential Social and Ecological Dangers of Biotechnology

The following general guidelines address the potential negative impacts that new biotechnologies may have if not carefully regulated in their development, testing, and use. Development of detailed guidelines at national, regional, and international levels should be a priority for the 1990s.

■ Countries should develop the capacity needed to monitor and control new biotechnologies in advance of their development and testing.

■ The dangers of releasing genetically modified organisms should be more carefully assessed, especially where genetic diversity is high.

■ The importation of genetically modified organisms, plasmids, and other materials to any country should be strictly regulated.

■ Biotechnology should be regulated to prevent excessive uniformity of plant and animal varieties that may arise through the use of new techniques, such as the clonal propagation of planting materials or embryo transfer in livestock.

■ Biotechnology should not be developed, tested, or used for military purposes, such as biological warfare.

■ Mechanisms should be established at both national and international levels to compensate and support farming communities and countries harmed when new biotechnology-based crops or products are substituted for existing ones.

■ An early warning network, monitoring the socio-economic impact of biotechnology and its effects on biodiversity, should be established to prevent further marginalization of small farmers.

■ An International Code of Conduct on biotechnology should be developed to regulate biotechnology at all levels.

Since few developing countries have IPR regimes for crop genetic resources, governments should establish or expand private-sector programs while recognizing farmers' rights over local genetic resource innovations. But new IPR regimes must be backed up by strengthened public agricultural institutions that can meet those farmers' needs unmet by the private sector, furnish unfinished germplasm to private breeders, train breeders, develop solid seed-certification programs, and enforce regulations.

To tailor IPR regimes to current needs, nations should draw on the experience of other countries and on such international conventions as the International Union for the Protection of New Varieties of Plants (UPOV). Gradually, countries should also harmonize their various IPR regimes, but technological and economic differences must be kept in mind here. IPR regimes designed for industrialized countries, for instance, may require levels of monitoring and enforcement not found in many developing countries, and countries may clash over ethical norms. (The United States allows the patenting of human genetic material, for instance, while many countries do not.) In any case, nations should adopt IPR regimes only after farmers, breeders, and the government carefully consider the programs' costs and benefits and only when such programs encourage both local innovation and the conservation and maintenance of genetic diversity.

Finally, countries should establish national review boards and an ombudsman office to monitor IPR regimes to help ensure that any negative impacts on either biological diversity or social welfare are addressed quickly. Since a mere handful of businesses and affluent market-oriented farmers could reap an unfair share of the benefits of biodiversity development, and small businesses could lose patent disputes just because they cannot afford legal assistance, such a public forum for airing disputes among non-governmental organizations, local communities, and the public sector is needed.

Action 13

Modify national income accounts to make them reflect the economic loss that results when biological resources are degraded and biodiversity is lost.

Currently, such ecosystems as forests and wetlands are treated as essentially "free goods," and their degradation does not count as depreciation of a nation's basic capital stock in calculations of Gross National Product (GNP). Moreover, much of the use and misuse of biotic resources takes place in the informal economy, which national income accounts do not monitor. The result is a distorted picture of a nation's economic health. *(See Figure 12.)* With this picture in mind, governments make ill-advised policies and back inappropriate development projects, the private sector receives the wrong market signals, and biodiversity loss accelerates. The EXXON-Valdez oil spill in Alaska, for example, actually *increased* the U.S. GNP: billions of dollars were spent on clean-up, and resource losses did not show up on the ledger.

More credible methods for assessing biodiversity's economic worth and for building the national capacity needed to carry out such analysis are sorely needed. While the valuation of biological resources is relatively straightforward, methodologies for assigning value to the *variety* of life itself are in their infancy. Universities, research institutions, non-governmental organizations, and others with appropriate expertise should redouble efforts to refine methodologies for quantifying biodiversity's contribution to local and national economies.

Within such a framework, economists could compare the value of conserving biodiversity on particular sites with the opportunity costs of deferring or foregoing investment in commodity production on that same area, or of converting that natural habitat to other uses. Planners could incorporate costs related to lost genetic resources, degraded watersheds, or species extinctions in calculations of the social benefits of various development options; policy advisors could better analyze market and policy failures that distort the relative merits and drawbacks of conservation and development.

Developing credible methodologies for "biodiversity accounting" is only a first step. National governments should by this decade's end revise their systems for calculating national income accounts to incorporate the values of biological resources and, where possible, of biodiversity itself. Governments must also revise their official cost-benefit calculus. Some 20 countries are already developing national balance sheets for the more easily "monetized" natural resources, such as soil and timber. Getting decision-makers to use them, however, remains a political challenge.

To back up national efforts, the United Nations should revise its System of National Accounts (SNA) to incorporate the value of biological resources, and it should help improve the methods used to set such values. Changes in the SNA proposed in 1991 already include a natural resources "stock account" balance sheet for assets that—like land, sub-soil minerals, fisheries, and timber—can be tangibly quantified as productive assets at any given time. While this is an important change, the SNA does not yet include the same "stock" information in its "flow" accounts (which reflect change in the natural capital stock between two dates). Unfortunately, the failure to fully incorporate the insights of recent research on natural resource accounting into the SNA decreases the whole system's accuracy and value.

Ideally, conservation decisions should never be made strictly on the basis of cost-benefit analyses because many ethical, aesthetic, and other values of biological resources elude measurement. Nevertheless, every effort must be made to develop a consistent and comparable valuation framework and to make methodologies for valuing biological resources more accurate.

Objective:

Reduce demand for biological resources

If current high rates of population growth and increasing rates of resource consumption do not drop, growing demand for resources will overwhelm even the best managed production systems. For example, despite the yield improvements of the Green Revolution, total world cropland area

---

FIGURE 12

Costa Rica's Agricultural Product Before and After Natural Resource Depreciation, which Accounts for Value Lost Due to Deforestation, Soil Erosion, and Overfishing

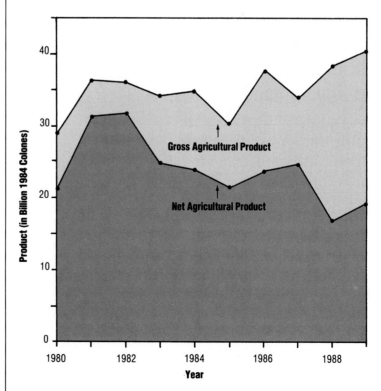

Source: Repetto et al. 1991

FIGURE 13

Energy Consumption Per Capita in Bangladesh, Japan, and the United States, 1987 (gigajoules)

280
Gigajoules

110
Gigajoules

1
Gigajoule

United States   **Japan**   **Bangladesh**

Source: U.S. Bureau of the Census 1990; World Resources Institute 1990

increased by 332 million hectares between 1950 and 1980, much of it at the expense of forests, wetlands, and natural grasslands, and a good deal of it on land that was unsuitable for agriculture. Since most countries have reached their arable land frontier already, more biologically productive but agriculturally marginal habitat will continue to be converted. Larger populations also require more energy, and in the developing world this need translates largely into fuelwood demand. Population and consumption growth also contribute to the over-harvesting of fisheries stocks, which are already yielding at near their calculated ceiling.

The message is clear. Unless growth in demand is slowed to levels in keeping with the capacity of technology and natural resources, the long-term prospects for biodiversity conservation and sustainable development are dim. In developing countries the essential need is for a mix of economic growth, efficient resource use and the stabilization of human populations at a level the environment can sustain. In developed countries, current wasteful over-consumption of energy and natural resources should be curbed, and this will in itself facilitate sustainable global development. *(See Figure 13.)*

Many of the actions needed to reduce resource demand are described in detail in *Caring for the Earth.*[48] Three of extreme importance to biodiversity include:

Action 14

Provide universal access to family planning services and increase funding to support their adoption.

A large gap exists between the demand for family planning services and their supply. Recent studies indicate that if quality family planning services were readily available, about three-fourths of all reproductive-age couples in most countries would use them, compared to about one-half today.[49] Improved access to family planning could greatly help nations reduce their population growth rates. If all women who wished to have no more children had access to family planning services, the number of births would be reduced by 27 percent in Africa, 33 percent in Asia, and 35 percent in Latin America.[50] Family planning services would also improve maternal and child health, and in smaller families children would enjoy increased educational opportunities and women would enjoy greater freedom.

Leadership is essential to raising awareness, eliminating legal obstacles, and building the infrastructure needed to dispense family planning services. Worldwide, current expenditures on family planning total approximately $4.5 billion. Providing family planning to 75 percent of people in developing countries in the year 2000 will cost an estimated $9 billion to $11 billion annually. Development assistance is needed to cover roughly half of the additional costs.[51]

Action 15

Reduce resource consumption through recycling and conservation.

Recycling and conservation can directly reduce demand for biological resources and can reduce incentives for destroying natural ecosystems. By one estimate, U.S. demand for wood could be halved simply by increasing efficiency in milling, eliminating construction waste, conserving paper, and increasing paper recycling.[52] *(See Figure 14.)* For perspective,

FIGURE 14

Potential Wood Savings in the United States through Demand Management. (Total Current Consumption = 460 million cubic meters.)

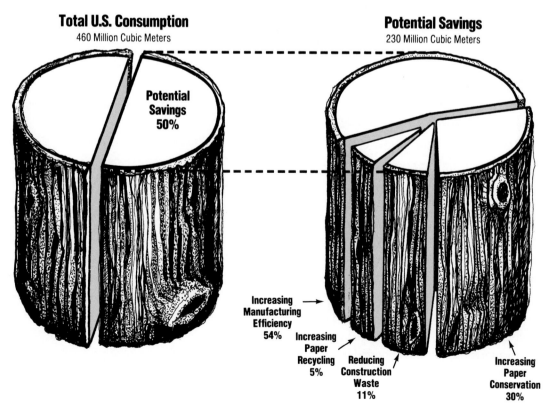

Total U.S. Consumption
460 Million Cubic Meters

Potential Savings 50%

Potential Savings
230 Million Cubic Meters

Increasing Manufacturing Efficiency 54%

Increasing Paper Recycling 5%

Reducing Construction Waste 11%

Increasing Paper Conservation 30%

Source: Postel and Ryan 1991

protecting all remaining old-growth forests in the Pacific Northwest would decrease U.S. timber production by only 2 percent.

Conservation and recycling of industrial products can help save biodiversity, too. Some of the most effective recycling programs involve glass, steel, and aluminum—all far more expensive to produce from raw than from recycled materials. Increased recycling of such energy-intensive products reduces the need for mining the raw material and—at least as important—the demand for the energy used in processing. These measures translate into fewer dams and powerplants destroying habitats, and fewer pollutants released into the air and water. Promoting energy conservation through energy taxes or public education can have similar salubrious effects.

One key step governments can take toward greater resource conservation and recycling is to remove subsidies for production based on virgin materials. In mining particularly, tax breaks are often given to companies to compensate for the depletion of mineral reserves. Since companies using recycled materials get no such breaks, tax policy encourages the use of virgin materials.

Action 16

Audit the consumption of biological resources to raise awareness of the balance between local consumption and production.

One of the most troubling aspects of the increasingly interconnected global economy has been the loss of immediacy in the relationship between humanity and the environment. For example, in much of the world, a local community loses its access to wood for construction or fuel if a forest is over-exploited. But where levels of income and infrastructure allow, wood is imported once the local forest is depleted—so consumers see a price increase but no break in supply.

In California, maximum sustainable timber

BOX 14

Resource Consumption Audits

In a path-breaking study, the Netherlands Committee of the World Conservation Union documented the role of the Netherlands' resource use on environmental quality in other nations. The Netherlands' population of 14.8 million occupies an area of 3.4 million hectares, a population density one-third higher than Japan's. It has the highest density of automobiles in the world, and a citizen of the Netherlands consumes on average forty times the resources of a citizen of Somalia. The Netherlands is host to four of the largest multinational corporations in the world: Shell, Unilever, Philips, and Akzo. Its foreign aid budget amounts to 1.5 percent of Net National Income, the highest percentage in the world.

Some 2.9 million hectares in the Netherlands are devoted to agriculture; yet, a further 13 million hectares outside the country—more than three times the country's size—are required to meet the demand for domestic consumption and for the export industry. A large percentage of the agricultural imports—particularly of tapioca and of soybean and palm-kernel-cake—are used to feed livestock.

Ninety-five percent of Dutch tapioca imports are from the uplands of northeast Thailand. Most soybeans come from Brazil and most palm oil from Malaysia. Dutch demand for tapioca—the dried roots of cassava—helped stimulate a growth in Thailand's cassava production from 100,000 hectares in 1965 to 1 million hectares today. Increased production of cassava may be responsible for up to 25 percent of the deforestation in north-east Thailand between 1965 and 1985. At the same time, cassava is a major source of income for poorer farmers in that region, providing 40 to 80 percent of the income of half a million families.

Soybean production in Brazil expanded from 432,000 hectares to 9.6 million hectares between 1965 and 1985. World-wide, Holland requires the import of roughly 2 million hectares of soybeans. The expansion of soybean farming in Brazil has led to forest clearance and substantial environmental damage from pesticides, and its mechanized production has led to the expulsion of labor.

Since 1957, oil-palm cultivation in Malaysia has increased from 55,000 hectares to 1.5 million hectares — almost all for the export market. In West Malaysia, some 20 to 30 percent of forest loss is attributed to oil-palm cultivation.

All told, the Netherlands' demand for agricultural imports has increased rates of conversion of natural habitats. At the same time, the Dutch market is providing significant economic returns to its trading partners.

The Netherlands' imports of tropical hardwoods increased fivefold from the early 1960s to 1988. *(See Figure 15.)* Wood imports in the Netherlands amount to one cubic meter per person annually —the highest in the European Communities. In the mid-1980s, 80 percent of imports came from Malaysia, 18 percent from South Africa, and less than 2 percent from Latin America. Less than 1 percent of imports are from timber plantations. Twenty-five percent of imports are re-exported. The Netherlands government has committed itself to restricting imports by 1995 to those coming from sustainably managed forests.

Other global biological impacts of resource consumption stem from the growing trade in cocaine and the impacts of oil, bauxite, iron ore, and coal extrac-

tion. Even nuclear power, supplying only 8 percent of Dutch needs, has significant impacts on developing countries. The major supplier of uranium to the Netherlands is Niger. Some 80 percent of Niger's foreign exchange earnings stem from the export of uranium; yet, the country is only a minority share-holder in all of the mining companies so its ability to negotiate for environmental controls and safeguards is weak. Massive disturbances to the landscape have resulted, accompanied by the modification of groundwater flow regimes, the leaching of toxic chemicals, and the release of radioactive material.

FIGURE 15

Annual Imports of Solid Tropical Hardwood in the Netherlands

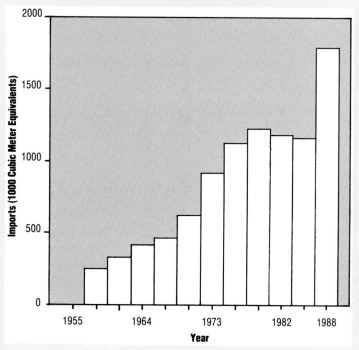

Source: Netherlands National Committee for IUCN, 1988; Wouter Veening, pers. comm., Sept. 1991

production is an estimated 4.5 billion board feet annually; current demand is some 10 billion board feet. Only 4 billion board feet are being harvested in-state annually, and officials may soon scale production back to less than 2 billion board feet to keep the forest ecosystems intact.[53] Californians are protecting their own forests by shifting, not reducing, demand. Similarly, Thailand banned logging in 1989 when the public protested the unsustainable forestry practices that exacerbated disastrous floods and mudslides; but here again, the burden was merely moved to neighboring countries. Often, shifting production to another region in this way makes economic sense since it allows each region to capitalize on its comparative advantages. But the danger is that people can lose all conception of how their purchases register on the lives and environments of others.

Governments or non-governmental organizations should take steps to restore the connection between the consumer and the environment by auditing demand for and consumption of key biological resources and by sharing this information with teachers and the communications media. A complete resource audit would indicate current consumption, the amount produced locally, and the location and intensity of the remainder of the production needed to meet local demand. Businesses using biological resources should also make available information on where they obtain materials for use in national or regional audits. The audit could be supplemented with information on the sustainability of resource harvest in regions supplying the resources. Such information could then be used to establish labeling programs indicating which products come from sustainably harvested material. To date, only the Netherlands has undertaken such an audit. *(See Box 14.)*

V

Creating An International Policy Environment That Supports National Biodiversity Conservation

The developed countries should practice what they preach and should be more serious about their own contradictions regarding biodiversity conservation before attempting to rule the international environment. They should also abolish the poisonous concept of donor with regard to biodiversity conservation. The response to global environmental issues should be based on real partnership for a common endeavor and not on a beggar-to-donor relationship.

MARC DOUROJEANNI, INTER-AMERICAN DEVELOPMENT BANK

The loss of biodiversity, and especially of genetic and species diversity, represents a loss to all people, today and in the future. Moreover, the impacts of ecosystem and habitat degradation reach beyond national boundaries. Climate regimes, river flows, sediment deposition patterns, and migratory species are all affected. The interconnections in the world environment mean that biodiversity loss in one area is liable to be felt widely.

These interconnections are the stronger because of the way the whole world shares crop plants, medicinal plants, and other living resources, and because of the increasing interlinkage of the global economy. Consider, for instance, that oil from Saudi Arabia fuels the machines and provides the feedstock for the fertilizers and pesticides that allow marginal land in West Africa to grow—on trees originating from South America—cocoa that the Swiss make into chocolate that is flown on American-made airplanes to Singapore for distribution in Southeast Asia and that the profit made by the West African farmer allows her to purchase a Japanese motorcycle, Ethiopian coffee, and Thai rice. No longer vulnerable only to local ecological and economic factors, this farmer's livelihood now depends on international commodity agreements, market forces, and many other factors that make the world economy function as a single system.

Although ecological and economic realities mandate a global response to biodiversity loss, global cooperation faces three obstacles. First, biodiversity is not a part of the "global commons" in the sense that the high seas and the atmosphere are. To the contrary, the bulk of genes, species, and habitats lie within the sovereign jurisdiction of individual nations. Second, threats to biodiversity are not evenly distributed among nations—the costs of conserving biodiversity globally will fall more heavily on some nations than on others. Third, the technical and financial abilities to respond to biodiversity loss vary greatly among nations. Indeed, Earth's most threatened natural ecosystems lie within the developing countries, which possess the least resources to conserve them.

Objective:

Integrate biodiversity conservation into international economic policy

Since 1950, measurable global economic activity has more than quadrupled to create a $20-trillion world economy. These large increases in economic activity and exchange have brought global market forces into once-remote areas that house the greatest remaining concentrations of biodiversity. The global economic system enables countries to exploit their comparative production advantages, and it provides each with access to a wider range of goods and services than it could efficiently produce alone. The challenges are to ensure that the health and diversity of Earth's life systems are not compromised in the process, and that economic power and benefits are equitably shared among and within nations. Realistically, these challenges cannot be met without major changes.

Action 17

Develop a principle and policy of "national ecological security" to ensure that international trade policies do not intensify biodiversity loss.

To buffer the negative effects of increasing economic globalization, governments should develop a policy of *national ecological security*. The three goals of such a policy would be: 1) to ensure that the integrity and diversity of a country's basic biological systems are not compromised by the rules and practices of international trade, 2) to protect the livelihoods of communities dependent on biotic resources, and 3) to equitably distribute the costs and benefits of trade based on living resources within the country.

Maintaining national ecological security is particularly important in developing countries. Currently, the relative terms of international trade work against the South, and many markets in the North are closed to the goods developing countries produce. Liberalizing trade without adjusting national policy frameworks often reinforces the trade disadvantages of developing countries, further diminishing biodiversity. At the same time, current trade patterns and prices for such commodities as tropical timber, prawns, and various cash crops often intensify pressures on forests and wildlands.

How can the principle of national ecological security acquire international legitimacy? An obvious possibility is through the General Agreement on Tariffs and Trade (GATT). Two GATT articles provide opportunities for countries to adopt strict environmental protection standards and to impose those standards on imports. Article 20(b) holds that countries can take measures to protect human, animal, or plant life or health. When drafted, however, the article's primary intent was to enable countries to impose quarantine procedures—not to address general environmental protection. Article 20(g) of the GATT exempts measures to conserve exhaustible natural resources so long as countries enacting such measures limit domestic consumption.

Article 20's scope vis-à-vis environmental protection has been hotly debated. The 1991 decision of a GATT panel to disallow a U.S. ban on tuna imports that had been designed to protect dolphins from the tuna fleets of other nations brought GATT's support for environmental provisions into wider question. However this specific case is resolved, national actions designed to protect the domestic environment or to ensure that domestic consumption does not degrade other nations' environments are likely to be challenged by trading partners as non-tariff trade barriers. Surcharges on the import of unsustainably produced tropical timber, for example, or even efforts to protect primary forests by reducing forest product exports appear subject to challenge as disguised protectionism.[54]

In fact, actions to protect the environment are no more disguised protectionism than actions to protect health and safety. The difference is that no machinery currently exists in the GATT for making judgments about trade's impact on the environment. A special committee set up by GATT in 1971 to discuss these issues—the GATT Working Party on Trade and the Environment—has never met, although its activation was being planned late in 1991.

Two decades after this false start, international guidelines on trade and environment should be developed within GATT. As a start, Article 20 should be clarified to make it explicit that trade restrictions for genuine environmental purposes are legitimate, so long as they are based on universally applied criteria. Second, a revitalized GATT Working Party on Trade and the Environment should develop criteria for judging the sincerity of environmental trade restrictions. To address trade's effects on biodiversity specifically, a protocol might be set up within the framework of the Biodiversity Convention and aligned with the general environmental criteria set up under GATT.

Action 18

Establish an International Debt Management Authority to purchase debt on the secondary market.

By 1989, the Third World's debt stood at $1.2 trillion—44 percent of its collective GNP. Nations of the South in that year paid $77 billion in interest and repaid $85 billion worth of principal. Net flows from South to North of some $32.5 billion annually make it difficult for many developing countries to increase investments in biodiversity conservation. (See Figure 16.) Indeed, indebted countries now feel compelled to increase exports, often at the expense of their natural resource base. And debt repayment absorbs a growing share of available development assistance revenues.

Increasingly large amounts of Third World debt (face value) can be purchased for a fixed amount of hard currency. This growing secondary debt market, the priority that many developing countries accord debt reduction, and the links between debt and biological resource degradation all suggest that debt reduction should be used to ease pressures on biological resources and to underwrite biodiversity conservation. "Debt for nature swaps" are one innovative method of linking debt relief to biodiversity conservation (see Action 28), though these have so far been too small to have much impact on either debt or biodiversity conservation.

To mount a larger-scale response, a consortium of aid-giving nations should establish an *International Debt Management Authority* to purchase some $100 billion of the debt obligations of selected countries on the secondary market over five years.[55] In return, the countries would adopt sustainable development policies and programs, including those based on the conservation and sustainable use of biodiversity.

Action 19

Facilitate the exchange and development of technologies for conserving and using biodiversity sustainably.

The principle of free access to genetic resources reaches back millennia to the casual exchange of seeds among farmers, and accounts largely for world agricultural patterns today. But

FIGURE 16

Net Transfer of Financial Resources 1980-88

(Sample of 98 Nations, Covering Private Direct Investments, Private Loans, Official Flows.)

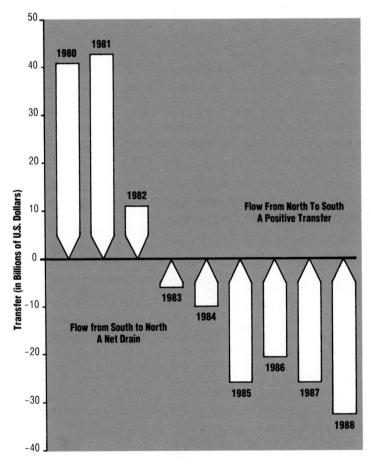

Source: UN Department of Public Information 1989

while genetic resources have tended to move relatively freely, the technologies for conserving them and exploiting their potential wealth have not. Currently, few effective mechanisms exist for exchanging technologies relating to biodiversity's conservation and use.

From the 1950s through the 1970s, the conventional wisdom was that technological progress in developing countries could best be achieved by transferring hardware from industrialized countries. Over these years, far too little attention was paid to the need of the country acquiring the hardware to learn to use it appropriately, and, more important, to define and develop new technologies tailored to local needs and realities. The entry barriers for developing countries are comparatively low in the biotechnology business since knowledge and innovation are more important than capital. But precisely because so much of the critical knowledge lies in the industrialized world, the industry simply cannot develop without international technical cooperation focussed on information and training.

Most of the technologies needed to conserve and use biodiversity wisely rest in the public domain. However, the lack of knowledge about available technologies, and the lack of developing countries' institutional ability to acquire that technology impede technological development. Developing countries need to define technological needs, seek and manage information on technology, adapt existing technologies, and develop their own. The international community should assist at each step of this process.

The role of international institutions, especially the International Agriculture Research Centers (IARCs), in providing training and access to public-domain technologies for developing-country scientists should be strengthened. In particular, greater funding is needed for training programs. Over time, the IARCs should increasingly channel information and technology to developing countries rather than carry out their own research.

International support for building national capacity to acquire technologies is vitally important in the 1990s and beyond. Rather than depending on the technological choices made in international centers, developing countries should be able to set their own priorities for technology acquisition. One means of doing this is for industrialized countries to help pay for the establishment of national "Biotechnology Trusts" in developing countries to promote technology exchange and serve as honest brokers between potential collaborators in the exchange of technology and technological information. The national Biotechnology Trust would also contribute resources toward joint research. The Trust could put forward genetic resources with specific economic values, while the biotechnology firm would supply the technology for using those resources. Patents and profits would be shared, and one condition of the agreements could be that local scientists receive training in the use of the technology.

One such project, developed by the U.S. Agency for International Development, involves enabling developing-country scientists to take part in joint research ventures with private companies to develop products of use in overcoming key agricultural constraints in developing countries. Patents on products resulting from the work—pest-resistant or drought-resistant sorghum, for instance—will be held jointly by the private company and by the scientist's home institution.[56] The National Biodiversity Institute (INBio) in Costa Rica, described in Chapter 10, is another model for enhancing technology transfer.

High priority for international support should be given to building information systems in developing countries in order to increase access to information on biotechnologies that may help save biodiversity or mobilize its benefits. Such mechanisms must ensure equity in access to these technologies. The same groups excluded from ownership and access to land, resources, education, and power—such as women, indigenous people, and minorities—are often also denied access to technology. Developing countries currently lack the technical capacity—including data bases and electronic mail systems—needed to exchange scientific and techno-

logical information with industrialized countries. Creating cross-border information exchange networks would allow for both mutual access in national and international databases and encourage developing countries to build up their own databases. Currently, most information collected on resources in developing countries is stored and utilized only in industrialized countries.

To complement such expanded facilities in developing countries, Third World "research outposts" established in the industrialized countries to promote collaboration and tap into public-domain information on biodiversity and biotechnology might be useful. A possible model for this kind of outpost is the African Centre for Technology Studies' newly established Biopolicy Institute located in The Netherlands.

Action 20

Ensure that the activities of transnational corporations (TNCs) that destroy biodiversity are curbed in the countries where they are based and where they operate, and that compensation for, or restoration of, damages is sought where applicable.

Transnational corporations (TNCs) are increasingly important and powerful actors in the international economy. They play a critical role in the economies of many countries, and they can potentially be a positive force in biodiversity conservation as well. In many countries, however, TNC-financed extraction, processing, and export of such natural resources as timber, crops, minerals, and petroleum devastates biodiversity. With no vested interest in the sustainability of regional production, TNCs may over-exploit one region, earn substantial profits, and then move on to unexploited regions. Some TNCs have minimized the environmental impacts of their operations, but many more have not. In Papua New Guinea, for example, a 1989 Government Commission of Inquiry concluded that foreign timber companies in New Ireland Province were "roaming the countryside with the self-assurance of robber barons; bribing politicians and leaders, creating social disharmony and ignoring laws in order to gain access to, rip out, and export the last remnants of the province's valuable timber."[57]

As sovereign guardians of their territories, national governments must take the lead in regulating and punishing this kind of behavior, and in seeking compensation for damages. Their best recourse is legislation that provides TNCs with tough but clear guidelines for environmental protection but also provides foreign investors with a certain and predictable legal framework. To enforce such legislation, the institutional and human capacity to monitor TNC activities and enforce the law also needs to be strengthened.

Many developing countries fear that stringent environmental laws will drive away foreign investment. But this problem is largely illusory since TNCs relocate to developing countries because of lower production costs, of which compliance with environmental laws constitute a small percentage, even when the law is relatively strict.[58] A tougher problem is that few developing countries possess the resources and capacities needed to control TNC operations within their own borders, let alone to police the transfer of profits offshore. Thus, international action is also needed to improve TNCs' environmental behavior.

Most of the attempts that have been made to develop international codes of conduct for TNCs have fallen flat. A more promising approach is for governments of the countries where TNCs are domiciled to develop and enforce legal norms and restrictions for TNCs' conduct overseas. In the same way that some countries (such as the United States) prohibit their corporations from engaging in corrupt practices abroad, standards covering the effects of corporate overseas investment practices on biological resources and biodiversity should be devel-

oped and enforced. Observing the laws of host countries should be a minimum standard, and home countries should set more strict standards where necessary. Such controls are not an unfair "cost" to the TNC any more than the benefits that they enjoy in their home country—among them, resort to its legal system and easy access to capital—are unfair "subsidies."

The potential positive contributions of TNCs to biodiversity conservation must also be cultivated. TNCs that take constructive steps to harmonize their activities with biodiversity conservation should be encouraged, and their experiences studied and shared to engender a more responsible industry norm. If a system for labelling tropical timber in international trade were developed, for example, it would allow consumers concerned about biodiversity loss to reward those TNCs that use only environmentally sustainable timber sources. TNCs can also be potentially valuable partners in developing technological capacity in the countries where they operate if an appropriate mix of positive and negative incentives are provided by home- and host-country governments.

Action 21

Ensure that countries are free to decide whether to adopt intellectual property rights protection for genetic resources and how strong that protection should be.

With technology exchange increasingly influencing economic development prospects, intellectual property rights have increasingly triggered trade disputes and negotiations among countries. In general, industrialized countries contend that differences in intellectual property rights regimes among countries should be viewed as potential barriers to free trade and should be dealt with in an international trade forum. For their part, developing countries argue that IPR regimes must be tailored to development needs and *not* be subjected to international control. Currently, many developing countries exempt pharmaceuticals and living organisms from patent protection, and only a small number grant Plant Breeders' Rights.

Whether and how these disputes over IPRs are resolved will profoundly affect the development of technologies for using, evaluating, and protecting genetic resources. The right IPR regimes will help developing countries tap their genetic resources sustainably and strengthen incentives for conservation. The wrong ones will exacerbate inequities in the distribution of benefits from the exploitation of genetic resources and undermine conservation efforts.

At the urging of industrialized countries, and after considerable resistance from developing countries, the Uruguay Round of negotiations of the General Agreement on Tariffs and Trade (GATT) established a negotiating group on Trade-Related Aspects of Intellectual Property Rights (TRIPS) in 1987. Industrialized countries are pressing for uniform patent standards in all countries on a par with their own standards. (These issues have also been raised in the World Intellectual Property Organization (WIPO), where a revision of the Paris Convention on Intellectual Property is being considered, but WIPO is likely to postpone action until GATT negotiations end.)

The merits of strengthened IPR protection notwithstanding, there is considerable reason to question the appropriateness of *uniform* patent standards given the widely differing circumstances in developing countries. IPRs are development tools. As such, they must reflect and change with each country's unique needs. Whereas patent protection may promote cutting-edge innovation in a developed country, IPRs may provide little in-country incentive for innovation in nations that lack basic technological infrastructure. The few developing countries that have recently joined the ranks of industrialized countries did so by building technological capacity through adaptive innovation, not by strongly protecting patents. Industries in many industrialized countries have followed this same

route; France did not begin to grant patents for pharmaceuticals until 1958, nor did Japan until 1976, or Switzerland until 1977. Clearly, strict patent protection can stifle low-cost imitation.

Another problem is that in the pursuit of uniform patent standards, genetic resources' unique ethical and economic attributes, distinct from most industrial products, receive short shrift. From an ethical standpoint, patenting living organisms raises serious questions, particularly if human cells or genes are involved. From an economic standpoint, the ability of agricultural genetic resources to self-reproduce and undergo evolutionary change raises difficult questions about both the enforceability and legitimacy of patent protection. In addition, IPR protection for agricultural genetic resources may be hastening the loss of genetic diversity (and threatening the livelihoods of marginal farmers) by promoting the adoption of a few uniform varieties of crops where great diversity formerly existed. Until some of these thorny issues are resolved, it would clearly be premature to adopt uniform global standards.

Countries should be able to adapt IPR protection to meet their development needs, particularly in the case of genetic resources. GATT negotiators should thus exclude biological materials from agreements under the TRIPS negotiation.

Objective:

Strengthen the international legal framework for conservation to complement the Convention on Biological Diversity

The Convention on Biological Diversity is a key element of the international legal framework for biodiversity conservation. *(See Action 1.)* A number of other legal instruments are also important. Current agreements cover a range of specific conservation issues, and should be reviewed and strengthened. In addition, proposed conventions or agreements on global warming and forests must also be crafted to support biodiversity conservation.

Action 22

Strengthen the effectiveness of existing international conventions and treaties covering the conservation of ecosystems, species, and genes.

Numerous treaties, conventions, and multilateral or bilateral agreements address aspects of biodiversity conservation, including protection of certain species and ecosystems, regulation of international trade in endangered species, and the conservation of plant genetic resources. *(See Box 15.)* Although the most well-known international agreements are global in scope, many regional agreements also contribute to conservation. Many of these are tailored to specific regional conditions and tend to be more comprehensive and sometimes more stringent than global agreements since the countries involved are politically and economically homogenous. Whether global or regional, international agreements are essential components for cooperation on biodiversity, because they provide a level of detail that could not and should not be incorporated in the Convention on Biological Diversity.

The various international agreements now in force could do a great deal more to conserve biodiversity. The Convention on International Trade in Endangered Species of Wild Flora and Fauna (CITES), for example, has made strides in limiting the trade in endangered species. However, too few people are trained in CITES procedures and species identification, the system would be stronger if it had population studies on the numerous species involved in commercial trade to draw on, penalties for violating CITES have not been collected, and the CITES Secretariat is underfunded.

While it is difficult to generalize about the large number of international agreements that promote biodiversity conservation, it can be said that they share some common weaknesses. Where parties lack either the political will or the resources to honor their commitments, their membership is a formality and has little effect. In other cases, the problem is simply that not enough states are parties to the agreement—a particularly crucial issue in agreements protecting migratory species. In other cases, the legal instrument itself is poorly conceived and drafted.

Critical reviews of conservation agreements are needed for three reasons. First, such reviews would pinpoint the reforms and strengthening needed to make each agreement more effective. Second, they could illuminate the search for workable mechanisms in the Biodiversity Convention. Third, they would make it easier to link existing agreements to—or incorporate them into—the Convention on Biological Diversity and its subsequent protocols.

BOX 15

Major Conservation Conventions and Agreements

The Convention on Wetlands of International Importance Especially as Waterfowl Habitat (Ramsar, 1971).

Contracting parties undertake to use wisely all wetland resources under their jurisdiction and to designate for conservation at least one wetland of international importance under criteria provided by the Convention. By 1990, the 61 contracting states had designated over 421 sites covering more than 30 million hectares. Nations facing economic constraints have had difficulty in meeting their obligations. As a consequence, in 1990 parties voted to establish a Wetland Conservation Fund, built on mandatory and voluntary contributions, with an annual budget of approximately $660,000. Parties meet at least every three years, and the Secretariat is provided by The World Conservation Union (IUCN).

The Convention Concerning the Protection of the World Cultural and Natural Heritage (Paris, 1972).

The Convention, in force since 1975, recognizes the obligation of all states to protect unique natural and cultural areas and recognizes the obligation of the international community to help pay for them. A World Heritage Committee, drawn from the 111 State Parties, establishes and publishes the World Heritage List of sites of exceptional cultural or natural value; as of January 1991, 337 sites were on the list, of which only 79 are natural, and a further 13 combine both natural and cultural values. Each party must contribute to a fund to support these sites and related research; contributions are set at 1 percent of contributions to the annual budget of UNESCO, currently totalling approximately $2 million. The World Heritage Committee's "List of World Heritage in Danger" covers sites threatened by serious and specific dangers. Its Secretariat is provided by UNESCO.

The Convention on International Trade in Endangered Species of Wild Fauna and Flora (CITES) (Washington, 1973).

The Convention, in force since 1975 and currently ratified by 111 States, establishes lists of endangered species for which international commercial trade is either prohibited or regulated via permit systems to combat illegal trade and over-exploitation. A Conference of Parties is held every two years; non-governmental organizations have been well-represented at Conference meetings. The Convention includes species in three appendices, with progressing levels of restriction on their trade. Inclusion of species in the most restrictive categories requires a two-thirds majority of the Parties to the Convention; the least restrictive inclusions may be made by a single party. National "Management Authorities" and "Scientific Authorities" must be designated by each state to grant and review the Convention permits; records of permits granted are supposed to be transmitted annually to the Convention Secretariat for review (though many parties are not complying with this provision). The Convention has financed population studies of particular species to attempt to curb further species endangerment. The Secretariat is provided by UNEP.

The Convention on the Conservation of Migratory Species of Wild Animals (Bonn, 1979).

The Convention, in force since 1983, obligates parties to protect endangered migratory species and to try to conclude international conservation agreements for the conservation of vulnerable species that are not yet endangered. No such agreements have come into force, but several are likely to be implemented by the mid-1990s. The 36 contracting parties do not yet include several countries of major importance for migratory birds. Some 51 migratory species are listed as "endangered" by the Convention, including four species of whales, several species of antelopes, 24 bird species, and six marine turtles. The Convention precludes commercial taking of listed species; it also encourages member states to conserve and restore habitat areas for migratory species. The Secretariat is provided by UNEP.

continued on page 64

The Convention on the Conservation of Antarctic Marine Living Resources (CCAMLR) (1980)

The Convention's primary objective is the conservation of marine resources in the Southern Ocean ecosystem. It entered into force in 1982, and as of 1990 has 27 contracting parties. It applies to all species in the Southern Ocean and stipulates that the ecological relationships between harvested and dependent populations must be maintained whenever resource harvesting takes place. It calls for minimizing the risk of irreversible change to the ecosystem and promotes an ecosystem management approach to conservation. It established a Commission that meets annually and its Secretariat is housed in Hobart, Tasmania.

The FAO International Undertaking on Plant Genetic Resources (Rome, 1983)

This voluntary agreement among nations is based on the principle that plant genetic resources are the common heritage of humankind. A Commission on Plant Genetic Resources was also established in 1983 to pursue actions pursuant to the International Undertaking. At its 1987 meeting, the Commission established an International Fund for the Conservation and Utilization of Plant Genetic Resources, based on voluntary contributions. The Undertaking initially attempted to ensure the free exchange of genetic resources (including breeding lines and finished varieties). However, at the 1987 meeting of the Commission, the right of plant breeders to protect their breeding lines was recognized, as were "Farmers Rights" to compensation for their contribution to the selection and conservation of genetic diversity of crops and livestock. As of 1991, 111 countries are members of the Commission and 101 have adhered to the International Undertaking. The Secretariat for the Commission is housed at FAO.

FIGURE 17

Trade in Live Parrots in 1988

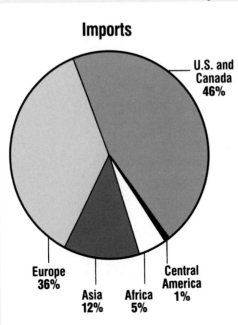

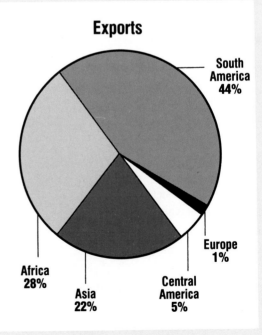

Source: World Conservation Monitoring Centre

Action 23

Ensure that international agreements on climate change and forests are compatible with the Convention on Biological Diversity and that they support biodiversity conservation.

International conventions or agreements on climate change and on forests are likely to be completed in the 1990s. These agreements and the Biodiversity Convention must be mutually supportive. Successful negotiations on the Climate Convention could reduce the threat that rapid global climate change may hold for biodiversity. At the same time, biodiversity could be destroyed by some of the strategies proposed for mitigating atmospheric carbon-dioxide buildup—among them, proposals to replace mature forests with younger, more rapidly growing ones. The provisions of both the conventions on climate and biological diversity should therefore prohibit global-warming prevention or adaptation strategies that involve the degradation or conversion of diverse natural ecosystems.

By the same token, any agreement or convention on forests should not work at cross-purposes with the Convention on Biological Diversity. To the extent that a forest agreement slows the loss of natural forests, it supports the objectives of the Convention on Biological Diversity and of this *Strategy*. But if the agreement uncritically mandates "net-afforestation" strategies without a strong commitment to both conserving natural forests and fostering biodiversity in planted forests, it may contravene the spirit and the provisions of the Convention on Biological Diversity. *(See Box 16.)*

FIGURE 18

Loss of Habitat in Selected Countries

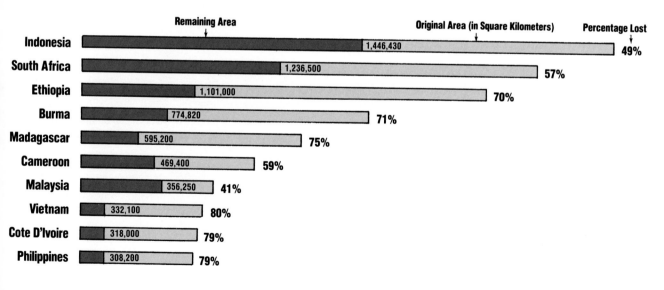

	Remaining Area	Original Area (in Square Kilometers)	Percentage Lost
Indonesia	1,446,430		49%
South Africa	1,236,500		57%
Ethiopia	1,101,000		70%
Burma	774,820		71%
Madagascar	595,200		75%
Cameroon	469,400		59%
Malaysia	356,250		41%
Vietnam	332,100		80%
Cote D'Ivoire	318,000		79%
Philippines	308,200		79%

Source: IUCN/UNEP 1986a, IUCN/UNEP 1986b

BOX 16

Principles for a Global Agreement on Forests

**States party to any global agreement
on forests should:**

■ recognize the rights of states to choose the means through which they shall sustainably use, manage, and conserve forests, consistent with all other principles in the Agreement;

■ recognize the duty of states to conserve the earth's remaining forests and restore previously forested land where possible;

■ fully protect all remaining primary forest if the state's primary forest cover is less then 20 percent of its original extent. If more than 20 percent remains, states should fully protect the maximum possible primary forest area, including large areas of all forest types;

■ restrict any conversion of primary or other natural forests to uses that are sustainable and directly fulfill tangible human needs that cannot otherwise be met;

■ modify development schemes—mining, hydroelectric, road-building, plantation, ranching, and colonization projects—to minimize their direct and indirect impacts on natural forests;

■ promote the regeneration of degraded forest lands to increase permanent global forest cover, reduce pressure on natural forests, conserve biodiversity, protect watersheds and soils, and stabilize climate;

■ modify systems of valuing forests to account for the broad range of goods and services that they provide, and reform policies that reward deforestation or otherwise promote inappropriate land use;

■ subject private companies operating in forested areas to monitoring, controls, and public accountability to prevent the use of environmentally or socially destructive practices;

■ relieve pressure on forests by decreasing waste in wood-processing, conserving energy to reduce the need for hydroelectric dams, increasing the efficiency of wood-burning stoves, and seeking alternative raw materials;

■ reduce demand for forest products, particularly in the industrialized countries and in urbanized areas of developing countries, to reduce pressures on forests;

■ develop markets for non-timber forest products as a mechanism for promoting ecologically sustainable and small-scale local economic development;

■ safeguard the rights, livelihoods, and cultural integrity of forest-dependent communities through policies and laws that protect their lands, intellectual property rights, and economic and cultural rights;

■ validate and develop the stewardship skills of indigenous peoples, extractivists, hunter-gatherers, small farmers, and other forest-dependent communities;

■ relieve forest encroachment pressures by providing land security to small and landless farmers through land tenure laws, land reform, or agrarian reform;

■ offset the revenue and employment sacrificed by forested countries—particularly developing countries—in conserving forests, through aid, direct financial compensation, technical assistance, and trade concessions; and,

■ ensure that the General Agreement on Tariffs and Trade (GATT) does not preclude states from taking steps to conserve their own forests or from adopting regulations restricting imports of timber from non-sustainable sources.

Objective:

Make the development assistance process a force for biodiversity conservation

Development assistance could play an important role in directly supporting biodiversity conservation efforts. All too often, development aid has contributed to the destruction of habitats and ecosystems, the over-exploitation of species, and excessive genetic uniformity in agriculture. The loss of biodiversity brings about social disruption and a reduction in the resource base for people's livelihoods, thus undermining the objectives of development efforts. While development aid forms a relatively small percentage of overall economic activity in most developing countries, it has transformed certain areas and communities. Perhaps more important, institutions such as the World Bank dominate development policy, deeply influencing the decisions of developing-country policy-makers.

If development-assistance institutions are to play a positive role in conserving biodiversity, they must follow two parallel tracks. First, development-assistance agencies must channel a greater proportion of their resources into projects that strengthen developing countries' capacity to save, study, and sustainably use biodiversity. Many of the actions suggested in the *Global Biodiversity Strategy* could be undertaken through development assistance. Second, and more important, development assistance agencies must reorient their "mainstream" assistance to incorporate biodiversity conservation objectives.

To these ends, development assistance agencies should create guidelines for assessing projects' impacts on biodiversity, dedicate special funds to initiating biodiversity conservation programs, develop in-house expertise and strategy statements on biodiversity conservation, and ensure that all sectors include biodiversity conservation among their objectives.

Action 24

Incorporate biodiversity values into the criteria for choosing, designing, and evaluating development assistance loans and projects, and for assessing developing countries' economic performance.

Development agencies should evaluate the impacts on biodiversity of all development projects—whether ongoing, in the pipeline, or planned. Projects should not be financed through development assistance if they violate the criteria listed in Box 17. Moreover, the addition of "green" projects to a development agency's portfolio should not be considered a substitute for deleting or revising "brown" ones. Increased funding of biodiversity-conservation projects is not an acceptable alternative to changing mainstream lending objectives and criteria.

To bring about these changes, development agencies should explicitly incorporate all quantifiable monetary values of biodiversity into their evaluation of proposed projects. These values should be considered separately and in addition to such hard-to-quantify biodiversity values as the preservation of species endangered by a project, the incursion of a proposed project into natural areas of local spiritual value, or the loss of a country's last major area of a particular ecosystem type. The promulgation of binding staff guidelines on these matters would help ensure that the value of biodiversity is adequately considered.

Donors making large sectoral and "structural adjustment" loans should also assess the impacts of their lending on biodiversity and biological resource values, using the same criteria used for projects. This test is particularly important where adjustment and sector lending promote the privatization and com-

BOX 17

Biodiversity Criteria for Evaluating Development Assistance Projects

Bilateral and multilateral development assistance agencies should support investments in the capacity to save, inventory, and analyze biodiversity and foster its wise use. They should not support projects that significantly contribute to the loss of biodiversity. To this end, projects should receive support from development assistance only if they:

Process Criteria

■ are planned for regions where basic surveys of plant and vertebrate taxa have been conducted, and for regions with an ecosystem classification system in place;

■ involve local people, especially women, in the initial biodiversity inventory and project planning, as well as in review and implementation;

■ provide ready access to biological survey information and planning documentation (in local languages) to local people;

■ include Environmental Impact Assessments that explicitly address the impacts of projects on genetic, species, and ecosystem diversity;

■ provide for a means of monitoring impacts on biodiversity and modifying project implementation based on that feedback;

Biological Criteria

■ do not destroy, degrade, or fragment habitat used by a species listed as globally threatened or endangered by the IUCN or listed on Appendix I of CITES and do not involve the harvest of such a species;

■ do not involve any exploitation of resources or disturbance of habitat in strictly protected areas (IUCN Categories I to III), including the core zone of Biosphere Reserves and World Heritage Sites;

■ do not take place in an ecosystem or biogeographic unit designated as a threatened site by IUCN or by the proposed International Panel on Biodiversity Conservation;

■ do not result in the conversion or degradation of primary forests;

■ do not engender the loss of genetic diversity of domesticated species without adequately supporting grassroots conservation groups financially and institutionally, or establishing national genebanks to ensure the *ex situ* preservation of that diversity;

■ do not destroy or degrade the habitat of migratory species listed as globally threatened by IUCN or by any country on their migratory route;

■ do not introduce species or varieties in violation of the IUCN guidelines for translocations of living organisms; *(See Box 12.)*

■ are consistent with the country's National Conservation Strategy or other similar conservation planning document or with any international convention to which the state is party;

Social Criteria

■ do not increase landlessness or resource needs without provision of alternatives suitable to the local people;

■ provide a substantial share of any increased economic benefits from biodiversity (through, for instance, tourism or exploration for pharmaceutical plants) to local communities;

■ do not degrade or encroach upon the ancestral domain of indigenous groups without their informed consent;

■ ensure that any research on biodiversity or biological resources makes full use of local and national expertise, significantly strengthens local and national research capacity, and helps the host country acquire the technologies involved in the research;

■ recognize and reward rights to traditional knowledge on biological resources and biodiversity;

■ provide the option to maintain traditional lifestyles or traditional uses of biological resources; and,

■ do not destroy or degrade the resources upon which women depend to maintain their families, nor increase their burdens inadvertently.

mercialization of natural resources, thereby often accelerating their consumption and degradation.

The multilateral development banks should also explicitly incorporate a "natural resources accounting" methodology into their often-influential country economic reports on borrowing countries. *(See Action 13.)* If the World Bank compliments or chastises a country in such a report for its policies' effects on biodiversity, the political will for change within that country becomes easier to mobilize.

Action 25

Open the development-assistance process—the design, implementation, and evaluation of projects and the policies that guide them—to public scrutiny, participation, and accountability.

Development-assistance loans and grants leave their mark on biodiversity, and all too frequently it has been negative. Stories of how "aid" has invited biodiversity losses and alienated rural communities from their natural resource base are legion. In the wake of such disasters, aid agencies and development banks must increasingly be held accountable not only to the governments they assist, but also to the communities touched by projects and programs and the general public in both the North and South.

Ultimately, development assistance uses public funds, provided by both the citizens of the countries lending or granting funds and by the citizens of countries that must repay development loans, whether they are utilized wisely or wasted. Yet development agencies—particularly such multilateral financial institutions as the World Bank and the International Monetary Fund (IMF)—often operate without an appreciable degree of public scrutiny, participation, or accountability, particularly within developing countries. Increased "openness" in the decisions and operations of these agencies would

enable local communities to reject projects that degrade their biological resource base or alienate them from it, and increase the leverage of citizens who do not want biodiversity destroyed in the name of development.

The first step in opening up the process is increasing public access to information on proposed projects, on the development of policies, and on operational guidelines, well before decisions are made. Development agencies should share the information they have and pressure governments to release more of the data now considered confidential.

Just as important, agencies must make sure that the information that communities and their advocates need reaches them in a form they can use. At the agencies' expense, draft terms of reference, appraisal reports, and feasibility studies should be translated into local languages and distributed to communities in planned project areas and their advocates. Local meetings may be needed to explain and defend any plans.

Regular consultations with non-governmental organizations and other public representatives on proposed policy changes are also needed. When specific projects are at issue, public comment should be built into the Environmental Impact Assessment process. In all consultations, agencies should *respond* to comments and concerns, not just listen to them.

Finally, development agencies need to come up with more participatory procedures for evaluating completed projects. Typically, agency staff or consulting technical experts carry out such evaluations. Rarely do they systematically involve the communities from the project areas, their advocates, or independent experts and critics.

Increasing participation in project and policy design, management, and evaluation may moderately increase initial project costs. But measured in terms of ultimate savings—avoidance of bad projects, needless disruption of lives, and biodiversity saved—it is a wise investment.

Action 26

Ensure that development assistance strengthens the role of women in the sustainable use of biological resources.

All too often, the vital contribution of women to the management of biological resources, and to economic production generally, has been misunderstood, ignored, or underestimated. Women are the sole breadwinners in one third of all households in the world. In poor families with two adults, more than half of the available income is from the labor of women and children. Furthermore, women direct comparatively more of their earnings to meet basic needs. Women produce 80 percent of the food in Africa, 60 percent in Asia, and 40 percent in Latin America.[59] *(See Figure 19.)*

FIGURE 19

Role of Women in Farming and Agricultural Extension

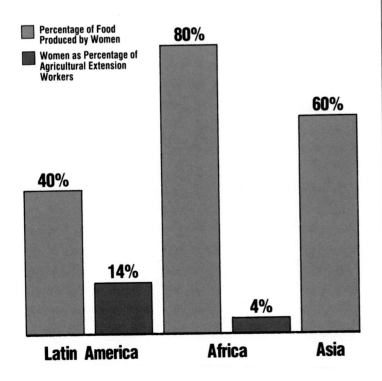

Percentage of Food Produced by Women

Women as Percentage of Agricultural Extension Workers

Latin America 40% 14%

Africa 80% 4%

Asia 60%

Women tend to be more actively involved than men in the "household" economy, which typically involves use of a much wider diversity of species for food and medicine than are traded in regional or international markets. *(See Figure 20.)* With primary responsibility for providing their families with food, water, fuel, medicines, fibers, fodder and other products, as well as often for cash income, women rely on a healthy and diverse ecosystem. As a result, rural women are often the most knowledgeable about the patterns and uses of local biodiversity. Yet, these same people are often denied access to land and resources. In many countries, such as Kenya, women have access only to the most marginal land—medicinal plants are collected along roadbanks and fencerows and fuel is collected in the *de facto* commons—land too far from villages for men to claim it.

Women's important role in the management of biodiversity and biological resources must be recognized, and their participation in decision-making must be ensured at all levels of resource management. Failed efforts and projects that did not acknowledge and include women—forestry schemes in Asia that ignored the myriad forest products gleaned by women, agriculture plans in Africa that overlooked the central role of women as farmers, and income-generating projects in South America that neglected the importance of women's income for family well-being—testify to the need for this action.

The capacities of women as biodiversity managers cannot be fully realized until women are freed from legal and social discrimination—a task still before many countries. Increased educational opportunities for women must be provided. They need mandatory primary schooling in rural areas, greater representation in secondary schooling, and more vocational training, including agricultural extension. They also need rights of access and ownership to land and resources. On all these fronts, development assistance can play a key role.

Development programs and projects must also promote equal participation by women in planning, implementation, and decision-making. Mere "consultation" is not enough. Often, obstacles to effective involvement must first be removed. In Madagascar, for example, few rural women speak French, so they may be shut out of political processes. Where consultation is needed, development agencies should seek input from women's organizations and should provide opportunities to meet with women separately from men. Development assistance agencies must also look inward, making sure that women have their fair share of decision-making authority within the agency.

Finally, development assistance agencies should recognize that the typical "project" approach to assistance is inherently biased against women in most countries. Where females have less access to power and less visibility in cash economies than males, development projects virtually always benefit men more than women. Alternatives must be provided to increase women's economic opportunities, including wider access to credit and help establishing and managing enterprises in their communities.

Objective:

Increase funding for biodiversity conservation, and develop innovative, decentralized, and accountable ways to raise funds and spend them effectively

Governments, which have always borne the main responsibility for biodiversity conservation and its costs, should not view biodiversity conservation as a burden or unrecoverable expense. Instead, it should be seen as an investment similar to that in public education or health. Indeed, many of the

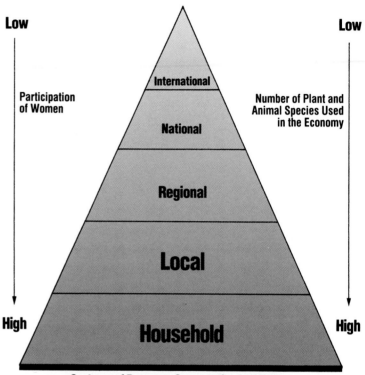

FIGURE 20

Women and Biodiversity

Source: Adapted from S. Hecht, unpub. figure

policy reforms needed to slow biodiversity loss, such as the removal of subsidies, can actually *save* money for governments. In other cases, the maintenance of key habitats and species provides economically valuable ecosystem services or forms the indispensable basis for such major industries as fisheries, tourism, and the harvesting of non-timber products. Since international funding for biodiversity conservation will always be limited, national governments themselves must make needed policy changes and increase their own investments.

Nevertheless, both the global benefits derived from biodiversity and the inability of many developing countries to invest heavily in conservation, demand that the international community provide financial support for conservation in many developing countries. That support must be provided in ways that surmount formidable constraints hampering the wise and effective use of conservation funding. In particular, the governmental and non-governmental organizations best suited to carry out conservation often cannot absorb rapid and massive investments efficiently. Moreover, it is difficult for international donors to target funds to those institutions and activities that can do the most good since donors are removed from the communities affected by their actions. Finally, throwing money at biodiversity conservation without simultaneously initiating the policy and institutional reforms discussed in other chapters will not be effective. Money in the wrong hands may merely strengthen inefficient or oppressive institutions and reinforce inappropriate ways of implementing biodiversity conservation.

Agencies that lend funds rather than grant them must also recognize that while investing in biodiversity has potentially large returns, those returns do not necessarily flow into the national treasury. Real economic benefits may flow to rural dwellers, for example, but not show up as government revenue. Accordingly, governments may be reluctant to borrow for some biodiversity projects at usual rates and terms. Thus, there is a clear need for additional and concessional biodiversity funding.

Action 27

Involve governments, multilateral development agencies, and non-governmental organizations jointly in establishing new biodiversity conservation funding sources and mechanisms, initially totalling at least $1 billion per year.

The 1988-1989 *International Conservation Financing Project* commissioned by the United Nations Development Programme (UNDP) and managed by WRI, called for $3 billion to be committed to conservation in developing countries over an initial 5-year period.[60] These funds would support projects in restoration and protecting genetic resources by using biological resources sustainably, maintaining national parks and protected areas, training, public awareness, promoting regenerative forestry, farming and fisheries, and energy conservation. The project estimated that at least $500 million could be invested in small-scale projects alone.

Based upon these analyses, and the estimates for investments required for those components of biodiversity already analyzed by other institutions, this *Strategy* proposes the need for at least $1 billion per year during the coming decade. Naturally, the results from the UNEP Biodiversity Country Reports, and other on-going studies will provide further refinement to these estimates.

Several international funding mechanisms for biodiversity conservation now exist or are under negotiation. Some regional or international conservation conventions include funding mechanisms (in all cases providing less than $2 million per year), and various international planning mechanisms have helped stimulate increased financial commitment to conservation. Bilateral and multilateral development agencies also have increased their financial support for biodiversity conservation over the past several years.

A new experiment in biodiversity-conservation funding is the Global Environment Facility (GEF) established in 1990 on a three-year pilot basis under the management of the World Bank, UNDP, and UNEP to provide concessional funding to developing countries. Twenty-two countries have contributed some $800 million. The GEF is expected to commit up to $400 million for biodiversity conservation projects during its three year life (1991-1993), and to provide experience upon which to base establishment of a more permanent funding mechanism or mechanisms.

A funding mechanism may be established as part of the anticipated Convention on Biological Diversity to provide additional support for biodiversity conservation activities in developing countries. In addition, the Fund for Plant Genetic

Resources was set up by members of the International Undertaking on Plant Genetic Resources under the auspices of FAO, though contributions are voluntary and have so far been minimal.

Existing funds for biodiversity conservation fall far short of estimated needs to slow biodiversity loss and ensure its sustainable use. The Keystone International Dialogue Series on Plant Genetic Resources estimated that $300 million per year in additional funds are needed to support urgent plant-gene conservation needs alone.[61] The cost of expanding the current network of tropical forest protected areas to better address biodiversity conservation needs is estimated to be roughly $1 billion, with $300 million annual recurrent costs.[62] *Caring for the Earth* estimates that over the next 10 years some $52 billion will be required to halt deforestation. This estimate includes calculations for reforestation and associated agricultural investments.

But while new funding is needed, mechanisms to manage and spend it effectively and equitably are still at a rudimentary stage of development. As a high-profile experiment, the GEF should be closely monitored to determine whether or not it is an appropriate model, and to promote dialogue on alternative models. Already, questions have been raised by both governments and NGOs about the lack of broad participation in GEF project development, difficulty of access to information about projects, the bias toward large projects run by central governments, and the concentration of control over funds by both the World Bank and donor country governments. Overcoming these problems will be the key test of whether GEF emerges as a viable model or prototype for managing international funding for biodiversity conservation in developing countries.

There is little consensus on what the governance and operations of a post-GEF global environment funding facility—or facilities—should look like, but some basic principles are becoming clear. First, funding mechanisms must reflect the needs and interests of both industrialized and developing countries, but must also attract unprecedented financial contri-

FIGURE 21

Estimated Growth Costs for Reducing Deforestation and Conserving Biodiversity in the 1990's

(Does Not Include Savings Achieved through the Removal of Inappropriate Subsidies or Benefits Gained from the Use of Biodiversity)

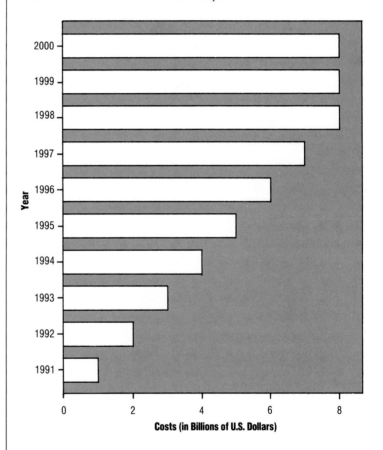

Source: IUCN, UNEP, WWF 1991

butions from the industrialized countries. In this regard, the Interim Multilateral Fund of the Montreal Protocol (on protection of the stratospheric ozone layer) provides a model attractive to the South: donor and recipient countries are equally represented when funds are allocated, and a two-thirds majority is required for decision-making. Both the donor and recipient blocs therefore have effective veto power over expenditures. On the other hand, donor governments have been slow to finance the Montreal Protocol Fund, and many would prefer a structure in which decisions are made in accordance with the size of a country's financial contribution. Striking a balance between these two models will require a great deal of negotiation.

Second, no global environmental fund is likely to attract widespread support unless its procedures provide for public accountability to the communities affected by the activities it finances, and to taxpayers in the countries that provide the funds. In practice, this means providing access to information on all aspects of the fund's operations, and formal procedures for public consultation on both individual projects and on the criteria for choosing and developing them.

Third, an increase in available funds will not actually conserve biodiversity unless capacities to design and manage biodiversity conservation projects are greatly enhanced. Biodiversity projects require more preparation to understand ecological processes, to gain community support, and to build managerial capacity than does, say, an energy conservation project for public utilities. Successful efforts typically start small, testing sustainable methods of resource use and community management models in a limited area, often through the efforts of local non-government organizations. And as this *Strategy* has repeatedly stressed, strengthening of in-country capacity to set priorities, develop, and manage projects, is an essential prerequisite for effectiveness.

Fourth, even if project preparation capacity can be bolstered, discrete biodiversity conservation projects are unlikely to have lasting impacts unless predicated on supportive policy and institutional reforms. A focus on money alone will inevitably overwhelm implementing agencies, and can often breed corruption.

There is no consensus on whether one "umbrella fund" or a diversity of mechanisms will best serve biodiversity conservation. Investment in biodiversity may well merit a diversity of funding sources and disbursement mechanisms. Centralizing all funding for biodiversity could stifle innovation

and accountability. Besides the three sources discussed above—the GEF, the Fund for Plant Genetic Resources, and a fund established under a Convention on Biological Diversity—a range of other mechanisms should be explored. A number of countries contribute project funds to the International Tropical Timber Organization (ITTO) for disbursement; ITTO could reinterpret its mandate and fund more biodiversity conservation projects in forests managed for timber. If the revised Tropical Forestry Action Plan gains the support of bilateral donors and conservation non-governmental organizations, it too could play a role. Finally, the need for international funding for country-level funding mechanisms should be emphasized.

Some donor countries may prefer to work bilaterally but within a general framework of global priorities and funding targets like those the proposed International Panel on Biodiversity Conservation would establish. International non-governmental organizations have limited financial resources, their close contacts in the field often put the projects they fund at the cutting edge. In addition, such organizations might be able to help disperse small grants.

Decision-makers must recognize that the additional funds needed for biodiversity conservation are miniscule in comparison to public spending in other areas. Reallocation of a tiny fraction of military budgets, for example, would more than fulfill biodiversity conservation needs in the 1990s. *(See Figure 22.)*

Action 28

Improve debt-for-nature swaps as a means of protecting biodiversity.

Since the mid-1980s, the "debt-for-nature swap" has been pioneered as a tool for generating additional funding for conservation in debt-ridden developing countries. *(See Figure 23.)* In a debt-swap of this type, the debt-holder forgives the indebted country's debt in exchange for the debtor government's commitment to invest (in local currency) in conservation projects in the debtor country.

Debt-for-nature swaps cannot solve the debt crisis; nor can they provide the lion's share of the funds needed for biodiversity conservation over the next decade. But they are a potentially useful way to raise new funds to address specific conservation needs. Indeed, since 1987, some 18 debt-for-nature swaps have been negotiated in the so-called secondary debt market. Some $98 million of debt (face value) has been relieved, and $61 million in conservation funds generated.

Despite their proven potential for supporting conservation, debt swaps have their shortcomings. Such swaps may appear to legitimize debts incurred under corrupt former regimes, abetted by undue pressure to borrow exerted by banks. On the other hand, swaps may benefit countries with poor economic and environmental management records. Some swaps have raised questions about national sovereignty, while others have incensed local communities whose homelands were "swapped" without their consent. Questions about how the funds are spent and who controls them also linger. But mistakes always trail innovations, and the challenge now is to refine debt-for-nature swaps, respecting their intrinsic limitations as well as their untapped potential.

Action 29

Promote the use of trust funds or endowments for biodiversity conservation.

Even if funding for biodiversity conservation doubles or quadruples in the coming decade, allocating funds to priority needs will still be a problem. Both public and non-governmental organizations responsible for carrying out new conservation activities have historically been financially strapped, so a sudden infusion of large sums of money could overwhelm them. Moreover, many long-underfunded organizations need long-term operating and maintenance funds more than they need project funds.

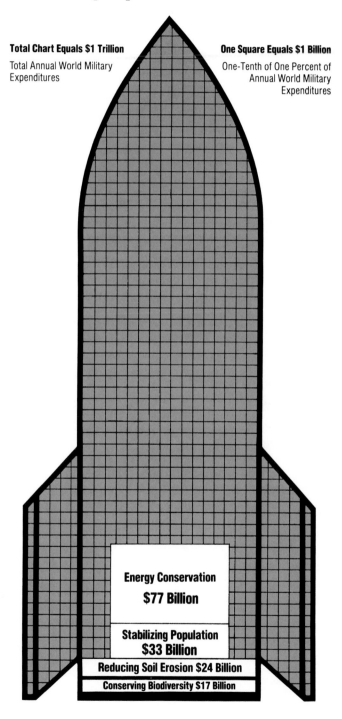

FIGURE 22

The Relative Cost of Ecological Security and Military Expenditure in 2000

Total Chart Equals $1 Trillion
Total Annual World Military Expenditures

One Square Equals $1 Billion
One-Tenth of One Percent of Annual World Military Expenditures

Energy Conservation
$77 Billion

Stabilizing Population
$33 Billion

Reducing Soil Erosion $24 Billion

Conserving Biodiversity $17 Billion

Source: IUCN, UNEP, WWF 1991

FIGURE 23

Simplified Structure of a Debt-for-Nature Operation

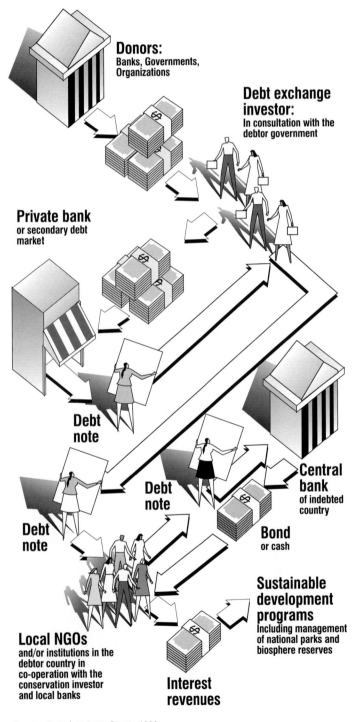

Donors:
Banks, Governments, Organizations

Debt exchange investor:
In consultation with the debtor government

Private bank
or secondary debt market

Debt note

Debt note

Debt note

Central bank
of indebted country

Bond
or cash

Local NGOs
and/or institutions in the debtor country in co-operation with the conservation investor and local banks

Interest revenues

Sustainable development programs
Including management of national parks and biosphere reserves

Source: Dogsé and von Droste 1990

One of the most promising ways to both boost absorptive capacity and satisfy the need for long-term financial support is thus to establish trust funds or endowments for biodiversity conservation.

Just such a trust fund is being established for conservation in Bhutan, with $10 million to $20 million dollars (funded in part through the GEF and WWF). UNDP invests the principal, and the interest will be used to fund training, inventory, protected areas system review, institutional support for government ministries, environmental education, and integrated conservation-development projects. The Fund's governing board consists of three members of the government of Bhutan, and one each from World Wildlife Fund (WWF) and UNDP.

The Bhutan Trust Fund experience should be closely followed to assess its strengths, weaknesses, and replicability in other countries. At the same time, smaller-scale trust fund mechanisms should be established. Individual protected areas, non-governmental conservation organizations, and research organizations would all be appropriate candidates for such arrangements.

Action 30

Develop mechanisms to fund grassroots organizations and initiatives.

Many innovative biodiversity conservation activities are taking place at the local level, initiated by thousands of small grassroots organizations throughout the world. But most funding for biodiversity conservation is channelled through large bilateral and multilateral aid agencies and the major private foundations, which are ill-suited to reach the grassroots. Some, such as the World Bank, are largely restricted by their own charters from working with anyone but central governments. Many others lack local staff or have procedural requirements that overwhelm most grassroots groups. Many see their business as moving funds, not ensuring they are well spent.

The answer to this institutional problem may lie in the development of national government/non-governmental organization consortiums that serve as clearinghouses and administrators for grassroots biodiversity funding. Such a consortium might be composed of officials from government agencies, national non-governmental organizations, and international conservation groups. It would represent local groups and projects with small but urgent funding needs to government agencies and large international and national donors. It would also help grassroots groups develop project proposals and meet donors' reporting and other procedural requirements.

Such a system could not work without the backing of governments and large donors. Governments might need to change some policies and regulations to clear the way for small grants funding, and donors would have to come up with core support for the consortium and amend their internal procedures to accommodate it. The establishment of a "small grants window" within the GEF is a step in the right direction, but alternative mechanisms should be developed as well.

VI

Creating Conditions and Incentives for Local Biodiversity Conservation

In and around the remaining centers of high biodiversity are also the poorest communities in the world. These communities—especially those of tribal peoples—have never shared in the bounties of the land, either during the days of colonialism or during today's era of local elite colonialism. The best way to liberate these communities from the vicious cycle of poverty is through empowerment—the control of their own natural resources, and access to information and technology. To support the advocacy of these issues is to support the cause of biodiversity conservation.

CELSO ROQUE, UNDERSECRETARY, DEPARTMENT OF ENVIRONMENT AND NATURAL RESOURCES, PHILIPPINES

Why should villagers respect a protected-area boundary that cuts off their access to resources? Why should a logging community support the protection of an endangered species' habitat? What is the appeal of "ecotourism" to a community if the profits from the venture go elsewhere? Indeed, people living in areas of high biodiversity value may have more convincing reasons to over-exploit resources than to conserve them.

Many communities simply have no economic incentives to conserve biodiversity. In these communities, the key to successful conservation is making sure that they share the benefits fairly and do not shoulder a disproportionate share of the costs. In many others where economic incentives do exist, local authorities and communities need to regulate the use of biodiversity within wider resource management plans and to apply technical skills to manage and conserve biological resources. Important here are legally recognized and enforceable rights to land, which give the communities both an economic incentive and a legal basis for stewardship.

Governments often misinterpret calls for greater community involvement in biological resource management as demands to turn the whole enterprise over to local people.

In fact, communities must manage their biological wealth within the wider context of obligations and responsibilities to the nation and the world, and local communities need various government services to be effective resource managers. In some cases, government should in fact assert more control over local abuses of the environment or intervene to correct local inequities in resource access. For these reasons, governments have a legitimate and important role to play in safeguarding national interests and in enforcing minimum standards of resource stewardship, even on private lands.

Objective:

Correct imbalances in the control of land and resources that cause biodiversity loss and develop new resource management partnerships between government and local communities

The longstanding trend in most parts of the world has been to transfer ownership of forest lands and coastal waters to the public domain and to vest centralized government agencies with their management. The rapid destruction of tropical forests and coastal ecosystems within the public domain—and the accompanying impoverishment of the tens of millions of people that depend on them—indicates that this approach has failed in both social and ecological terms. Returning a measure of control over public lands and resources to local communities is thus fundamental to slowing biodiversity loss in many threatened ecosystems. Such restitution is particularly appropriate in the biologically rich ancestral domains of the world's indigenous peoples.

In some parts of the world, however, excessive local or private control of natural ecosystems is a cause of biodiversity loss, largely because of the lack—or loss—of a social structure and resource management tradition conducive to sustainable use and stewardship. In such situations, governments should enforce basic norms of stewardship on behalf of the wider society and future generations. States need not and should not take over private or communal property rights except in extreme situations; dialogue, education, zoning or other forms of regulation, and technical assistance are more appropriate vehicles for promoting stewardship. The ultimate goal of government in such cases should be to promote the restoration or creation of a social, technical, and ethical basis upon which each community can take the leading role in managing its resources sustainably. *(See Chapter 7.)*

The concentration of productive land in too few hands also creates serious economic, social, and environmental problems. Correcting any of these imbalances in the ownership and control of land and resources presents daunting political challenges; no issues are more politically charged in many countries than land reform, the return of public lands to local communities, or the restriction of private land management by government. But these changes are needed not only for biodiversity's sake, but also to increase agricultural productivity, address inequities, and create political stability.

Restoration of balance in land rights and resource access, however, is only the first step in developing more sustainable systems for managing living resources. The second is to establish new resource-management partnerships between local communities and the state to maintain biodiversity and productivity.

Action 31

Reduce pressure on fragile ecosystems and wildlands by using land already under cultivation more efficiently and equitably.

In many agricultural countries, skewed distribution of land ownership greatly intensifies the pressures that degrade natural ecosystems. *(See Figure 24.)* When a small minority controls the most productive agricultural lands, many landless rural people have no alternative but to seek their livelihoods in forests and fragile upland areas, many of which cannot sustain agriculture.

In Guatemala, for example, the economy is dominated by the production for export of a limited number of cash crops grown on extensive lands held by a tiny minority (2 percent) of farmers. This skewed pattern of land ownership forces poor people denied access to fertile valleys and lowlands to

FIGURE 24

Distribution of Agricultural Land in Selected Countries of Latin America and the Caribbean

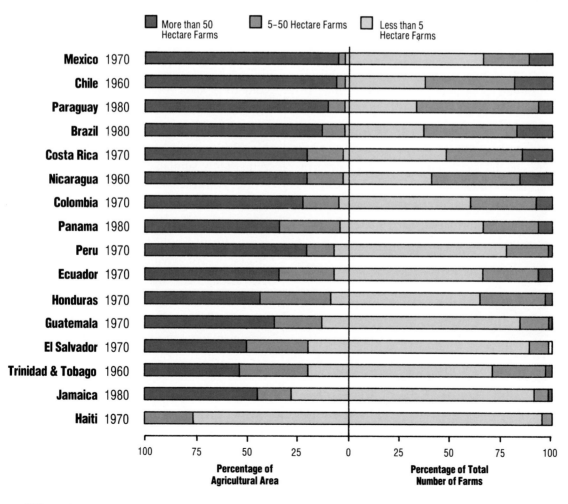

Source: WRI and USAID 1991

cultivate marginal lands inappropriate for agriculture. Meanwhile, half of the land held by the landholding minority is almost unused. The results for the country's biologically rich forests are devastating: Guatemala's forest cover has dropped from 77 percent in 1960 to less than half in 1991, and 90 percent of this deforestation is due to colonization for agriculture and ranching.[63]

The situation is much the same in many other Latin American countries, in the Philippines, and to a lesser extent in many other parts of the world. Even where land seems to be more equitably distributed, as in parts of Africa, women may be denied rights to land or resource ownership.

Some analysts have concluded that land reform would do more to relieve pressure on forest lands than any other single policy intervention.[64] But the politics of making access to productive lands more equitable can be tortuous. Most large landowners are well-connected and powerful, and impetus for change is most likely to come from below, through popular movements and their advocates in non-governmental organizations. Researchers, development-aid agencies, and international organizations can also play a role, however, by exposing the social and environmental costs of inequitable land ownership, convincing governments that land reform is in the countries' long-term best interest, and supporting organizations and movements struggling for fair access to the land, forests, and waters.

Action 32

Increase incentives for local stewardship of public lands and waters.

In the many parts of the world where livelihoods depend directly on natural resources, state ownership and control over large stretches of land and water has often created incentives for overexploiting these resources. In the developing countries, more than 80 percent of the closed forest area is public land.[65] The global figure for coastal resources (near-shore fisheries, coral reefs, mangroves) may be even higher since few countries allow individuals or communities to own reefs and near-shore fisheries.

This widespread policy of blanket state ownership sometimes creates an "open access" situation in which governments do not have the resources to control access and exploitation, but no one else has the legal right to try. Spoils therefore go to the quickest and the strongest, and nobody has an incentive to maintain ecosystem productivity and biodiversity. Local resource-harvest limits set by customary law are legally voided, state controls cannot be enforced effectively, and a wide range of outsiders—migrants, timber concessionaires, commercial trawlers, and others—grab resources in a "first-come, first-serve" free-for-all. Traditional communities frequently join in the frenzy when so many competitors arrive on the scene. The degradation of tropical forests, depletion of fisheries, destruction of coral reefs, and conversion of mangroves to unsustainable aquaculture and woodchip production all contain legacies of open access.

While the effects of public ownership are remarkably similar throughout the developing world, constructive alternatives must be tailored to the local situation. In some cases, privatization and secure individual property rights may be the most effective policies. In others, especially in coastal areas, reviving moribund common-property management systems, or inventing new ones, may make sense.

In all cases, however, governments should retain ownership of certain core land and sea resource areas (including national parks) and control of others (including timber concessions and critical watersheds). In these "public" areas, more effective state management and enforcement systems are necessary, along with increased financial support.

Action 33

Recognize the ancestral domains of tribal and indigenous peoples and support their efforts to maintain traditional practices and adapt them to modern pressures and conditions.

Some 200 million indigenous peoples (4 percent of the world's population) live in and have special claims to territories that, in many cases, harbor exceptionally high levels of biodiversity. Their claim rests on their long occupation of a particular place; their cultural, spiritual, and economic ties to the area; and their ability, in most cases, to manage it sustainably. At the same time, the cultural diversity inherent in the world's indigenous groups is imperilled by the encroachment of dominant societies and economies. Preserving indigenous territorial rights thus protects biodiversity and the local culture, including knowledge and resource-management skills with potentially wide applications, as well as spiritual ties to the environment that could provide direction for the development of a biodiversity ethos in the wider society.

Indigenous peoples do not, however, have all the answers; nor do they want to be left alone in some kind of "human zoo." Many traditional strategies have already yielded to contemporary economic and social pressures, and most indigenous communities need government support and services if they are to develop their territories sustainably.

Governments should legally recognize and demarcate tribal and indigenous territories under national law, help indigenous communities defend their land against incursions, and permit indigenous peoples to develop organizations to directly represent them in national and international fora. Governments and development agencies should also—through a sustained dialogue without intermediaries—determine what kind of development indigenous groups want, providing information on options, funding, and support services. Ultimately, the indigenous peoples themselves should determine their own future.

Action 34

Compensate individuals and local communities who own or depend on land or resources taken for public purposes.

Recognizing local rights to land and resources does not make these rights absolute. All governments must from time to time take land from individuals or communities—or restrict their access to its resources—to build a road, create a protected area, or serve some other public purpose. In such cases, the recognition of local rights implies that just compensation should be paid to those whose land rights are diminished or extinguished.

Compensation—whether cash, alternative tracts of land, or services—directly supports biodiversity conservation. Where the creation or expansion of a protected area or restrictions on the use of particular species constrains ownership or use of land, compensation helps garner local support for conservation objectives. Where land is needed for other development purposes (such as a road or dam), compensation can reduce the need for displaced people to invade fragile forest or upland areas. In all cases, however, compensation must be perceived as fair, and must reach the hands of affected communities.

To qualify for compensation, occupation of land and reliance on its resources should be enough. In much of the world, the poor simply do not have land title (even though they may have customary rights). Standing on legal formality would only obstruct attempts to equitably share the costs and benefits of biodiversity conservation and management.

Action 35

Manage living resources on public lands through new forms of community-state partnership and cooperation.

Living resources such as forests and coastal ecosystems cannot be sustainably managed exclusively by communities or states. The state must recognize the interests and rights of the community, and the community must recognize that it is part of a larger political and economic framework that not only imposes responsibilities and limitations, but also provides opportunities. "Co-management"—the sharing of power and responsibility between the government and resource users—provides a middle ground upon which the two can meet and cooperate.[66]

The success of co-management depends on six basic requirements. First, government agencies and officials must acquire new attitudes and skills, learning to respect local communities' needs and

---

BOX 18

Conserving Amazonia's Biodiversity: The Perspective of the Coordinating Body for the Indigenous Peoples' Organizations of the Amazon Basin (COICA)

We, the Indigenous Peoples, have been an integral part of the Amazon Biosphere for millenia. We used and cared for the resources of that biosphere with respect, because it is our home, and because we know that our survival and that of our future generations depend on it.

Our accumulated knowledge about the ecology of our home, our models for living within the Amazonian biosphere, our reverence and respect for the tropical forest and its other inhabitants, both plant and animal, are the keys to guaranteeing the future of the Amazon Basin, not only for our peoples, but also for all of humanity.

Our experience, especially during the past 100 years, has taught us that when politicians and developers take charge of our home, they are capable of destroying it because of their short-sightedness, their ignorance, and their greed.

We are concerned that the Amazon peoples, and in particular the indigenous peoples, have been left out of the environmentalists' vision of the Amazonian biosphere. The focus of concern of the environmental community has typically been the preservation of the tropical forests and its plant and animal inhabitants. Little concern has been shown for its human inhabitants who are also part of that biosphere.

We are concerned that the indigenous peoples and their representative organizations have been left out of the political process which is determining the future of our homeland. The environmentalist community has at times lobbied on our behalf; it has spoken out and written in the name of the Amazonian Indians. While we appreciate those efforts, it should be made clear that we never delegated this power to the environmentalist community nor to any individual nor organization within that community.

The most effective defense of the Amazonian Biosphere is the recognition and defense of the territories of the region's Indigenous Peoples and the promotion of their models for living within that Biosphere and for managing its resources in a sustainable way.

Source: Adapted from COICA, "To the Community of Concerned Environmentalists," 1989

knowledge, and seeing them as part of resource management rather than an obstacle to it. Second, co-management requires the empowerment of weaker social groups within local communities—particularly landless people and women. Third, local communities as a whole must be sufficiently organized to bargain with state agencies on terms of relative equality. Fourth, co-management implies blending new and old knowledge and technologies; neither "traditional" nor "modern" ways of doing things can be viewed as intrinsically superior. Fifth, co-management schemes must generate tangible economic benefits for the community and satisfy state management objectives. Finally, the co-management regime must be supported by a clear assignment of legal rights and responsibilities, including tenurial rights, contractual agreements, and processes for resolving disputes.

State resource-management agencies generally resist recognizing the need for cooperation with local communities. The traditions and skills of foresters, for example, stress timber-stand management, soil and water conservation, and silviculture, and few foresters want or know how to work with local people to manage forest lands. Accepting the need for formalizing community forest management has sweeping implications for forestry agencies' policies, personnel, and attitudes. Many local communities are likely to be either suspicious of or hostile to co-management proposals as well, since they have years (sometimes centuries) of conflict with government authorities to overcome.

Government agencies generally have to take the first steps toward co-management, but other actors can encourage them to do so. Policy-makers, development agencies, and non-governmental organizations who want to promote co-management can forge alliances with sympathetic agency personnel to lobby for decentralization and new approaches. When enough agency personnel finally accept these ideas, they can begin to push for the internal changes in policy, training, and organization that co-management requires; pilot efforts can than be launched. One of the most powerful forces of change in the

U.S. Forest Service, for example, is the Association of Forest Service Employees for Environmental Ethics (AFSEE)—individuals tired of being forced by policies beyond their control to make management decisions that violate their professional ethics. The support network created by AFSEE has empowered individuals to take actions that might have gotten them fired only a few years ago.

Research on the social, economic, and ecological dimensions of a community's relation to its resource base can sometimes serve as the opening wedge to institutional change and the breakdown of mistrust between state and community. Government officials often harbor negative and inaccurate stereotypes about rural people that good research can challenge. For rural people, the experience of being asked how they live and interact with their environment is generally a welcome break from being told what to do. And baseline information on local resources and their management is an essential foundation for a co-management effort in any case.

Attempts at co-management are under way in societies of northern and southern hemispheres. No single initiative can be called an unqualified success, and some have failed. But taken together they point the way toward a more sustainable paradigm for managing living resources and thus for conserving biodiversity.

"Social forestry" initiatives in which communities and government foresters cooperate to reforest degraded state lands have been under way for at least a decade in Indonesia, the Philippines, Thailand, and India.[67] These experiments have illustrated the promise of co-management—even under conditions of extreme poverty, high population densities, and strong pressures for commercial exploitation. But they have also revealed the considerable obstacles to be overcome, including the fragility of government commitment to co-management, the tendency of local elites to monopolize benefits, and the strength of external commercial pressures.

In Brazil, "extractive reserves"—in which communities hold rights to harvest rubber and other non-timber forest products in specified areas of state-held forest—have been established by law in parts of the Amazon. Fourteen extractive reserves covering about 3,000,000 hectares have been created in four states.[68] Although the establishment of the reserves shows a promising change of heart in the federal government, the long-term economic viability of these reserves is uncertain, some state governments are opposed, and local elites continue to use violence against extractivists seemingly with impunity.

Efforts to co-manage particular species have also been pioneered. In northern Canada, conflicts between government and Inuit hunters over management of the large Kaminuriak caribou herd led to development of a Joint Management Board. The board formulates policy, proposes research, and circulates an educational bilingual newspaper to all households.[69] Finally, some protected areas are also being co-managed. In Costa Rica, community and local organizations constitute a regional board for the Guanacaste Conservation Area that has authority and responsibility for its management.

Co-management of the marine environment has received less attention than forest-based initiatives, but its potential is perhaps even greater. Governments simply cannot police and manage thousands of miles of reefs and nearshore waters, and no centralized agencies for coastal environments exist.[70] Recent developments in the Philippines illustrate the potential for co-management in coastal and marine areas. *(See Box 19.)*

Objective:

Expand and encourage the sustainable use of products and services from the wild for local benefits

Local communities have long exploited nature, reaping a wide variety of subsistence and market products, often without substantially degrading the ecosystem. Throughout the world, much of the management and use of wild products is done by women, with great benefits for the family and local economy. The benefits to local communities from wild products could be increased, and it makes both ecological and economic sense to do so. Yet no product is inherently "sustainable," so safeguards against over-exploitation are required. The flow of benefits to local communities rather than outsiders must also be protected.

Action 36

Recognize and quantify the local economic value of wild products in development and land-use planning.

Development planners have systematically undervalued the economic importance of the local use of wild products, many of which are consumed directly and never enter markets. Examples include vegetables, meat, fibers, bamboos, canes, grasses, medicines, spices, seeds for oil and propagation, gums and resins, dyes, honey and wax, and wood.

The value of these products can be far higher than that of timber harvest or land conversion to pasture or agriculture. For example, over 50 years, harvesting such forest products as fruit and latex in

BOX 19

Co-Management of Marine Resources in the Philippines

A community marine resource management program called the "Marine Conservation and Development Program" (MCDP) was conceived and initiated in 1984 by university researchers in three fishing communities in the Visayas Islands of the Philippines. The program was designed to promote conservation and sustainable use of coral reefs and associated fisheries through community-based efforts to stop over-fishing and destructive fishing techniques using dynamite, cyanide, and bleach and practiced by both local residents and outsiders.

Basically, MCDP seeks to establish reservation status for large portions of the reef and, within the reserve zone, sanctuary status for the smaller areas. The reserve area functions as a limited access buffer zone in which ecologically sound fishing is permitted. The sanctuary is a specially marked, cordoned area of the reef where all forms of exploitation and entry are forbidden. The sanctuary functions as a fish-breeding and habitat-rehabilitation area—a natural hatchery—to increase overall fish yields to local islanders.

The results of the program have been environmentally and socially impressive: the species richness and abundance of selected coral-reef fish per unit area has significantly increased, and the condition of the reef itself has improved.

The most striking aspect of MCDP was its manner of implementation. Local fishers helped design and implement the reserve and sanctuary systems at all levels. Collaborating with community organizers, they designated the portions of the reef to be governed as a reserve, as well as the more strictly protected sanctuaries, and they physically laid the marker buoys themselves. The local communities also formulated regulations prohibiting fishing, the anchoring of motorized boats, and the collection of giant clams within sanctuaries. Within the larger and less restrictive reserve areas, they prohibited dynamite fishing, spearfishing using scuba gear and cyanide, and the use of small-mesh gill nets. These guidelines were subsequently recognized by local government authorities.

Enforcement is also carried out by the communities. Young local men formed a group called Guardians of the Sea that confronts and chases away violators (locals as well as outsiders)—sometimes with the help of the Philippine Constabulary—and initiates public hearings for local perpetrators, who are tried and punished according to an indigenous system of public justice.

In 1990, a draft Philippines Fisheries Code was proposed to put the principles of marine co-management into practice nationwide. This code would transfer basic operational authority to local groups of fishers and to bay-wide councils of fishers or municipalities, though the central fisheries agency would still supervise the exploitation of fishery and aquatic resources, issue permits, formulate policy, and establish and operate a national fisheries information system.

The MCDP experience shows that local efforts must be actively supported by the wider political institutions and legal structures in which they are imbedded in order to prevent local elites from capturing a disproportionate share of the benefits of conservation and management programs. The MCDP relies on assistance from local police, legislators, universities, activists, and international development-assistance institutions, and on the ingenuity and commitment of the local communities themselves.

Source: Zerner, 1991

one forest in Peru could yield more than twice as much money as either cattle ranching or conversion to timber production.[71] In Southeast Asia, at least 29 million people depend on the harvest of non-timber forest products for daily needs and cash income.[72] The export value of non-timber forest products in 1987 totalled $23 million in Thailand and $238 million in Indonesia. In India, so-called minor forest products—produced mostly by women—account for 75 percent of net export earnings from forest products.[73]

FIGURE 25

Exports of Non-Timber Forest Products from Thailand in 1982

(Total Value Approximately U.S. $15 million.)

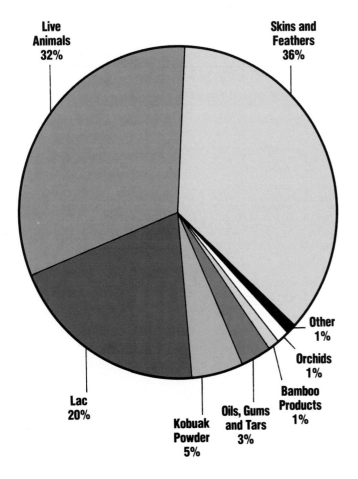

Live Animals 32%

Skins and Feathers 36%

Other 1%

Orchids 1%

Bamboo Products 1%

Oils, Gums and Tars 3%

Kobuak Powder 5%

Lac 20%

Source: DeBeer and McDermott 1989

So long as products like these are undervalued in development planning, land and potentially renewable biological resources will be sacrificed to quick profits. Determining the value of wild products to local economies can be time-consuming, and care must be taken to evaluate differences between men and women in their use. But unless such studies are made, local communities and development planners will not be able to evaluate the costs and benefits associated with various development options.

Action 37

Encourage local communities to explore opportunities for developing a larger market share for wild products harvested sustainably.

Rattan, a vine often used to make furniture, is a non-timber product of great economic importance in Southeast Asia. Before 1986, when it banned shipments abroad, Indonesia exported $63 million of unworked rattan annually. But rattan production also exemplifies the risks of exploiting valuable wild species. In Peninsular Malaysia, 35 percent of rattan species may already be threatened; in Sabah, 25 percent; in Sarawak, 30 percent.[74]

Because high market values provide incentives to exploit wild products, markets for these goods must be developed carefully to ensure that the harvest rate doesn't exceed the regeneration rate. Equally important, markets should be developed *by* local communities, not *for* them. All too often in the past, the people who harvest the resource have been abused—in the worst cases, virtually enslaved—along with the resource.

Numerous efforts are now under way to develop new products from tropical forests or to maintain economies based on wild products. Brazil nuts harvested in the Amazon are finding their way into ice cream consumed in North America, and oils and essences of tropical forest plants are used in health and beauty products. Currently, many of the industries using these products try to "cut out the middle-man" to ensure that the raw materials fetch a fair price. As these ventures expand, however, less socially conscious entrepreneurs are sure to enter the field. One response is to add value to the products locally. Of course, developing business in ways that will promote conservation instead of in ways that will ultimately transform the landscape and culture is difficult. But the choice has to be made within the local community—not outside. *(See Box 20.)*

Action 38

Increase the local benefits of tourism in natural areas—"ecotourism"—and ensure that tourism development does not result in biodiversity loss or cultural conflict.

Natural attractions have always drawn crowds, but recent years have seen a boom in "ecotourism" as more tourists seek alternatives to traditional vacations and a deeper understanding of the natural environment. Tourism entrepreneurs and officials have taken note of this trend, opening ever wider natural areas to both independent travelers and package tours. Ecotourism can, in theory, increase the value of maintaining ecosystems in their natural state, thereby providing both governments and local communities with incentives for conservation. In practice, however, the benefits accruing to local communities have not been great, while the negative impacts on local ecosystems and cultures have often been high—a combination that discourages conservation.

Typically, the ecotourism industry employs personnel from outside a region or country for all but the lowest-paid positions, and any government entrance and concession fees charged go to the government, not the community. Meanwhile, local residents pay ecotourism's price. Residents' rights to use the natural "attraction" are often restricted,

tourism sparks local inflation, and the local culture is tested, if not undermined, by the consumerism and hedonism that modern tourism entails. Meanwhile, heavy tourist traffic in forests, game parks, and on coral reefs can degrade these resources directly.

If ecotourism is to contribute seriously to conservation and development, rather than simply drive a wedge of well-heeled tourists into biologically rich pristine areas, certain basic guidelines should be followed. In general, ecotourism should:

- provide significant benefits for local residents;
- contribute to the sustainable management of natural resources;
- incorporate environmental education for tourists and residents; and,
- be developed and managed to minimize negative impacts on the environment and local culture.

Few ecotourism programs have followed these principles scrupulously. To put them into practice, government and industry should involve local communities as equal partners in all phases of ecotourism planning and development. Concrete financial benefits are obviously an important part of such a partnership. Most important, local communities must have the final say about how much and what kind of tourism develops in their areas.

This new partnership should be based on a commitment to hire local residents as managers in protected areas and tourism operations. In addition, programs for providing credit for rural enterprises should be initiated or expanded so that more local entrepreneurs can develop tourism-related businesses. It could also mean offering "on-the-job" training and scholarships to tourism and park management schools abroad, leasing rather than buying land from local residents, and purchasing more goods and services for ecotourists locally.

BOX 20

Principles for Developing Markets for Non-Timber Forest Products

Start with what is already on the market.

Marketing efforts should focus initially on products for which markets already exist. New products face both market uncertainty and a substantial time lag for development and acceptance, particularly in the international market.

Diversify production and reduce dependence on a few products.

The diversification of products being sold is absolutely essential to the overall viability of non-timber forest product strategies, though diversification can take decades and should be undertaken for one product at a time. Products for which there is already a market and a high volume or value of production should be used to create possibilities for lesser-known commodities to be marketed.

Diversify the number and type of end uses for any particular product.

More end users for a particular product mean less risk for producers. Brazil nuts, for example, can be sold for use as snacks, as ingredients in ice cream, baked goods, candies, cereal, oil, and flour, thereby cushioning producers from market fluctuations in any one of these so-called end uses. Risk can be further

reduced by penetrating regular as well as specialty markets and a mix of local, national, and international markets.

Determine the best way to capture the value that is always added to a product as it leaves the source, and value that is added farther from the source.

Value can be added locally by transporting the product farther into the market to eliminate other traders and by local processing. Each attempt to add value can often double income from the product. As a rule of thumb, progressively greater values are added to a product as it moves away from the source or undergoes a further stage of processing. Producers and their supporters should therefore work to capture value at as many steps as possible in the commercial chain from source to consumer.

Ensure that extractivist marketing strategies are sustainable and replicable.

Particular "pet" projects or products should not be highly subsidized by conservation organizations and other supporters of extractivism or promoted as financial panaceas; no single model will work everywhere, and excessive subsidies ensure that a particular project will not be widely replicated.

Action 39

Strengthen local capacity for maintaining and benefiting from crop and varietal diversity.

The diversity of crops and livestock grown in a region is a source of economic and ecological secu-

rity, as well as a cultural inheritance. Even where modern varieties have largely replaced traditional ones, farmers often maintain traditional varieties for their better flavor or higher local market price, or as insurance against the failure of the modern varieties. Many "informal" conservation networks of farmers, non-governmental organizations, and horticulturalists maintain local crop and livestock

Promote cooperation among producers for greater power in the market.

If extractivist producers wish to target commercial firms in the international market—and in many cases this is the most profitable strategy—they have no choice but to band together. The M&M Mars candy company, for example, could utilize the entire annual production of the Brazil nut shelling plant in Xapuri, Brazil, in one eight-hour production shift. Economies of scale can also benefit producers. Where producers' cooperation commands a large market share of a particular commodity, producers may also be able to influence the entire market.

Certify the environmental sustainability for the "Green Market."

"Green consumers" in urban areas and industrialized countries are generally more concerned about plants and animals than about the livelihoods of local communities in far off places. Because of this orientation, the sale of commodities from the wild must be linked with credible monitoring systems to ensure that the quantity of products taken does not destroy the very forests, reefs, or other wild places that consumers are paying to protect.

Source: Cultural Survival, 1991.

---

genetic diversity and provide crop options and varieties to local farmers.[75]

These grassroots conservation networks also fill gaps in the formal system of genebanks, universities, and research institutions by focusing on regionally important crops, marginal areas, and traditional agricultural practices. Because they are decentralized by nature, non-governmental organi-

FIGURE 26

Value of Coffee Exports and Tourism in Kenya

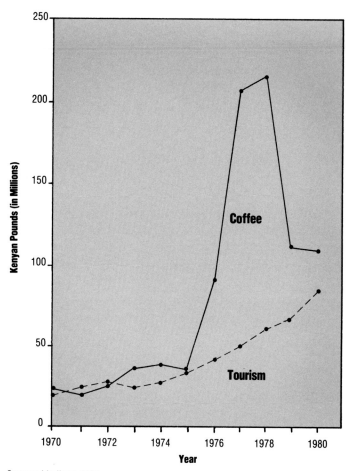

Source: Lindberg 1991

zations are often better suited than national institutions to save local genetic diversity and make it available for local needs.

Informal genetic resource conservation networks already figure prominently in germplasm conservation. Brazilian non-governmental organizations, for example, are spearheading efforts to link the conservation and breeding of maize by farmers; non-governmental organizations and farmers' organizations in Peru and Bolivia are conserving traditional varieties of potatoes.[76] In the United States, of the 1799 heirloom and standard varieties of beans held by a non-profit network of farmers and gardeners (the Seed Savers Exchange) only 147 are found in the government-supported collections. In a 1991 survey of twelve grassroots seed-conservation groups in the southwestern United States, roughly one half of the groups maintained over 1,000 accessions of seeds each.[77]

Unfortunately, the potential of informal conservation networks is severely constrained by lack of funds. One Filipino farmers' organization surveying and collecting hundreds of traditional varieties grown on the island of Mindanao could raise only $15,000 for the program. Indeed, the single biggest obstacle to the development of community-based plant genetic resource systems in both developing and developed countries is funding.[78]

As for other key obstacles, the most important are lack of facilities (freezers, office space, grow-out plots, etc.) and trained personnel, the rapid loss of traditional varieties, and the financial constraints facing farmers who might be involved in the work. In some countries, legal barriers to the conservation of genetic resources also exist. According to reports from non-governmental organizations, as recently as 1984 the Indonesian government burned traditional rice cultivars planted by farmers. In many countries, farmers planting traditional varieties cannot obtain agricultural credit.

The formal genetic-resource-conservation network needs to collaborate more with farmers and nongovernmental organizations. A wise first step might be setting up national advisory boards on traditional crops and varieties, adding grassroots representatives to advisory boards for other crops, or involving grassroots conservation groups in national agricultural planning. In addition, national agricultural research institutions should provide training, guarantees of access to genetic resources, and research tailored to the needs of small-scale farmers.

The payoffs from such collaboration can be significant. In Thailand, one non-governmental organization, Technology for Rural and Ecological Enrichment (TREE), launched a rescue operation to save plant-genetic resources from being lost as the Thai government aggressively introduced new seeds backed by agricultural loans and extension services. TREE collected more than 4,000 accessions of rice and almost 3,000 accessions of other food crops in two years and gave duplicates of these collections to the national gene bank.[79]

Action 40

Develop the role of traditional medicines and ensure their appropriate and sustainable use.

The sustainable use of plants and animals for their medical value is an important use of biodiversity often overlooked by policy-makers. The full benefits of this use must be calculated in the context of both traditional and "industrialized" medicine.

Both Western health-care systems and traditional systems have much to offer—medically, economically, and culturally—and countries should seek to integrate these systems rather than try to replace one with the other. One way to do this is for health care workers to screen traditional medicines using procedures developed to test the efficacy of "modern" pharmaceuticals. An example of such a program is TRAMIL in the Caribbean, which assesses the effectiveness of traditional remedies through ethno-pharmacological surveys and classifies traditional herbal remedies as either toxic, indeterminant, or beneficial/innocuous.[80] The program has produced a manual, "Elements for a Caribbean Pharmacopeia," that health-care workers use as a guide to the region's many useful traditional medicinal treatments.

Such applied medical research can help decrease the cost of medicinal therapy by drawing on local practical knowledge of the treatment of common ailments and by putting local remedies within the reach of all. But such programs do have drawbacks. The people who evaluate traditional therapies have little understanding of, or training in, the traditional health care systems. A solution here would be to familiarize people already involved in traditional health care systems with western medicine, through extension programs, enabling these individuals to choose among systems as they see fit.

From an environmental standpoint, the use of traditional medicines can threaten biodiversity. Accordingly, strengthening such systems requires taking steps to ensure the sustainability of resource use. In Africa, many villagers can no longer find medicinal plants in part because commercial collectors have overharvested them to meet the demand in cities. In East Asia, the use of the rhinoceros in traditional medicine has helped bring several species to the brink of extinction. (Rhinoceros horn and horn powders are used as cures for ailments ranging from high blood pressure to impotence, and other medicines are derived from hide, bones, meat, and blood.) The cure-all reputation of bear gall bladders in Southeast Asian markets has helped endanger the Asiatic black bear and is now pressuring other species of bears around the world.

For medicinal plants, the best insurance against over-exploitation is generally to promote their sustained cultivation, looking to agricultural extension, botanic gardens, and arboreta for information and advice. For many vertebrates, however, solutions are much harder to find. The Convention on International Trade in Endangered Species (CITES) has helped reduce pressure on some species overexploited for medicinal uses, but this must be buttressed by public education on the problems created by some medicinal uses and by national bans on the sales of medicines derived from endangered or threatened species.

Objective:

Ensure that those who possess local knowledge related to genetic resources benefit appropriately when it is used

For well over a decade, international debates over genetic resources have centered on questions of equity in the distribution of benefits from the use of genetic resources. On the one hand, developing countries question the fairness of granting a plant breeder a "patent" for a new crop variety while not legally recognizing the work of generations of farmers who created and nurtured the traditional plant varieties that the breeder used. On the other hand, industrialized countries have stressed that patents (or, more generally, intellectual property rights—IPRs) are not a form of compensation but rather a necessary incentive for commercial innovation.

This debate was partially resolved in 1987 by the Commission for Plant Genetic Resources. It revised the FAO International Undertaking for Plant Genetic Resources to recognize both breeders' rights (exclusivity in selling a specific variety under a specific name) and farmers' rights (reflecting the contributions of local communities in the creation and maintenance of genetic resources).

While the recognition of farmers' rights represents a significant conceptual advance, it has proven extremely difficult to turn the concept into a reality. A practical problem is that if an international fund is set up, as many experts recommend, it may not be able to reach local communities. A more fundamental problem is that the central issue addressed by the concept of farmers' rights, is not restricted to farmers. A wide variety of people who work in agriculture or forestry or use natural products to practice traditional medicine, have valuable knowledge of the location and use of genetic resources. They may also have directly contributed to the breeding and conservation of specific agricultural genetic resources. Their knowledge, as well as their crop and livestock varieties, must be treated as a resource that cannot be obtained, much less used, without a contract or formal agreement.

Moreover, the issue is broader than the question of "just compensation." The recognition of intellectual property rights should be considered a basic human right and an incentive for innovation within local communities just as much as it is within the commercial sector.

To legally recognize the intellectual property rights of local communities and individuals vis-à-vis genetic resources is to break sharply with the historic treatment of these materials as the "common heritage of mankind." Under that seemingly lofty doctrine, however, the custodians of genetic resources have not received benefits for conservation, so the resource is being lost. Certainly, it is better to restrict access to a stable resource than to allow free access to a dwindling one.

Action 41

Promote recognition of the value of local knowledge and genetic resources and affirm local peoples' rights.

Significant problems plague attempts to establish and enforce IPR protection for the broad range of actors who manipulate genetic resources—particularly the farmers and medicinal healers farthest removed from formal market systems. Currently, IPR protection is narrow precisely because so few of these actors have any political and economic power. If medicinal healers had the economic clout of large multi-national corporations, then their intellectual contribution to pharmaceutical development would certainly be respected. As it is, farmers and traditional healers cannot control access to the resource, and they are not financially able to challenge IPR claims made by others.

Resolving these problems will take decades. But recognizing the rights of farmers and local experts on genetic resources would help establish a legal basis to ensure that collection of genetic resources or local knowledge will directly benefit local communities in the future. The first step in the evolution of such an expanded IPR regime must be recognizing farmers' and medicinal healers' right to refuse information or access to genetic resources. Codes of conduct for genetic-resource collection notwithstanding, only with such rights of refusal will local communities have much influence over the form and amount of compensation owed.

Action 42

Base the collection of genetic resources on contractual or other agreements ensuring equitable returns.

Compensation for information about genetic resources or for a farmer's traditional varieties need not be financial, especially since the sums paid would very likely be small. Potentially more important are non-financial benefits: community empowerment, new information, and the exchange of genetic resources. Moreover, the recognition of community or individual rights provides an incentive for adding value to genetic resources as more is learned about their chemical activity or growth characteristics. And as value is added locally, the local bargaining position for negotiating royalties also improves.

As discussed in Chapter 4, regulations or codes of conduct governing the collection of genetic material should be predicated on local rights to genetic resources. Any collection agreements should reflect the concepts of just compensation and accountability, and codes of conduct should apply to genetic resource collectors, anthropologists, or other researchers studying local peoples or local resource management. In some cases, contracts may be needed to ensure the return of royalties or other benefits to local communities or individuals. Model contracts should be developed and circulated widely through non-governmental organization networks and indigenous peoples' organizations.

For their part, local groups should—as those in many countries already do—copyright the use of local or tribal names that might be used to market products developed from local genetic resources. Increasingly, entrepreneurs are profiting from the use of tribal names to sell unique foods, such as "Hopi Blue Corn" in the southwestern United States. With copyright protection, local groups would have the legal basis to argue for just compensation for any such use.

Recognizing the rights of local communities is but a small step toward achieving actual equity in the use of genetic resources. The resources available to industry for negotiating agreements on genetic resources or for fighting claims of infringement dwarf those of communities and even some nations. Still, on principle and for economic reasons, it is better to seek just compensation than to abrogate legitimate rights, and governments could help level the playing field by establishing ombudsmen and public legal-support offices staffed by experts in intellectual property law. Ombudsmen would hear complaints from local groups or individuals and attempt to mediate disputes or bring complaints to the attention of appropriate officials. Legal-support offices would provide the financial and technical resources needed to challenge the illegal use of physical or intellectual property.

VII

Managing Biodiversity Throughout the Human Environment

This land is the place where we know where to find all that it provides for us—food from hunting and fishing, and farms, building and tool materials, medicines. This land keeps us together within its mountains: we come to understand that we are not just a few people or separate villages, but one people belonging to a homeland.

THE AKAWAIO INDIANS, UPPER MAZARUNI DISTRICT, GUYANA

Even if most of Earth's remaining natural ecosystems could be protected from development, they could not adequately maintain biodiversity. The remaining wild is simply not large enough to meet all species' habitat needs or to provide important ecological services, and many of these still-natural ecosystems will inevitably be transformed by human use in coming decades.

Clearly, the success of biodiversity conservation will depend upon how well the *overall* landscape is managed to minimize biodiversity loss. Human needs and activities must be reconciled with the maintenance of biodiversity, and protected areas must be integrated into natural and modified surroundings. Farms, forests, grazing areas, fisheries, and villages belong on the same planning grid as land restoration projects, protected areas, and species-conserva-

tion efforts. The scale of such efforts must be tailored to both ecological processes and the needs and perceptions of local communities. This integrative approach is here termed *bioregional management*. [81]

The Meaning of Bioregional Management

A bioregion is a land and water territory whose limits are defined not by political boundaries, but by the geographical limits of human communities and ecological systems. Such an area must be *large* enough to maintain the integrity of the region's biological communities, habitats, and ecosystems; to support important ecological processes, such as nutrient and waste cycling, migration, and stream flow; to meet the habitat requirements of keystone and indicator species; and to include the human communities

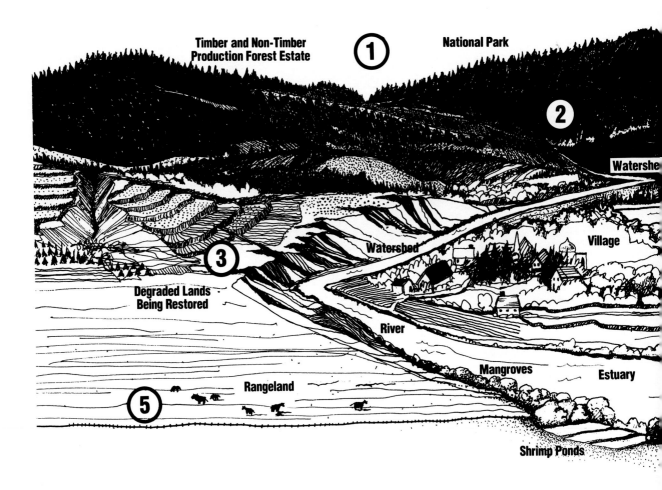

Timber and Non-Timber
Production Forest Estate

① National Park

②

Watershe

Watershed

Village

③

Degraded Lands
Being Restored

River

Mangroves

Estuary

Rangeland

⑤

Shrimp Ponds

BOX 21

Elements and Dynamics of a Bioregion

1. A variety of protected area types are used in a bioregion: strictly protected nature reserves, national or state parks, areas for the controlled extraction of non-timber forest products, privately owned conservation areas, and areas of permanent forest estate managed for timber production.

2. Watersheds are managed in their entirety, from ridgetop to blue water, and across a range of uses from strictly protected uplands to estuarine fisheries.

3. Degraded lands are restored to a variety of uses, including soil and water conservation, coastal protection, wood production, agriculture, pasture, and protected areas expansion.

4. Coastal and marine areas are managed to conserve key coral reefs, mangroves, beaches, and other elements, maintain fisheries productivity, and provide local economic opportunities through carefully managed tourism development.

5. Rangelands are managed within their carrying capacity to maintain native flora and fauna, raise livestock, and ensure the livelihoods of any nomadic pastoralist peoples.

6. Agricultural lands are managed to optimize long-term productivity and support biodiversity by minimizing

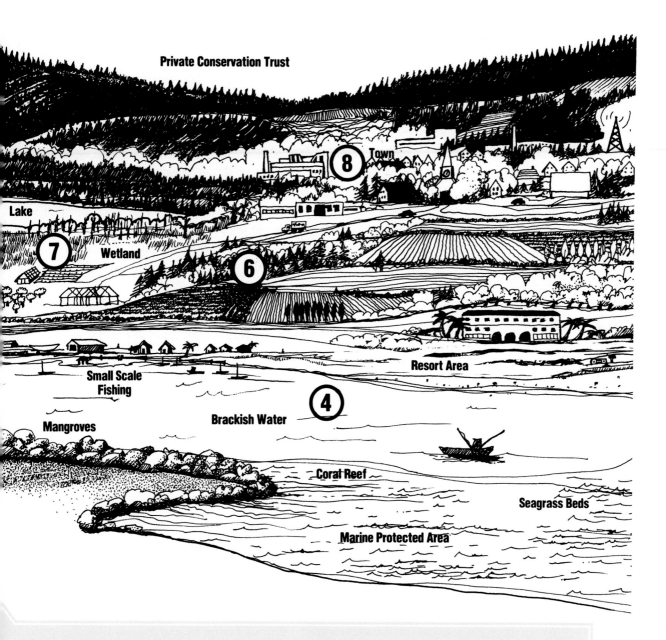

Private Conservation Trust

⑧ Town

Lake

⑦ Wetland

⑥

Small Scale Fishing

Resort Area

④ Brackish Water

Mangroves

Coral Reef

Seagrass Beds

Marine Protected Area

use of chemical pesticides and fertilizers, using local as well as introduced crop varieties, and including trees, hedgerows, community woodlots, and wildlife corridors within the agricultural landscape.

7. A range of community-based institutions support biodiversity conservation, including community seedbanks, agricultural extension services, and biodiversity inventory and research stations.

8. Larger towns within the bioregion provide a range of supporting institutions. These include zoos, aquaria, and botanic gardens to conserve endangered species and educate the public; schools, places of worship, and media outlets to build awareness; non-governmental organizations to provide support and information for both communities and government; and biodiversity information centers to serve as a focal point for bioregional dialogue, information sharing, and collective action.

involved in the management, use, and understanding of biological resources. It must be *small* enough for local residents to consider it home.

A bioregion would typically embrace thousands to hundreds of thousands of hectares. It may be no bigger than a small watershed or as large as a small state or province. In special cases, a bioregion might span the borders of two or more countries.

A bioregion is also defined by its people. It must have a unique *cultural identity* and be a place in which local residents have the primary right to determine their own development. This primary right does not, however, imply an absolute right. Rather, it means that the livelihoods, claims, and interests of local communities should be both the starting point and the criteria for regional development and conservation. Within that framework many other state, investor, and other economic interests must be accommodated.

Within a bioregion lies a *mosaic* of land or aquatic uses. Each patch provides habitats in which different species survive and flourish, and each has its own particular relationship to the region's human population. All the elements of the mosaic are interactive; the management of a watershed affects riverine habitats, farms, estuaries, fisheries, and coral reefs. The components are also dynamic; each changes over time as rivers change course, fallow fields regenerate, storms batter coasts, and fires ravage forests. This dynamism gives a well-managed bioregion the resilience and flexibility to adapt to natural evolution and human-induced activity—be it changing climate or changing markets.

Within this ecological and social framework, governmental, community, corporate, and other private interests share responsibility for coordinating land-use planning for both public and private land and for defining and implementing development options that will ensure that human needs are met in a sustainable way. Innovative forms of institutional integration and social cooperation are needed to meet these needs. Dialogue among all interests, participatory planning, and great institutional flexibility are essential. A wide range of conservation tools and technologies must also be

brought to bear—among them, protected-areas management, *ex situ* technologies, landscape restoration, and sustainable management of such resources as forests, fisheries, and croplands.

The *biosphere reserve* concept, launched by UNESCO's Man and the Biosphere Program in 1979, provides one useful model and starting point for bioregional management. In the model reserve, a protected "core area" is surrounded by a "buffer zone" and then a "transition area." Use of the buffer zone is limited to activities compatible with the protection of the core area, such as certain research, education, training, recreation and tourism, while development activities are permitted in the transition area.[82]

The biosphere reserve network, consisting of 300 reserves covering some 12 million hectares in 76 countries, represents a tentative commitment by governments to develop bioregional approaches.[83] However, in the field most biosphere reserves have been far from the bioregional ideal. Most biosphere reserves were superimposed directly on existing national parks and forest reserves without the mandates, resources, inclination, or capability to address overall rural development issues at the bioregional scale. As a result, the change of status is in name only, with little obvious change in emphasis or philosophy. For example, little has been done to promote sustainable development in the buffer areas of most reserves.[84]

Some countries have begun to address the gap between the concept and its application through legislative reform. Indonesia's Basic Law on Conservation of Living Resources and their Ecosystems (1990), for example, establishes the biosphere reserve as a legally recognized category of conservation area. Costa Rica is trying to remove the institutional obstacles to managing its La Amistad Biosphere Reserve on a truly bioregional basis. *(See Box 22.)* Similarly, the Mapimí Biosphere Reserve in Mexico has successfully involved researchers, political leaders, and local residents in cooperative management and project design.[85] If these efforts continue, the model for a global network of biosphere reserves can serve as one basis for bioregional management.

Objective:

Create the institutional conditions for bioregional conservation and development

Bioregional management has clear ecological, economic, and social advantages. To begin with, it provides a spatial and social scale that makes sense to most people. But since governments, communities, economic-production systems, and conservation programs were not organized with bioregions in mind, bioregional management will not work unless institutions change the way they do business, nurturing innovative forms of social cooperation and action.

Two basic problems stand in the way of bioregional management. First, bioregional approaches require greater decentralization, access, and even-handedness than most of today's institutions possess. Planning and management are over-centralized, sectoral divisions and specialization are over-emphasized, and most laws and administrative structures reinforce these shortcomings. Second, the diverse actors within any particular bioregion possess varying degrees of wealth, power, and access to information, so they are not able to participate with equal effectiveness. Unless the weaker actors are empowered, their interests are likely to be slighted.

Action 43

Develop new methods and mechanisms at the bioregional level for dialogue, planning, and conflict resolution.

The transition to bioregional management is bound to involve considerable social adjustment. The long-term availability of resources, the preservation of habitats and species, job and food security, the distribution of costs and benefits, the maintenance of culturally important areas, and access to and control over resources are all matters of political debate. Fortunately, models abound for the communication, cooperative-planning, and dispute-resolution mechanisms needed to contain conflict.

In some areas local governments, non-governmental organizations, or business consortiums may best facilitate dialogue. In others, religious organizations, tribal councils, town meetings, or chambers of commerce may be more effective. Of course, individuals experienced in conflict resolution and mediation can be of help initiating the dialogue regardless of where it takes place, especially if none of the other participants appears objective. Developing guidelines for the dialogue process may also help.

Bioregional dialogue has to involve all concerned parties within the bioregion. Interests from outside, however, also need to participate. Corporations and other business enterprises with interests and activities in the region should be brought into the process. So should the government agencies that create the policy framework within which bioregional management must fit. In biologically rich or threatened regions, institutions working to stem the global loss of biodiversity should also be involved.

The first agenda items in bioregional planning are likely to involve issues such as public health, access to such critical resources as fuelwood and water, employment generation, and the need for collective decision-making. At this point, the many connections between these issues and biodiversity and natural resource conservation should be introduced. When the discussion turns to preliminary planning for biodiversity use and conservation, the key factors are access to good information, clear goals and priorities, and mobilization of financial, human, and technical resources from both within and outside the region. Locally accountable monitoring and evaluation procedures must also be developed.

Financial and other supports for biodiversity conservation can often be secured internally if those

BOX 22

From Biosphere Reserve to
Bioregional Management: La Amistad

La Amistad Biosphere Reserve, located in the mountainous region of Talamanca in southeastern Costa Rica, contains some of the richest and more diverse ecosystems of Central America. A complex of protected and inhabited natural areas covering approximately 600,000 hectares, La Amistad encompasses 12 percent of the country's land and a significant fraction of Costa Rica's plant and animal species. La Amistad also encompasses the lands of the two largest Amerindian groups in Costa Rica, the Bribi and the Cabecar.

Rugged terrain and infertile soil have kept much of La Amistad undeveloped relative to the rest of the country, but pressure on the region is growing. Mineral concessions granted within the biosphere reserve, roads and hydroelectric plants slated for the region, and population growth and intensive land use in surrounding areas have exacerbated pressure to expand the agricultural frontier within La Amistad, placing the mosaic of protected areas at risk.

Development is needed in the region. Although they are endowed with extraordinary biodiversity, the people of La Amistad are extremely poor and have little access to social services. Inadequate health care, transportation, and education facilities have resulted in the highest mortality, malnutrition, and illiteracy rates in the nation. This poverty impels people to move into protected forest lands or invade areas reserved for Amerindian communities.

These pressures have confounded attempts by the Costa Rican government to manage national parks, forest reserves, and other protected areas and to supply basic services to the indigenous communities. Recognizing the links between security within these areas and social and economic factors throughout the region, in 1988 the government created the La Amistad Biosphere Reserve Coordinating Commission, made up of representatives from national institutions charged with managing the reserve's lands. The commission has looked for ways to address development pressures while maintaining the integrity of its conservation areas.

A major activity of the commission has been to devise and implement a strategy for institutional development in the biosphere reserve. Produced with the technical assistance of the Organization of American States and Conservation International, the strategy facilitates the design of management plans and identifies priorities for sustainable development in the region. The strategy heavily emphasizes regionally integrated planning under the auspices of the powerful Ministry of National Planning and Economic Policy. It also contains proposals for securing indigenous people's land rights, compensating landowners for expropriated land in the reserve's core, formulating agricultural and forestry policies to improve land-use practices in consultation with the region's agro-industries and inhabitants, and conducting environmental-impact analyses for development projects within the reserve.

The strategy allows Costa Rica to realize its commitment to the socioeconomic development and conservation of selected wildland areas. Staff of the biosphere reserve and of adjacent protected and reserve lands in Panama are negotiating a cooperative agreement to bring nearly 1.1 million hectares in both countries into the reserve.

The strategy presents an enormous challenge. Instituting integrated management policies will require the commission to engage in frequent negotiation and conflict resolution. In addition, having exhausted its agricultural frontier, the country is struggling to cope with a heavy burden of external debt. Since the strategy was formulated in 1988, the epicenter of the terrible April 1991 earthquake fell within the biosphere reserve, destroying roads and homes and further isolating communities. Visionary planning to accommodate these needs while ensuring conservation will have to guide reconstruction.

However, a number of factors suggest that integrated regional planning may succeed in La Amistad. The strategy does, for instance, provide the means to secure financial, technical, and political support from other government agencies, from communities within or near La Amistad, and from international organizations. The nation as a whole has a long history of respect for its natural heritage and enjoys one of the world's finest systems of protected areas. Costa Rica's major political parties are firmly behind the project, which has also gained international support. Finally, the people of La Amistad support the program because they maintain access to their land and are able to adopt models of development consistent with their lifestyles.

Source: Ministry of Natural Resources, Energy, and Mines of Costa Rica et al., 1990.

FIGURE 27

Bioregional Management Involving Eight Conservation Areas in Costa Rica. (Each Conservation Area Includes a Variety of Land Use Categories)

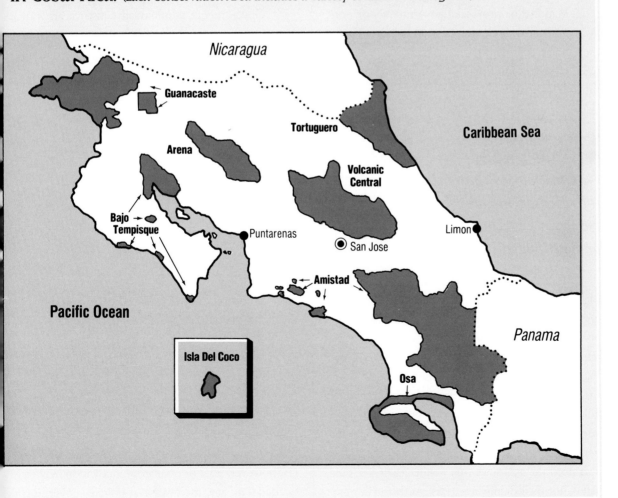

who depend on a bioregion's wealth see the value of investing in its maintenance. Timber companies or tourism operators, for instance, may be persuaded to fund local actions that help preserve their business. Local communities may cooperate to reforest denuded hillsides. The possibilities are endless, though some funding from either national or international sources will probably be needed (and justified), especially where costs are high and local natural resources are of national or global interest.

Finally, the parties involved in bioregional dialogue and planning must develop a political strategy for gaining the support and cooperation of government agencies, external funders, and others from outside the region. This strategy may involve cultivating sympathetic officials, approaching the media, and developing alliances with activist and conservation groups.

National or provincial governments or nongovernmental organizations should help to catalyze bioregional planning by providing funding, facilitators, or technical information to interested communities or regions.

Action 44

Give weak and disenfranchised groups the means to influence how the bioregion's resources should be managed and distributed.

True dialogue and collective action can take place in a bioregion only when all parties listen to and respect the interests of all others. Yet, diffuse groups of poor people cannot compete with the wealthy and the well organized as decisions are made about how resources are used and who benefits from such use. In the many places where their voices are routinely ignored or suppressed, the poor, women, minority groups, and indigenous and tribal peoples all need help pressing their interests. They also need the assurance that neither their personal safety nor their dignity are at risk as they try.

In many cases, non-governmental organizations and local citizens' organizations can help empower these often-disenfranchised groups by providing access to information, demystifying the institutions and language of power and policy, and encouraging local organization. But governments must do their part too. As the ultimate guarantors of basic human rights and the due process of law, they must observe these basic norms themselves and make sure that the strong and wealthy do not violate them.

Action 45

Establish intersectoral and interagency task forces to facilitate bioregional planning and action.

Governmental administrative districts are usually incongruent with ecological or community boundaries. Government agencies are generally divided along sectoral lines—forestry and agriculture departments, for example, are rarely required to work on a common plan—and governments usually centralize administrative power and staff resources in capital cities. These facts of life hinder bioregional planning, and they are not likely to change rapidly in most countries. Ways can be found, however, to make institutions more receptive to bioregional management *if* governments are willing to make the commitment.

Government agencies will be most disposed to such change where they know that an ecologically or economically important resource is threatened and that current government approaches are not working, where staff within agencies and administrative districts are willing to innovate and to coordinate new activities, and where the people of a bioregion have organized themselves and developed sound proposals. In many cases, government's participation in a bioregional dialogue is enough to scale many administrative and sectoral hurdles. In others, however, legal or regulatory innovation may be needed—in, say, the laws and policies governing land ownership and use. Where external funding is sought, donors can sometimes catalyze discussion among disparate government agencies and local communities.

Action 46

Establish bioregional information centers to heighten public awareness and support biodiversity conservation.

A bioregional information center can be a repository of data on a region's biodiversity, biotic resources, and their economic and cultural importance. It can help local communities, resource managers, businesses, farmers, and other residents of the region plan and implement conservation activities and mobilize biodiversity's economic potential. Most important, it can help citizens become more aware of their own region, its issues and problems, and opportunities for getting involved.

Such centers must be established by and for the community. The people of a region should be the final arbiters on how the centers function and on the type of information they provide. A wide range of educational resources and technologies will probably serve best. Information should be organized and formatted to meet the needs of educators and students, commercial fishermen and subsistence farmers, grassroots leaders and local government, and both local inhabitants and outside interests. Locally-based industry can contribute by providing equipment, technical expertise, and internships that enable local young people to help gather and analyze data, make presentations to the public, and prepare exhibits. Such centers could also be linked to local *ex situ* collections, research institutions, national and international biodiversity centers, and provincial, state, or national databases.

Frequently, bioregional centers can be added on to a local institution—a government office, nature appreciation center, school, place of worship, health clinic, non-governmental organization office, or community meeting place. In the Sierra Nevada de Santa Marta project in Colombia, for example, a small center has been developed to serve as a forum for all local affairs. As an integral part of community development, biodiversity can be discussed wherever community development issues are aired.

Objective:

Support biodiversity conservation initiatives in the private sector

Conservation initiatives have traditionally focussed on publicly owned or managed lands, but substantial opportunities exist for conserving biodiversity on private lands kept wild or semi-wild. A bioregional approach to biodiversity conservation requires that conservation on private lands become an integral part of the strategy.

To date, governments have controlled or dictated land use on private lands primarily through regulations or outright purchase. A complementary approach is to provide incentives for private sector conservation. The private sector can often protect land at a lower cost and with less political opposition than can government.

In most countries, law already allows any number of private interests to share access to the same area. Oil and gas rights may belong to one party, mineral and surface rights to another, hunting rights to others, and easements for power lines, pipelines, and railroads to still others. By law, private parties can take actions to promote their mutual interests without interference from the government or undue delay. Given these clear advantages, private conservation action can be an important adjunct to governmental action.

Action 47

Establish tax incentives for conservation.

Throughout the world, the growth of urban centers has transformed land use in surrounding regions. As land values and property taxes go up, pressure on rural landowners to sell to urban or industrial developers or to increase production by more intensive monocultural agriculture mounts. Indeed, if taxes rise high enough, a once-profitable woodlot operation or small farm may become a losing venture.

Hoping to preserve some traditional land uses and to keep some space open in urban areas, many individuals and communities have pioneered "conservation easements" whereby landowners sell or donate in perpetuity the development rights to their land to an agency that holds such easements in the public trust. In exchange, the landowner receives a tax deduction based on the decrease in the assessed value of the land.

Without conservation easements, land conversion becomes likely, if not inevitable, as soon as the assessed value of developed land exceeds the value of nearby land in its natural or rural state. But a mix of developed and undeveloped land better serves community and national interests. Developed land may provide more tax revenues, but undeveloped land obviously contributes more to biodiversity conservation, and this contribution should be reflected in the appraised value or the tax assessment.

Critics of conservation easements argue that they deprive communities of tax revenues because tax assessment on lands with conservation easements drops. In fact, though, open space generally *increases* the property values of the adjacent land, which means net revenue gains.[86]

As an alternative to easements, covenants between land owners and fiscal authorities can oblige the owner to hold a parcel in wild state under a specified management regime for a number of years (usually ten), during which taxes would be reduced. But should the owners decide to change land use—by, say, logging a forested area or draining wetlands—they would immediately have to repay all the tax forgiven since the covenant was initiated. Such covenant options can be renewed indefinitely and made permanent, with the owner retaining full legal title.

Action 48

Support the establishment of private Biodiversity Conservation Trusts.

Local land trusts—non-profit organizations dedicated to preserving open space—are playing an ever greater role in conservation in many parts of the world. Between 1980 and 1991, the number of land trusts in the United States doubled from 429 to nearly 900. Collectively, these trusts are responsible for protecting more than 1.1 million hectares of land—equal to approximately 3 percent of the land in the U.S. National Park System.[87]

The work of these local and regional land trusts is complemented by national organizations. The Fundación Reservas para Colombia, though not technically a land trust, creates private reserves with a portion of the donations that it receives. It also establishes community centers within these reserves to foster sound conservation practices and to offer assistance and services to local communities. The Nature Conservancy, an example of a national land trust in the United States, has protected over 2.2 million hectares.[88]

Bioregional management could best be strengthened by fostering the development of small, locally operated land trusts. Large trusts are also important, but dollar-for-dollar the most effective action is likely to be taken at a smaller scale. Each of these independent trusts would be administered by local trustees whose fiduciary responsibilities would be carefully defined in the trust's charter. Each charter would be broadly directed toward sustainable development and specifically toward conservation. Trusts have several advantages over regulation, government ownership, or acquisition by large centralized private organizations:

■ overhead costs are minimized; (Trustees are volunteers, and all staff are "on-site.")

■ usually, local efforts are more acceptable and effective than the activities of "outsiders;"

■ creating hundreds of land trusts insures a diversity of action and approaches; and,

■ trusts involve local people who become a local constituency for biodiversity conservation.

Local conservation trusts could be funded by one-time government grants, conservation organizations, or business. The trustees would be authorized to spend the income from the funds for the purposes described in the trust declaration. The trust could form non-profit corporations to hold and manage its property. The trust would pay no federal or state taxes, and contributions to the trust would also be tax exempt. The public could use property owned by the trust only if such use was compatible with maintaining biodiversity. The trust could use any instrument normally available to other private parties to protect biodiversity, including purchase, lease, easement, and rent. It could fund educational activities, communication, environmental mediation, and applied research.

As an example, in 1971, the Federal Government of Canada granted the Nature Trust of British Columbia $3.2 million to conserve areas of provincial ecological significance. The trust is certified as a charitable federal and provincial foundation and has a 13-member volunteer board and a staff of four. In 20 years, it has sponsored 180 species-protection, habitat-conservation, research, and education projects at a cost of $14.1 million and has conserved 11,650 hectares.

Objective:

Incorporate biodiversity conservation into the management of biological resources

The essence of the bioregional approach is to incorporate biodiversity conservation into *all* land and resource uses, including those aimed mainly at economic production. That means integrating biodiversity-conservation objectives into forest management, rangelands, fishing grounds, and agricultural fields; into decisions about developing wetlands, tundra, deserts, and high mountain areas; and in policies for reclaiming wastelands.

Techniques and strategies for conserving biodiversity in these varied landscapes and resource uses exist, but they need to be refined and applied much more broadly. In many parts of Africa, for example, raising native grazing animals instead of cattle is both ecologically and economically sound. Relying on native species helps maintain the natural diversity of the animals themselves and the local grasses. It also raises landowners' and communities' net revenues compared to what they would be with cattle.[89] Similarly, coastal wetlands are often far more commercially valuable in their natural state—as shrimp-breeding grounds, for instance—than they are when converted to other land uses.

Significant opportunities for better integrating biodiversity conservation into resource management also abound in forestry, agroforestry, agriculture, and ecological restoration. In each case, conserving biodiversity within the production system is the key to the resource's sustainability, and often provides short-term benefits as well.

Action 49

Incorporate biodiversity conservation practices into the management of all forests.

Forests and woodlands cover nearly 40 percent of the earth's land surface,[90] and they are the most biologically-diverse ecosystems in most parts of the world. The protected-areas network will never expand enough to include the bulk of the world's natural forest areas. Within most regions, some forests will be strictly protected and some managed for such generally low-impact uses as tourism and non-timber forest products. But in many private and public forests extraction of timber will likely remain a dominant use—whether in Canada, Indonesia, or Colombia.

Almost all current logging practices significantly reduce biodiversity, and it is doubtful that more than a fraction of commercial-scale logging operations in the humid tropics are sustainable.[91] Nevertheless, areas dedicated to timber production are part of many bioregions, so the management challenge is to minimize biodiversity loss.[92]

If forests managed for timber are to contribute to biodiversity conservation, three steps are especially important. First, since many species depend on the complex physical structure of natural forests, some key habitats (including mature trees, snags, and decomposing logs) should be left in place following harvest in production forests. This will help to maintain the "legacy" of the natural forest in the new forest that develops.

Second, populations of keystone species should be maintained as a high priority. These indispensable species control the structure of the community and help determine which other species are present. In many tropical forests, figs are keystone species. So are trees that provide habitat or food for pollinators and such seed dispersers as bats, fruit-eating birds, and hummingbirds.

Finally, the fragmentation of natural forest areas that occurs when they are used intensively should be kept to a minimum. In most situations, highly selective logging, careful extraction of trees from large forest blocks, and the use of long rotations (70 years or more) keep the problem within bounds. Logging should be staggered so that various areas are at various stages of succession following disturbance and mature stands lie in close proximity to each other. A rule of thumb, then, is that all of the land covered by a particular forest type should not be logged at the same time and forest corridors should be maintained among unlogged and regenerating blocks. During logging, care should be taken to minimize the damage from felling, road-building, and log extraction.

Native tree species should be given priority over introduced species in forest regeneration, as well as in agroforestry and the restoration of degraded lands. This holds true even in plantation forestry, where indigenous species are most often overlooked on grounds that "exotics" grow faster. Recent work with native species punctures many such myths and shows that indigenous trees can often be *more* productive than the exotics that replace them. But the myths will live on until information to the contrary is available. Indeed, in many forestry programs the greatest obstacle to the increased use of indigenous trees is lack of information.

As increasing knowledge on the role of natural disturbances in forest dynamics becomes available, forestry and other human activity can be made to better mimic the disturbances to which forest ecosystems are adapted. Knowledge of the "tree gap dynamics" that govern the natural regeneration of trees in mature tropical forests is especially important. In the Palcazu project in Peru, strip-cutting that mimicked this natural process maintained a high level of natural species diversity.[93] In temperate and boreal forests, such natural disturbances as fires and storms are integral parts of ecological processes in forest areas and should inform silvicultural practices.

Action 50

Promote agricultural practices that conserve biodiversity.

More people are hungry today than ever before. Population growth still outpaces rapid growth in food production, and closing that gap will require both growing more on currently cultivated land and converting more uncultivated land, as well as increasing the poor's access to food. Unfortunately, the productivity gains of recent decades have been attained at a great cost to future generations. Modern agriculture and the overuse of pesticides engenders unsustainable losses of topsoil, soil fertility, genetic resources, and natural predators. From now on, productivity gains must be achieved in ways that do not degrade agriculture's potential.

Biodiversity is an important resource for achieving sustainable production increases. People often think of the role of biodiversity only in terms of its potential contributions to biotechnological advances in agriculture, and in fact new biotechnologies could make environmentally sound gains in productivity possible by developing crops that do not need pesticides, herbicides, and fertilizers. But current trends are worrying: the first commercial biotechnology products to reach the market will probably be herbicide-resistant crops that work only in high-input agricultural systems. Moreover, technological solutions to agricultural problems have left a legacy of concentrated land ownership, marginalization of indigenous people and small farmers, rural impoverishment, and other social problems.

Biodiversity has another, more promising contribution to make to agriculture. The diversity of crop species and the diversity of varieties within a species have traditionally strengthened the resilience of agriculture and this role can be enhanced *if* agricultural research practices change. Currently, national and international systems of agricultural research are geared to solve the problems of farmers by introducing uniform "improved" crop varieties. This must change. The objective of research must increasingly be to give farmers the technology and know-how to solve problems themselves.

In many regions, farmers face ruin as their diverse and usually well-adapted cropping systems are replaced by modern agricultural systems that shift the responsibility for food security to the state, which may not be prepared to handle it. Between 1977 and 1986, for example, an average of 42 percent of land planted in wheat in the Punjab of Pakistan and India was sown with "improved" varieties which in fact were no longer approved because of susceptibility to disease.[94] In most agricultural research programs, farmers' traditional knowledge—of enormous value where fertilizers, irrigation, and pesticides are out of economic reach—is ignored or lost, along with crop varieties and food plants that are often far more suited than the modern varieties to local conditions and dietary preferences.

To promote greater diversity in cropping systems, national agricultural research and breeding programs need to be strengthened and decentralized, and farmer-based research must be increased substantially. *(See Figure 28.)* Agricultural production gains in most developing countries will be far more cost-effective and equitable if traditional breeding techniques are strengthened than if modern biotechnology is unreservedly embraced. Indeed, the benefits of biotechnology cannot be realized without a strong public program in crop breeding—one that meets the needs of marginal farmers as well as those of farmers on irrigated and good rain-fed land. *(See Box 23.)*

Backed by the international agricultural research network, national agricultural research programs should also institute "genetic diversity checks" for major crop varieties to minimize the risk of crop failure. With rigorous data in short supply, it is hard to size up the current threat posed by genetic uniformity.

Although billions of dollars have been spent responding to the threat of genetic uniformity, no attempt has been made to monitor genetic diversity in agriculture—the single best indicator of the status of crop genetic-resource management and the most relevant indicator of vulnerability to crop failures.

To fill this gap, national agricultural research programs should develop indicators of the status of crop genetic diversity in farmers' fields. At a minimum, the number of species and varieties grown in defined regions and the genetic diversity of varieties grown in defined regions must be determined.

To develop such indicators, national agricultural research institutions should obtain and publish data on the area planted to specific varieties of crops in each province or state. Alternatively, plant variety protection (PVP) offices should require that breeders make available (at least confidentially) the entire pedigree of new varieties. National boards or the PVP office should also publish yearly measurements of the genetic diversity of crops, and

FIGURE 28

Research Budgets of the CGIAR International Agricultural Research Centers, Monsanto Corporation, and all National Agricultural Research Programs in South America

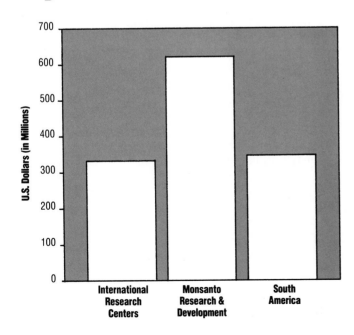

Source: Collinson and Wright 1991; Pardey and Roseboom 1989

review boards should establish guidelines to follow when such indicators reveal dangerous trends.

Action 51

Restore degraded lands in ways that enhance their productivity and biodiversity.

Few countries have tried to restore degraded lands for either agricultural production or biodiversity conservation. Agriculture has generally expanded onto wild frontiers while conservation has focussed on preserving remaining natural habitat. As the availability of lands ideally suited for either agriculture or protected area status shrinks under population and production pressures, and as the area of degraded land increases, the widespread adoption of techniques to restore the earth becomes a necessity.

The problem is widespread. At least one third of Java's cultivated mountainous areas are seriously eroding.[95] In India, 175 million hectares, half of the country's area, require special treatment to restore the land to productive and profitable use.[96] Human-induced soil degradation, primarily water erosion and nutrient decline, affects approximately 14 percent of South America's land area.[97] Worldwide, six to seven million hectares of productive agricultural land are lost to soil erosion annually and another 1.5 million hectares are degraded through waterlogging, salinization, and alkalinization.[98]

Degraded lands can be restored to meet a variety of objectives, each of which may be best served by different techniques. In some places, increasing the production of food crops, trees, and other products for human use may be paramount, and the use of fast-growing monocultures may be appropriate. In others, protecting environmental services (such as water cycles) may be most important, indicating a different mix of techniques. In still others, the objectives may be to return the degraded area to a near-natural state, which requires a quite different approach. All of these approaches can support bio-

---

BOX 23

On-Farm Landrace Conservation and Enhancement in Ethiopia

Since 1988, the national Plant Genetic Resources Center/Ethiopia (PGRC/E) has been implementing a revolutionary new approach to plant genetic resource conservation and use. It is revolutionary not because its activities are new—farmer seed conservation and breeding has been the norm for millennia—but because it reverses the standard interaction between national breeding programs and farmers. On a network of 21 farms in drought-prone areas of two provinces, PGRC/E is involved in on-farm landrace conservation and breeding programs focussed on sorghum, chickpeas, teff, field peas, and corn.

From seeds collected in the region and the seeds they were already growing, farmers associations have selected the best varieties. Together with PGRC/E scientists, they have also undertaken simple forms of mass selection to improve each season's crop production. Representative samples of the original seed stock are planted alongside the selected material to help farmers critically evaluate their selection, and maintain the original stock in its natural environment. The on-farm work also helps scientists understand the farming systems used with each of the varieties that are being collected. Certain

types of cultivars that were adapted by the farmer but later abandoned to reduce risks of crop failure or avoid marketing problems are also saved in the PGRC/E genebank.

Farmers have also helped maintain and select elite indigenous material being developed by national agricultural researchers. Farmers receive a number of lines of indigenous wheat varieties that breeders are developing for specific conditions. From these, the farmers select and then multiply the seeds that best meet their own needs. PGRC/E provides guidance on conservation, selection, use, and distribution.

PGRC/E plans to increase the number of farmers involved in its work and to expand the program to cover a broad range of agro-ecological conditions in the country. Eventually, it hopes to extend the program to cover other aspects of genetic-resource conservation, including *in situ* conservation of forage species and wild relatives of cultivated plants. A substantial amount of the *in situ* conservation work pays for itself since the farmers prefer the landraces to the input-intensive modern varieties. But the program requires financial and other inputs to help farmers assume a custodian role for genetic diversity.

Source: Worede, 1991

---

diversity conservation by taking pressure off natural ecosystems or extending natural areas.

Returning degraded lands to production is necessarily the major thrust of restoration work in many places, particularly in poorer, densely populated areas. While few degraded lands in such areas can be returned to their virginal state, such lands can still contribute greatly to biodiversity conservation. Restoration efforts can draw heavily on diverse local species to provide varied benefits to the community and weave diversity into the structure of

the restored areas, mixing annual crops, fruit trees and other perennials, woodlots, grasses, livestock, fishponds, and other features. Over some large areas, in contrast, timber plantations or pasture reformation make sense.

India has become a leader in reclaiming degraded farmland. Between 1982 and 1986, in the states of Haryana, Punjab, and Uttar Pradesh alone, nearly 200,000 hectares of alkalinized land were rehabilitated using low-cost methods and hand labor. Alkaline-tolerant species recolonized the area, improving the site for less tolerant species. Nearby villages saw such increases in farm productivity that many were able to bring electricity into homes for the first time.[99]

It has been widely assumed that commercial cattle-ranching operations are inherently unsustainable in the Brazilian Amazon and inevitably lead to severe land degradation. Recent research in Pará state suggests, however, that production can be sustained with the right management practices and that degraded pasture can be revitalized to support sustainable production for approximately $260 per hectare. To restore these lands, they must be cleared, tilled, fertilized, and planted with the forage species *Brachiaria bryzantha*. Once reformed, these pastures generate about $50 per hectare per year in profits, compared to $10 per hectare per year for unimproved pastures. While reformed pastures would require periodic fertilization, present indications are that they are economically viable. (Unfortunately, the capital for restoration is currently coming from timber sales on the forested portions of ranch holdings.)[100]

In some places, especially industrial countries, the dominant objective may be to restore natural conditions rather than to optimize production for direct human consumption. Regenerating natural ecosystems is in fact gaining popularity in industrialized countries, often as a way to partly offset the development of a pristine natural area. Although some such efforts fail because many natural conditions are beyond human control or knowledge, these projects may lay the foundation for reintroducing species preserved *ex situ*, and for redistributing species and biotic communities in the wake of climate change.

Since, in some cases, restoring a complex natural ecosystem can require great amounts of time and money, not degrading it in the first place is clearly more cost-effective. (The return of the Kissimmee River to its original meandering channel in South Florida will cost more than $100 million.) But the restoration of natural ecosystems can sometimes support biodiversity conservation

and save money as well, as the innovative work of the São Paulo Electric Company in Brazil attests. *(See Box 24.)*

Sometimes "preventive restoration"—through the removal of roads in areas under threat of degradation—is the best strategy for conserving biodiversity. In logging areas or other natural forests where roads have been built, closing and re-seeding the roads decrease human pressures on the land and helps the forest recover.

Restoration efforts can be crucial in the expansion of protected areas and the development of "buffer zones" around them. Many protected areas are too small to sustain the species they contain, but cannot easily be extended onto nearby productive lands. One alternative is to develop adjacent degraded lands for agroforestry and other production systems that can support local communities that would otherwise need to use land, wood, and other resources in the protected area. Another is to incorporate adjacent degraded lands into the protected area and restore them.

For example, Costa Rica's Guanacaste Conservation Area is being enlarged through the restoration of former pasture and agricultural land. In this case, rather than attempting to replant over 700 square kilometers of the degraded land, restoration resources are focused on fire control. If fires can be prevented, a closed-canopy forest will return within fifty years. Cattle are also permitted to continue grazing the area; because they eat grass but not tree seedlings, their grazing reduces competition and allows the tree species to grow faster, and they spread organic matter and disperse seeds as well. Guanacaste's survival odds over time are increased by efforts to integrate the component protected areas economically and culturally into the life of local communities. The protected areas maintain local watersheds and provide jobs and tourist income for local residents, and an active education and outreach program makes the protected areas "living classrooms," re-establishing the traditional ties of local people to their native environment.[101]

The traditional land-use practices of many

indigenous peoples afford insights into how agricultural and habitat restoration can be combined. Commonly, for instance, these people introduce useful native species into a regenerating forest clearing, which allows natural succession to occur and yields

a crop that does not require fertilizers, pesticides, or other agricultural inputs. The HIFCO project in the Peruvian Amazon illustrates the potential of indigenous approaches to restoration. *(See Box 25.)*

BOX 24

Restoration of Degraded Watersheds with Native Species

**The Experience of the Power Company
of São Paulo, Brazil**

The construction of dams, the flooding of reservoirs, and the subsequent changes in land-use practices in their surrounding areas usually impoverish local plant and animal communities. In the state of São Paulo, where only 5 percent of the original forest cover remains, hydroelectric power accounts for 89 percent of the state electricity needs. The São Paulo Power Company (CESP) oversees 22 hydroelectric plants with reservoirs covering 7,500 km² and a combined shore length of 15,000 km, all within the state of São Paulo. CESP's current power-generating capacity is close to the total potential hydroelectric capacity of the state's major rivers. Further expanding capacity will require building many smaller dams and reservoirs that could undermine regional flora and fauna.

Since 1989, CESP has run an innovative program with the University of São Paulo's Institute for Forestry Research using secondary succession principles as a basis for restoring degraded lands bordering its hydroelectric dams and reservoirs to their natural condition. Although the company has been involved in restoration activities since the mid-1970s, its previous attempts to rehabilitate disturbed lands have been hampered by high costs and limited success in reintroducing native plant species. As a result, the restored ecosystems differ significantly from the original ones.

The first step in the new, improved restoration process now under way is the evaluation of the area's regeneration capacity. This involves quantitative and qualitative analysis of the existing seed bank, an assessment of germination constraints, the evaluation of remaining vegetation and its stage of succession, the identification of dispersal poles, and a determination of the level of degradation suffered by the area. Then, researchers re-introduce plant species, taking care to use species appropriate for specific successional stages and to optimize the timing of planting. Once the reforested areas have stabilized, animal reintroduction activities are initiated and these include studies to identify pollinators and understand their interrelationships.

As of July 1991, CESP had restored 5,000 hectares of publicly held shorelines and islands and had plans to rejuvenate 500 hectares per year. In addition, the company has helped restore 294 hectares of private lands (with a target of 1,000 hectares per year) and 900 hectares of bulldozed land (with a goal of 300 hectares per year). CESP maintains five nurseries that can produce 8.5 million seedlings per year.

The cost of restoring degraded areas ranged from $8,980 per hectare for completely bulldozed land, to $3,450 per hectare for agricultural lands. CESP realized a 50-percent savings by using the secondary succession techniques instead of traditional reforestation methods. Time savings have also been considerable: traditional reforestation had taken up to five years, compared to two to three with the new method.

Source: Galli and Goncalves, 1991

BOX 25

Restoration in the Peruvian Amazon: An Indigenous Response

AIDESEP, an association of 28 federations of indigenous peoples from Peru, has launched a program to restore the productivity and diversity of degraded fields and forests in their ancestral domain.

The project site is near Pucalpa, which lies at the end of the Pucalpa-Lima highway, the only road linking the Amazon Basin to the rest of Peru.

Since the highway was built during the mid-1960s, waves of colonists and land speculators have cleared the forests for farming and cattle ranching. In the process, the local indigenous peoples lost access to their ancestral lands. In response, AIDESEP has launched a campaign to secure land titles for those still living in forested areas and to reclaim their ancestral domain, much of which is now a wasteland of abandoned farms and low-productivity cattle pastures.

In 1985, AIDESEP launched the HIFCO project to reclaim a 7.5-hectare parcel of abandoned cattle pasture—an experiment in wresting food crops from marginal lands. German ecologists provided technical assistance during the first year. Since then, HIFCO has been totally managed and developed by the indigenous community, with modest international financial support. The abandoned pasture has become an ecological "Garden of Eden" that enjoys year-round production. Acidic soils have been restored, and crop yields have increased each year, surpassing those of nearby farms employing "modern" non-organic agriculture.

The HIFCO farming system is best described as a "hybrid," built on a model of the forest canopy's strata, but also drawing on both modern and traditional agriculture. It focuses on improving soil structure and nutrient content through a system of raised beds and drainage canals. Rejecting the recommendation of extension agents from the Ministry of Agriculture to scrap the whole project, HIFCO began working organic

matter—crop residue, leaf litter, and animal manure—into the planted beds. By 1990, farmers' experiments with different mixes of traditional and cash crops with trees had turned 4.5 hectares into productive agricultural land.

The species diversity of the beds is very rich, with a kaleidoscope of 42 annuals and perennials intercropped among trees. The system is laced with leguminous plants (e.g., various "pole" beans and pigeon-pea bushes) that serve as green mulches and soil enrichers. Trees in the system support "climber" crops (various beans), fix nitrogen, bear fruit, and provide timber and specialty products. By integrating trees into the system, especially as "live" posts, both vertical and horizontal spaces are optimized, so yields per hectare are high. The immediate area encircling the garden is being replanted with trees to mimic a natural forest. To date, 62 different tree species have been tried, most of them endemics from local forests.

A number of aromatic plants and spices are cultivated among the food crops to repel insect pests, and the HIFCO staff also brews its own "agrochemical"—a reportedly effective fertilizer and pest repellent made from more than 14 local ingredients mixed together in precise ratios. Fish stocked in the water-filled ditches also help out by eating insect eggs.

Eighteen varieties of fish raised in ponds and ditches, along with a variety of domesticated animals, are also part of the HIFCO system. Guinea pigs, geese, ducks, pigeons, and guinea hens are raised in stalls. Residual food crops and aquatic plants provide feed for the animals, which in turn provide the manure that fertilizes the raised beds. (HIFCO has exiled cattle, pigs, goats, and chickens —all environmentally notorious—from this Eden.)

The project even has a crop-improvement program. Seeds are collected from the most promising crop varieties, dried in a solar oven, and stored in the project's seed bank for out-planting and field trials. They are sowed in germination flats and later transferred to raised nursery beds made of logs and located under the forest canopy or to containers fashioned out of cross-sections of hollow plantain stems, palm trunks, or bamboo. Once planted in the soil, the containers decompose quickly.

The HIFCO demonstration farm serves as a training center for AIDESEP's member federations. By 1990, four intensive training courses had been held for 36 families from 18 federations. The training program spans three months of classroom instruction, conducted entirely with graphic materials, and field practice. Entire families—mothers, fathers and children—participate in the course, residing in the HIFCO farm "dormitories." So far, graduates have launched five "mini-HIFCO" demonstration projects in their communities.

AIDESEP hopes eventually to do away with the centralized training center in Pucalpa, and instead help each federation to train its members locally. To this end, AIDESEP initiated a scholarship program in 1985: the 20 students currently enrolled, are working toward degrees in agronomy, engineering, and law.

The mere fact that AIDESEP has been able to bring degraded lands back into agricultural production and maintain it has wide-ranging implications. Continuing high rates of tropical deforestation is producing an ever-increasing amount of degraded and unproductive land. Reclaiming these lands to feed a growing population and support biodiversity conservation presents a major global challenge. The HIFCO project appears to offer one creative and perhaps replicable solution.

Source: Cabarle, 1990

VIII

Strengthening Protected Areas

We must make every effort to preserve, conserve, and manage biodiversity.
Protected areas, from large wilderness reserves to small sites for particular species,
and reserves for controlled uses, will all be part of this process. Such systems of protected areas
must be managed to take account of a range of ecological and human-induced changes.
This is no small task; yet humans must be equal to this challenge, or risk becoming irrelevant.

PETER BRIDGEWATER, NATIONAL PARKS AND WILDLIFE SERVICE, AUSTRALIA

Protected areas—legally established sites managed for conservation objectives—are an essential means for saving biodiversity. Worldwide, 8,163 protected areas cover over 750 million hectares of marine and terrestrial ecosystems, amounting to 1.5 percent of Earth's surface or 5.1 percent of national land area.[102] These areas are managed for objectives ranging from strict nature preservation to controlled resource harvesting.

All protected areas already contribute to conserving biodiversity, but modifying the management and selection of protected areas will enhance their contribution. Explicit biodiversity conservation objectives need to be established for each protected area, and in most cases they need to be better integrated into the fabric of social, environmental, and economic welfare. Though many governments and non-governmental organizations throughout the world would like to expand protected areas and enhance their role in conserving biodiversity, serious obstacles must be overcome.

First, the establishment or existence of a protected area often creates conflicts with local people. When an area is protected, people living near or within it must generally restrict their use of its resources; in some cases, they must leave their homes. Too often, society at large reaps the benefits of protected areas while local people bear the costs.

In extreme cases, open conflict may erupt between hunters, gatherers, loggers, miners, fishermen, or tourism operators and protected area staff or environmental advocates.

Second, protected areas are often institutionally unstable since the agencies administering them are vulnerable to changing policies and budget cuts. The battle for conservation is perpetual, while the fight for exploitation need be won only once. Mining, forestry, or fisheries interests may lobby for "opening" protected areas; transportation departments may want to chart a road through a protected area's "free" land; tourism departments may drum up more visitors than a protected area can support; and industrial development policies may stimulate encroachment, trans-boundary pollution, and even climate change.

Third, many protected areas are insufficiently or ineffectively managed. Rarely can a protected area be managed well in a "hands-off" fashion. Most need intensive management to meet the needs or respond to the impacts of those who use the protected area or to mitigate impacts of development on surrounding lands, the pollution of air and water, and changing climatic conditions. Unfortunately, the trained personnel and ecological knowledge needed for such intensive management are in short supply.

Fourth, funding for most protected areas is either scanty or insecure. Most such funds come from national budgets, which are declining in real terms in most countries. Often, protected areas bear the brunt of budget cuts even when they are highly profitable. Moreover, economic benefits from protected areas are rarely channeled into protected area maintenance or community develop-

FIGURE 29

Growth of World Coverage of Protected Areas

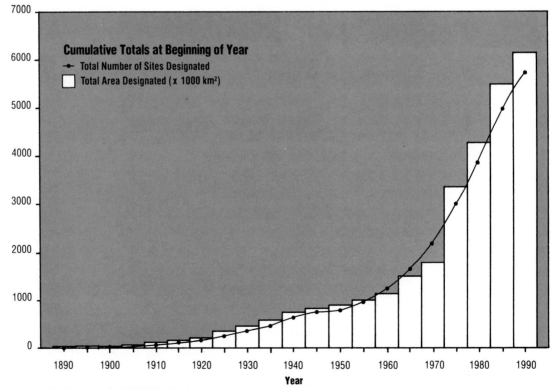

Source: World Conservation Monitoring Centre

ment on nearby lands. In Kenya, for example, nature tourism—the nation's second leading source of foreign exchange—generates some $500 million annually,[103] but only a small portion of this revenue is reinvested in the protected area system. Similarly, tourism in New Zealand earns $1.5 billion each year, while the annual budget of the country's Department of Conservation—which manages the protected areas that draw many of the tourists—totals a mere $58.2 million.[104]

Finally, most people take a narrow view of protected areas, so public support is comparatively weak. Protected areas are often seen only as exotic vacation spots or remote wilderness, not as essential elements of sustainable development. In fact, protected areas contribute to society in many ways and a broader constituency is both necessary and justified.

Objective:

Identify national and international priorities for strengthening protected areas and enhancing their role in biodiversity conservation

Since professional and financial resources are limited, priorities must be determined in ways that reflect both scientific criteria and local, national, and international needs.

Action 52

Conduct national reviews of protected area systems.

All nations should review their existing and proposed protected areas to evaluate their status, needs, and effectiveness. While no individual protected area can meet all management objectives, a carefully designed national *network* of protected areas can encompass the diversity of local and national conservation goals. *(See Box 26).*

A well-designed protected area system review should provide:
■ a comprehensive national statement of the objectives, rationale, definitions, and future directions for the evolving network of protected areas in a country;
■ an assessment of the existing system's viability and completeness;
■ a procedure for systematically identifying the additional areas most suitable for meeting national conservation objectives; and,
■ a clear statement of national priorities and a plan of action for achieving national conservation objectives.

A system review can help researchers, conservation organizations, and international institutions identify priorities for field work, wage public awareness campaigns, raise funds, and carry out conservation activities. It can help the protected area management authority win larger budgets, more land, more personnel, and greater public support. A plan springing from this review can help integrate the many approaches being taken to conserve biodiversity.[105] It can form the foundation of a strategy for funding priority actions or helping governments and others choose among investments in protected areas. And it can be the vehicle for presenting those choices to politicians, administrators, non-governmental organizations, and development assistance agencies. Finally, a system review provides a means of assessing the contribution of existing protected areas to biodiversity conservation. *(See Box 27.)*

A number of planning procedures have been proposed, tested, and proven effective.[106] *(See Box 28.)* Indeed, national protected-area system plans have already been prepared by such countries as Bangladesh, Botswana, Brazil, Canada, Chile, Costa Rica, Indonesia, Madagascar, Sierra Leone, and Peru, and regional system reviews have been prepared by IUCN for Indo-Malaya, Oceania, and Sub-Saharan Africa.[107]

In a protected area system review, some form

BOX 26

Protected Areas Management Categories

Protected areas fall into two main groups. In *strictly protected areas* (such as scientific reserves, national parks, natural monuments, and wildlife sanctuaries), natural landscapes dominate. These are characterized by relative freedom from exotic species, cultivation, and human settlement. In *extractive protected areas* (such as national forests, hunting and fishing zones, and protected rural landscapes) limited harvesting of natural resources is allowed, generally under government control.

Protected areas are given a great variety of names by the nations establishing them, but IUCN has classified these sites into five categories according to their management objectives.

Strictly Protected Areas

1. *Strict Nature Reserves.* Generally smaller areas where the preservation of important natural values with minimum human disturbance are emphasized.

2. *National Parks.* Generally larger areas with a range of outstanding features and ecosystems that people may visit for education, recreation, and inspiration as long as they do not threaten the area's values.

3. *Natural Monuments.* Similar to National Parks, but usually smaller areas protecting a single spectacular natural feature or historic site.

Extractive Protected Areas

4. *Habitat and Wildlife Management Areas.* Areas managed to protect and utilize wildlife species.

5. *Protected Landscapes.* Areas consisting of publicly or privately owned lands that may be subject to resource extraction—including farms, forests, freshwater areas, and coasts—and their associated human settlements, where the objective is to maintain the quality of the overall landscape, harmonious human interaction with it, and the biological diversity it contains.

	IUCN Cat. I-III		IUCN Cat. IV-V		TOTAL	
	Number	Area (ha)	Number	Area (ha)	Number	Area (ha)
Africa	260	88,722,877	381	35,918,296	641	124,641,173
North and Central America	610	170,344,290	1,073	91,415,737	1,683	261,760,027
South America	289	58,190,622	291	56,182,497	580	114,373,119
Asia	410	35,397,425	1,762	66,025,886	2,172	101,423,311
Europe	289	8,056,879	1,635	32,031,759	1,924	40,088,638
Soviet Union	175	23,908,331	38	465,995	213	24,374,326
Australia and S. Pacific	443	67,872,385	494	16,481,489	937	84,353,874
Antarctica	12	220,649	1	36,700	13	257,349
Total	2,488	452,713,458	5,675	298,558,359	8,163	751,271,817

Source: IUCN/CNPPA, 1990; World Conservation Monitoring Centre, U.K.

of "gap analysis" drawing on data on the distribution of species and communities and the location of protected areas is usually needed to make sure that coverage of biodiversity is adequate. But such analysis requires basic inventory data on the distribution of species and community types that many countries simply do not have. At a minimum, data on vegetation types and plant species distributions can provide a rough assessment of protected area gaps, especially if complemented by studies targeting other species, such as birds. *(See Figure 31.)*

The benefits of a protected area system review easily justify the time and expense. Experience shows that national planning and review teams drawn from the public management agencies, non-governmental organizations, universities, and local communities can usually carry out system reviews without conducting new research or taking on new staff. If outside help is needed, neighboring countries or international organizations can usually provide it.

Action 53

Propose immediate and long-term action to establish and strengthen protected areas.

Guided by national system plans, governments should work closely with non-governmental organizations and local communities to propose new protected areas or ways to strengthen existing ones. International support is now becoming available for biodiversity conservation, but because funding was scarce for decades few studies of funding needs exist and few projects are pending. As a result, donor and international non-governmental organizations are called upon to suggest funding priorities that should instead be set through broad-based national planning exercises. *(See Chapter 3.)*

Although basic priorities are clear—action should address threats to protected areas and the needs of economic development in surrounding com-

---

BOX 27

Ensuring the Coverage of Biodiversity in a National Protected Area System

For a national protected area system to effectively conserve biodiversity it must include:

■ two or more large samples of each of the nation's ecosystem types (biogeographic provinces, Holdridge Life Zones, or other ecological classification systems);

■ habitats containing viable populations of economically important genetic resources (wild relatives of industrial crops, vegetables, fruits, pharmaceutical plants, and traditional medicines, etc.);

■ transition zones (ecotones) in all major ecosystem types across altitudinal, moisture, salinity, and other gradients in the landscape (mountain slopes, wet to dry ridges and valleys, marsh and estuary sites, coastal zones, etc.);

■ a matrix of protected areas, corridors, and private land that ensures the survival of indicator and keystone species in the ecosystem; and,

■ sites containing locally endemic species.

---

munities—more specific priorities should be determined through systematic assessments. Commonly, it is assumed that the "priority" needs are obvious and that the only obstacle is funding, so not even a basic assessment of urgent funding needs—fuel for transportation or boots for park guards—is made.

Action 54

Undertake an international assessment of present and future protected area needs.

The IUCN Commission on National Parks and Protected Areas (CNPPA) and the associated IUCN Secretariat should be authorized and funded

BOX 28

Guidelines for Preparing Protected Area System Plans

The unique conditions of each country call for different approaches to preparing a system plan, but the following guidelines can help any country.

Objectives and Priorities

■ Establish national objectives for the protected area system through broad-based participation and debate.

■ Establish specific objectives for each protected area in the system, responding to input from all affected institutions and groups. Spell out the kinds of development permissible in each category of protected area.

■ Identify and establish priorities for better managing existing protected areas, as well as for creating new areas. Identify and establish priorities for research and resource needs, including personnel, funding, training, and materials.

Design Elements

■ Prepare or adopt a classification system of biogeographical units covering freshwater, coastal, marine, and terrestrial ecosystems.

■ Map the distribution of biogeographical units, species of particular concern, human populations, and existing protected areas.

■ Define options for expanding protected area systems using buffer zones, corridors, private land easements, resource management policies, or other options outside the control of area management agencies.

■ Determine the most cost-effective means of achieving the protected area system objectives.

Science and Information

■ Establish a monitoring system, based on information collected during planning for the whole protected area network, to measure the network's effectiveness.

■ Develop an explicit plan to manage key species (keystone and indicator species or species of particular economic or aesthetic value); include population and area requirements. Use this analysis to determine which habitats and species are insufficiently protected.

■ Include a strategy for promoting the system plan to government agencies, the general public, and non-governmental organizations.

Links to Surrounding Lands and Other Sectors

■ Promote the inclusion of protected areas in national land-use policy.

■ Use the system-wide planning process to involve all sectors that contribute to or benefit from protected areas.

■ Quantify direct and indirect benefits, and ensure that local communities are deriving benefits from the system.

Institutional Issues and International Linkages

■ Review legal and institutional systems and identify the changes needed to achieve national conservation objectives, including measures to increase local people's responsibility for protected area management.

■ Identify areas to be recognized under international programs and agreements.

■ Establish mechanisms for periodically reviewing and modifying the system-wide plan.

Source: McNeely and Thorsell, 1991

to coordinate the assessment of regional and global protected area needs.[108] The mandate for such a review could be given by either the proposed International Panel on Biodiversity Conservation (IPBC) *(see Action 3)*, or the secretariat of a ratified Biodiversity Convention. Working with the World Conservation Monitoring Centre (WCMC), national ministries (of environment, agriculture, forestry, and fisheries), scientists, communities, and non-governmental organizations, IUCN should establish a mechanism to document the status of the world's protected areas, provide criteria and guidelines to governments preparing national assessments, and help identify priorities for establishing or strengthening protected areas.

This work should build on regional assessments and investment analyses prepared for the IV World Congress on National Parks and Protected Areas (February 1992), as well as on existing national system reviews and regional studies undertaken by other governmental and non-governmental organizations. The FAO/UNEP Protected Areas Network in Latin America and the Caribbean has facilitated work by regional experts to evaluate existing protected area coverage and to identify gaps in coverage.[109] Similarly, the "Parks in Peril" program sponsored by Latin American organizations and The Nature Conservancy has identified 200 sites in Latin America needing emergency technical and financial support. Building upon these efforts and the World Heritage In Danger List, a list of sites requiring support should be prepared and national, community, and non-governmental organization efforts of high priority should be endorsed.[110]

Currently, IUCN's regional teams of governmental and non-governmental scientific and managerial experts advise governments and international organizations on protected area establishment and management. But IUCN would need a much larger budget to mobilize the local and regional expertise, conduct the field evaluations and consultations, and prepare the reports and publications needed to refine site selection and develop detailed regional lists of priority sites. To expand its reach and ser-

FIGURE 30

Vegetation and Protected Areas of Madagascar

Protected Areas Key
- ● Natural Reserve
- ○ National Park
- ■ Special Reserve
- □ Private Reserve
- ▲ Biological Site
- △ Protected Forest
- ✪ Ranger Station

Vegetation Key
- Dense Humid Forest
- High Altitude Forest
- Dense Dry Forest
- Bush
- Mangrove
- Savanna

Source: Stuart and Adams 1990

FIGURE 31

Endemic Birds in the Albertine Rift Mountains in Africa

(Shaded Areas Cover the Geographical Distributions of 22 Locally Endemic Birds.)

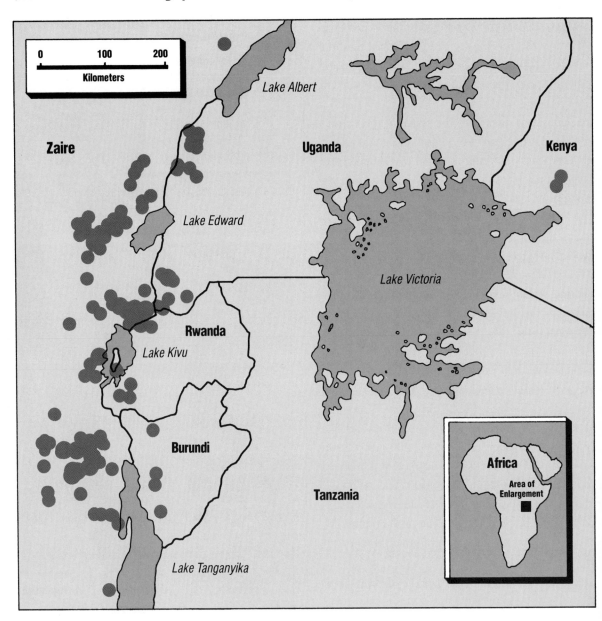

Source: International Council on Bird Preservation

124

vices, IUCN would also need to relate to a far broader range of groups interested in and affected by decisions on protected area priorities.

Action 55

Provide incentives for establishing private protected areas.

Protected areas established by private or non-governmental organizations already play a major role in the conservation of biodiversity and could play a greater role in the future. Community and private groups are purchasing lands for private reserves, donating private lands to public protected area systems, and helping maintain and manage public protected areas. *(See Actions 47 and 48.)*

To help carry out their vital work, changes in tax law are needed. The tax incentives described in Chapter 7 would both encourage resource conservation on private lands and encourage strict protection of such lands. Further tax reductions should be granted to landowners who commit lands to permanent nature reserve status to non-governmental organizations that provide financial or in-kind support to public reserves, and to donors to non-governmental organizations involved in establishing private reserves.

Action 56

Promote international cooperation on protected area management.

Protected areas established in different countries are often physically or biologically linked. Whether "transboundary" protected areas are contiguous (those along international borders) or non-contiguous (networks of sites utilized by migratory species), the need for and obstacles to international cooperation are similar.

To maximize the contribution of such protected areas to biodiversity conservation, governments of transboundary protected areas should establish joint commissions to formulate management plans that seek to reconcile conflicting management practices and establish approaches that are in each country's interest. Where governments resist such cooperation on grounds that their sovereignty might be breached, unofficial planning by protected-area managers may be the answer.

Transboundary protected areas need not have identical objectives—each country stands to gain even where protected areas are managed for somewhat different purposes. But to facilitate coordination, countries should also try to standardize protected area definitions. The Amazon Treaty nations, for example, are now consolidating varying definitions, nomenclatures, and management criteria for protected areas.

To manage non-contiguous protected areas maintained for migratory species habitat, multilateral arrangements are often required. Often, international non-governmental organizations can catalyze cooperation among countries and provide the information needed to make management decisions. For example, The International Council for Bird Preservation (ICBP) and the Western Hemisphere Shorebird Reserve Network (WHSRN) have helped identify critical habitats for migratory species, promote the creation of protected areas, and coordinate protected area management. *(See Box 29.)* Similarly, the international program to protect and restore the green turtle *(Chelonia mydas)* has led to the establishment of areas protecting nesting grounds in several countries.

Objective:

Ensure the sustainability of protected areas and their contribution to biodiversity conservation

How viable a protected area is over the long term depends on how well it is ecologically, socially, and economically integrated into the surrounding region. For protected areas to be sustainable, they must move beyond both the appearance and practice of "fortress parks." As David Hales notes, "Because we believed that our walls would protect our parks, we are now at risk of finding them to be prisons rather than fortresses."[111] To change this situation, increased economic benefits must flow from protected areas to local communities. At the same time, resource management on surrounding lands must be meshed with the needs of the protected area through buffer zones and habitat corridors.

Action 57

Broaden participation in the design of protected area management plans and expand the range of issues addressed by those plans.

The view of protected areas as "islands in a sea of development" reigns among the public and protected area managers alike. As a result, management plans are too often narrowly focused, making this view self-fulfilling. The only way to make sure that protected areas mesh with the local communities is to involve local people in planning and management. Indeed, all protected area management plans should be jointly assembled by protected area management authorities, non-governmental organizations, and community representatives and should address the following issues:

■ *the internal management of each site.* The management objectives for a protected area should be determined through system-wide planning, but surrounding communities and other interested constituencies should have a say in how those objectives are met. Local residents should help decide, for instance, whether to use herbicides to control forest regeneration or whether to establish a recreational facility in a multiple-use area;

■ *human use of and influence on the protected area.* Protected areas should not be designed to keep humans out, but rather to manage human uses of the areas to meet specific objectives. If surrounding communities participate in management planning, opportunities for new human uses of a protected area that are entirely consistent with the area's objectives can often be found. Once a year, more than 100,000 villagers collect tall grasses for house construction and thatching from Royal Chitwan National Park in Nepal. A boon to local people, the annual harvest reinforces the park's justification and in no way diminishes the park's effectiveness;

■ *policies influencing development and resource use in the bioregion.* Conflicts between local residents and managers of protected areas often stem from agricultural, forestry, fisheries, land-tenure, transportation, and trade policies and laws that are beyond the authority of either the park or the surrounding communities;

■ *the study and use of components of biodiversity.* Management plans should regulate inventorying, collecting, research, and monitoring on protected lands. These activities can contribute information for protected area management, and simultaneously help mobilize potential benefits from the biodiversity within the protected area;

BOX 29

International Cooperation on Shorebird Conservation

The Western Hemisphere Shorebird Reserve Network (WHSRN) was established in 1985 in response to declining shorebird populations and disappearing wetlands. The network brings together wildlife agencies, land owners, private conservation groups, and others to solve conservation challenges. Membership in WHSRN is voluntary; management decisions and priorities remain the prerogative of the land administrator. To be included in the network, a site must meet certain biological criteria. Hemispheric Reserves are used by at least 500,000 shorebirds annually (or 30 percent of the flyway population). International Reserves host at least 100,000 shorebirds annually or 15 percent of a flyway population. Regional Reserves host 20,000 shorebirds annually (or 5 percent of a flyway population). Endangered Species Reserves are of critical importance to the survival of one or more endangered shorebird species. As of September 1991, a total of 17 reserves have been included in the network, protecting 30 million shorebirds and 4 million acres of land.

Source: WHSRN, unpublished data, 1991

FIGURE 32

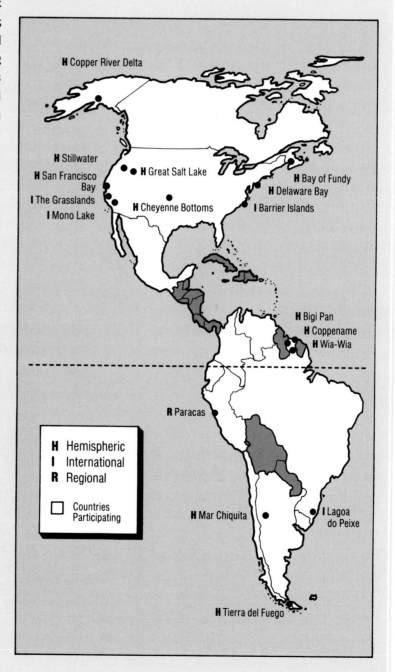

H Copper River Delta

H Stillwater
H San Francisco Bay
I The Grasslands
I Mono Lake

H Great Salt Lake
H Cheyenne Bottoms

H Bay of Fundy
H Delaware Bay
I Barrier Islands

H Bigi Pan
H Coppename
H Wia-Wia

R Paracas

H Mar Chiquita

I Lagoa do Peixe

H Tierra del Fuego

H Hemispheric
I International
R Regional

☐ Countries Participating

■ *financial needs.* Protected areas require stable long-term financial support. In addition to direct contributions from the national budget, other sources might include two-tiered entry fees (lower for local or national residents), hotel taxes, or tour taxes;[112]

■ *employment of local residents.* To the extent that surrounding communities get jobs and other economic benefits from the protected area, its effectiveness in meeting local needs will be enhanced.

In many countries, not all of these issues are considered in management planning, and they will not be until protected area agencies place less emphasis on policing and enforcement, and more on extension, education, and mediation. However, limited funding forces protected area managers, unable to afford outreach and education programs, to adopt a defensive position. Even when change does take place, it will take time to win the confidence of people who have been shut out of past decision-making.

Action 58

Expand the management objectives of protected areas to include the full scope of biodiversity conservation.

All protected areas contribute to the conservation of biodiversity, and through proper management this contribution can often be enhanced without detracting from other objectives. One of the most effective techniques for strengthening the biodiversity conservation role of a protected area is through zoning. For example, the Great Barrier Reef Marine Park, a multiple-use protected area in Australia, zones the park into four broad categories: 1) preservation zones exclude all human use except for strictly controlled scientific research; 2) scientific Research zones allow scientific use; 3) marine National Park zones allow scientific, educational, and recreational use; and 4) General Use zones place

almost no restriction on activity, including commercial and recreational fishing, for example. *(See Figure 33.)* Within each zone, other restrictions may be applied to enhance their role in conservation. For example, within General Use zones, small areas used by animals for breeding or nesting sites may be given special protection from time to time. Similarly, certain recreational zones allow floating hotels while others do not.[113]

In general, however, managing multiple-use protected areas with biodiversity conservation as one objective among several will not succeed unless clear criteria are established for guiding resource management. Without such criteria, unsound policies can be justified in the name of biodiversity conservation. Some forestry ministries, for example, have argued that because forest harvest often increases local species richness (by fomenting species-rich successional vegetation), logging *"enhances"* species diversity. In fact, this *local* increase in richness is typically accompanied by the loss of *overall* species richness since some species can exist only in the "climax community" that is lost to logging. *(See Box 30.)*

Action 59

Enhance the ecological and social value of protected areas through land purchase and zoning outside the protected area and by providing financial incentives for conservation on adjacent private lands.

Developed ecosystems are rarely separated from protected areas by neat hard lines. Zoning within protected areas may allow human activities in some areas while maintaining others in a wilderness state. Similarly, some surrounding land uses contribute more than others to maintaining ecological attributes of the protected area and the services the area provides. Given the importance of the management of surrounding resources to the success of a protected area, the concept of "buffer zones" or "transition zones" is an essential complement to pro-

FIGURE 33

Zoning in the Great Barrier Reef Marine Park, Capricornia Section

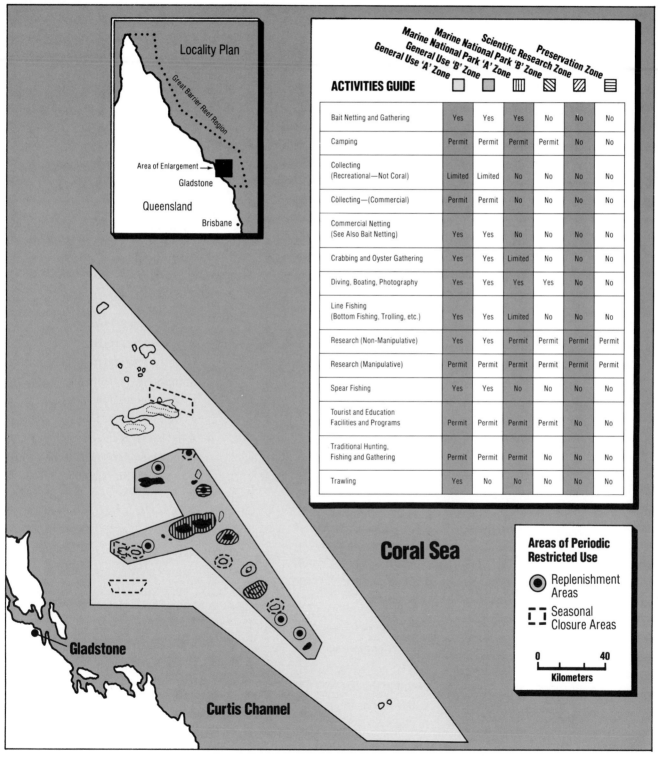

ACTIVITIES GUIDE	General Use 'A' Zone	General Use 'B' Zone	Marine National Park 'A' Zone	Marine National Park 'B' Zone	Scientific Research Zone	Preservation Zone
Bait Netting and Gathering	Yes	Yes	Yes	No	No	No
Camping	Permit	Permit	Permit	Permit	No	No
Collecting (Recreational—Not Coral)	Limited	Limited	No	No	No	No
Collecting—(Commercial)	Permit	Permit	No	No	No	No
Commercial Netting (See Also Bait Netting)	Yes	Yes	No	No	No	No
Crabbing and Oyster Gathering	Yes	Yes	Limited	No	No	No
Diving, Boating, Photography	Yes	Yes	Yes	Yes	No	No
Line Fishing (Bottom Fishing, Trolling, etc.)	Yes	Yes	Limited	No	No	No
Research (Non-Manipulative)	Yes	Yes	Permit	Permit	Permit	Permit
Research (Manipulative)	Permit	Permit	Permit	Permit	Permit	Permit
Spear Fishing	Yes	Yes	No	No	No	No
Tourist and Education Facilities and Programs	Permit	Permit	Permit	Permit	No	No
Traditional Hunting, Fishing and Gathering	Permit	Permit	Permit	No	No	No
Trawling	Yes	No	No	No	No	No

Locality Plan

Great Barrier Reef Region

Area of Enlargement

Gladstone

Queensland

Brisbane

Coral Sea

Gladstone

Curtis Channel

Areas of Periodic Restricted Use

Replenishment Areas

Seasonal Closure Areas

0   40
Kilometers

Source: Great Barrier Reef Marine Park Authority

BOX 30

Managing Protected Areas for Biodiversity Conservation

A protected area (or the management of biological resources more generally) contributes to biodiversity conservation to the extent that it:

■ maintains viable populations of all native species and subspecies, subject only to environmental changes that may naturally alter abundances or distributions;

■ maintains the number and distribution of communities and habitats, subject to environmental changes that may alter such distributions;

■ maintains the genetic diversity of all species in the protected area;

■ excludes human-caused species introductions;

■ enables distributions of species to shift in response to climatic or other environmental changes;

■ fosters the study of the taxonomy, distribution, and ecology of species and biogeographic units;

■ allows, but regulates, exploration for valuable genetic resources and other types of biodiversity information; and,

■ ensures that any use of biological resources is in keeping with the above criteria.

tected area design—witness the inclusion of such zones in many recent plans and proposals for protecting natural areas and managing tropical forests.

Increasingly, protected area planners also look outside the protected area proper to develop corridors of natural or semi-natural habitat—pathways by which plants and animals can migrate or disperse as seasons or climate change.[114] Of course, such corridors can be two-way streets, allowing the spread of disease, pests, or fire among the last representatives of certain communities or species, but careful management can reduce these risks.

Used strategically, corridors and buffer zones can fundamentally change the ecological role of pro-

tected areas. Instead of merely maintaining representative samples of ecosystems, protected areas linked by corridors become means of maintaining functioning natural or near-natural ecosystems over large regions. In Central America, a proposal has been made to develop a network of protected areas, linked by corridors and semi-natural habitats, that could maintain ecological continuity from Panama through Mexico. Similarly, a grassroots non-governmental organization, Preserve Appalachian Wilderness, is pressing for the establishment of linked and expanded protected areas running the length of the eastern United States and Canada to keep ecosystems healthy and allow species to migrate as climate changes.

Despite their promise, corridors and buffer zones have faced serious problems in practice. Attempts to establish buffer zones outside of protected areas often fail because the protected area managers do not have legal authority over the lands involved.[115] And few attempts have been made to establish buffer zones *inside* protected areas since managers believe that the loss of natural habitat that would ensue outweighs any benefits that might be gained through better integrating the protected area with surrounding communities. In the case of corridors, the cost of buying land can be high and the difficulties of managing long narrow habitats—with their extensive borders—insurmountable.

Buffer zones or corridors are most likely to work where population density is low, the benefits of the protected area to surrounding areas is clear, and restrictions imposed on resource use are outweighed by the local benefits of such limits. *(See Box 31.)* More generally, these conservation methods are more likely to succeed in countries with relatively small populations and high living standards. The best way to establish a buffer zone or corridor is for the government to purchase the land involved or its development rights, zoning the land surrounding the protected areas to ensure its semi-natural state, or by providing financial incentives for conservation on private lands.

Action 60

Enhance the ecological and social value of protected areas by increasing the benefits to people in and around them.

Establishing a protected area facilitates such resource uses as tourism and endangered species conservation but prohibits others, such as agriculture. It is thus crucial for the long-term success of a protected area that it is perceived as an asset rather than a liability.

Three general strategies can be adopted by governments and non-governmental organizations to

---

BOX 31

Making Buffer Zones Work

A buffer zone in name *and* practice is slowly being developed around Saguaro National Monument, near Tucson, Arizona, in the United States. With population growth in the region averaging 2 percent per year, development pressure on the land adjacent to the monument has been increasing rapidly. Protected area staff are working closely with the surrounding communities in regional planning initiatives to ensure that development does not undermine the protected area's objectives. They are following two approaches:

Project-specific agreements. One approach to ameliorating the ecological impacts of changing land use is exemplified by a recent agreement reached involving a proposed development of 4,400 acres adjacent to the protected area with four resort complexes, 10,000 housing units, and related commercial units. The developer recognized that the nationally significant natural and scenic resources in the adjacent protected area would contribute to profitability and was thus willing to institute environmental safeguards. The agreement reached calls for:

■ setting aside half of the project site (which includes key wildlife corridors) as protected open space;

■ restoring stream habitat that had been degraded through decades of farming and grazing;

■ establishing an independent non-profit institution—the Rincon Institute—to manage the open space for educational, scientific, conservation, and recreation value; provide environmental education to area residents; and make sure that the developed portion of the land is man-

aged sustainably. The Rincon Institute was given $240,000 of start-up funding by the developers, and deed restrictions requiring payment of fees and hotel taxes will provide continuing funding.

Zoning. The city of Tucson has adopted new zoning ordinances creating an "Environmental Resource Zone" around local and federal protected areas, and the county government is creating a "Buffer Overlay Zone." In each case, the zoning ensures the maintenance of migratory corridors, restricts the density of development near protected areas, promotes restoration of degraded habitat, and promotes the use of native species in landscaping and re-vegetation. The Buffer Overlay Zone applies to parcels of land of 80 acres or more located within one mile of any public reserve. The Board of Supervisors is using a map of Critical and Sensitive Biological Communities to site developments, and it has set standards for fencing, building color, and lighting to ensure that development blends with the natural environment. The Board also developed an "approved plant list"—consisting only of native plants—for landscaping areas removed from buildings, and a list of plants prohibited even in private yards. Most important, buffer overlay zoning requires that 50 percent of any future development must be maintained as natural open space.

Source: Propst and Carothers, 1991; Bill Paleck, Pers. Comm., July 1991; Ordinance 1988-116. Pima County Board of Supervisors, Arizona; Ordinance No. 7450. City Council of the City of Tucson, Arizona, July 3, 1990.

enhance the local value of protected areas, particularly in developing countries: compensation, local social and economic development, and promotion of sustainable resource extraction. The first two of these strategies have become standard elements of the many "integrated conservation and development projects" now supported by bilateral donors or international non-governmental organizations.[116]

As discussed in Chapter 6, compensation for loss of access to resources or work can be money, substitute resources, or jobs in new fields. The key is letting those affected help determine what constitutes "just" compensation and getting governments to make good on their promises. (In Kenya, the government drilled watering holes for the Maasai pastoralists as partial compensation for restricting their access to Amboseli Park, but after the park was established, the funding for maintaining the water sources was cut.)

Encouraging local social and economic development, the second strategy, is in keeping with the bioregional approach to conservation advocated here. *(See Chapter 7.)* Integrated conservation and development projects are only now beginning to be implemented, so it is too early to say authoritatively which designs work best. But though the projects now under way have stumbled on some fronts, many also contain successful components worth emulating.[117] These include:

■ improving natural resource management outside the protected area;

■ improving product marketing;

■ providing employment related to the protected area;

■ increasing local benefits from nature tourism; and,

■ providing community social services (schools, health clinics etc.).

Finally, governments and non-governmental organizations should seek opportunities to establish protected areas in which resource harvesting compatible with biodiversity conservation objectives is permitted (IUCN's Protected Landscapes Category)—as it is in Brazil's extractive reserves.

(See Chapter 6.) Harvesting impinges far less on biodiversity conservation in the region than would many alternative land uses. Considering how undervalued non-timber forest products are in many regions, significant opportunities may exist in other countries for similar types of reserves.

Action 61

Restore degraded lands within protected areas and in adjacent lands and corridors.

Where habitats have been fragmented or disturbed, ecological restoration techniques should be used to re-establish natural ecosystems. Beyond protected area boundaries, adjacent sites should also be restored wherever possible to increase the habitat available for species and to help maintain the protected area's integrity. Re-vegetating watersheds, re-establishing woodlots, and improving hunting and fishing outside of protected areas can all contribute to the sustainability of the protected area itself.

IX

Conserving Species, Populations, and Genetic Diversity

If Charles Darwin were alive today, his work would most likely focus not on the origins but, rather, on the obituaries of species.

MOSTAFA K. TOLBA, UNITED NATIONS ENVIRONMENT PROGRAMME

By almost any reckoning, the most effective and efficient mechanism for conserving biodiversity is to prevent the destruction or degradation of habitat. For conserving the diversity of landscapes and ecosystems, there is no alternative. But to conserve individual species, populations, and genes, habitat protection will have to be complemented by a wide array of other techniques. The options range from species-management programs in the wild to off-site protection in botanic gardens, zoos, genebanks, and aquaria. An integrated approach to conservation—one that utilizes this entire range of techniques—is a cornerstone of biodiversity conservation. *(See Figure 34.)*

A particular species or population may become a conservation target for various reasons. Many species face unique threats from over-exploitation, pollution, or introduced predators or competitors. So-called keystone species with particularly important roles in ecosystems may also need to be singled out for conservation. So may wild relatives of domesticated crops or livestock and the wild and semi-domesticated species used in local economies. As for such "flagship" species as the giant panda, great whales, redwoods, and barrel cacti, action on their behalf pays double dividends: the habitat of these well-loved species is also home to a wide diversity of less charismatic species for which it is difficult to garner public support. Finally, targeted conservation efforts are also needed to maintain crop, tree, livestock, and microbial genetic diversity.

Although targeted conservation programs are vital in efforts to save key species or genes, they may be even more important in making biodiversity "pay". The conservation of wild relatives of domesticated crops and the off-site conservation of crop varieties or cultures of micro-organisms provides breeders and genetic engineers with a ready source of genetic material. Plants and animals conserved in botanic gardens and zoos can be used to restore degraded lands, reintroduce species into the wild, and restock depleted populations. Finally, zoos, botanic gardens, aquaria, and other such facilities can give the public a window on the natural environment and expand opportunities for basic and applied research.

Objective:

Strengthen capacity to conserve species, populations, and genetic diversity in natural habitats

The protection of habitats and the careful management of resource-use can save a large fraction of the world's diversity of species and populations from extinction. But habitat and ecosystem conservation provide no guarantee that any particular species will be conserved. It is possible to conserve an ecosystem and still lose individual species or to save the species and lose genetically distinct populations. If saving particular species or populations is critical, it may be necessary to establish special conservation areas (such as genetic reserves, gene sanctuaries, and wildlife reserves) or to create optimal habitats for the species within protected areas or other components of the landscape. Species-focused conservation plans may rely heavily on protected areas (as in the case of elephants) or minimally (as in the case of whales).

Action 62

Integrate the conservation of species, populations, and genetic resources into regional management and protected area reviews.

Because a wide range of actions may be needed to conserve species, populations, and genetic diversity in the wild, conservation requires careful planning and close integration with regional conservation and development plans. Often, saving a species means taking action in many different ecosystems and intervening in various land uses.

Priorities for conserving species, population, and genetic diversity must be established and strategies adopted to ensure that habitat protection efforts and resource management regimes support those priorities. The IUCN Species Survival Commission (SSC) has completed conservation action plans for 16 groups of species—among them, primates, antelopes, and rodents—and plans are now afoot for 15 others. In cooperation with Botanic Gardens Conservation International, SSC is also planning survival strategies for plant species.

The development of species-focused plans provides governments with guidance on key conservation needs. Implementing the highest priority projects in the species action plans prepared to date would cost roughly $200 million. For Africa, such species-specific plans have been synthesized with assessments of protected area needs in the study, *Biodiversity Conservation in Sub-Saharan Africa and its Islands*.[118] Similar regional biodiversity assessments should be prepared for other parts of the world.

Conservation needs related to specific species or genetic resources are often overlooked when protected area systems are designed. Experts on the distribution of wild relatives of domesticated species, for example, should routinely be included in protected area system reviews.

Conservation of specific species or genetic resources may not necessarily require a hands-off approach; indeed, disturbance is desirable in some cases. The management plan for the Sierra de Manantlán Biosphere Reserve in Mexico, established in part to protect *Zea diploperennis*, an important relative of maize containing valuable germplasm for disease resistance, incorporates some traditional agricultural systems since this species occurs only in or near cultivated fields.[119] Similarly, since the wild cattle of Southeast Asia (such as the Gaur, Banteng, and Kouprey) thrive in the early successional habitat created by shifting cultivation, conserving the species may require continuing these practices.

To date, most habitat protection efforts aimed at saving particular species have been geared to such economically or culturally important animals as waterfowl or large mammals. But efforts to conserve such species as wild crop relatives, fruit trees, and orchids in their natural habitat should be greatly expanded. Unfortunately, serious institutional problems stand in the way. Too often, the people experienced in habitat conservation and management work on conservation and protected areas projects, while experts in sampling and handling genetic resources work in agriculture and forestry. Furthermore, in most developing countries, species recovery programs are limited to species listed as endangered by the U.S. Fish and Wildlife Service—a small selection of those actually threatened.

To begin widening the conservation net, nations should use national and international assessments to identify threatened species, monitor their populations, and launch recovery programs for them. Most developed countries have prepared lists of their threatened plants and animals, often in the form of "Red Data Books." But few of these countries have the basic field information on individual species needed to create such rosters. Still, where all threatened species cannot be listed, it is usually possible to list by group birds, mammals, amphibians and reptiles, fish, and medicinal plants.

FIGURE 34

Integrated Approaches to Biodiversity Conservation

Ex Situ Conservation

Field Genebanks

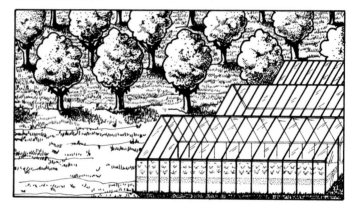

In Situ Conservation

Action 63

Use flagship species to increase support for conservation.

Some species that cross many political boundaries (such as migratory birds) or figure prominently in cultural lore (such as large cats and birds) have the potential to stimulate comprehensive conservation programs that protect many other species and larger ecosystems. To capitalize on this public support, a Global Heritage Species Program should be developed at national and international levels. Internationally, the Species Survival Commission of IUCN should designate certain species as globally important to the world's heritage. National environment ministries and non-governmental organizations should collaboratively develop lists of species of significance for the national heritage as well. Information on the status and conservation needs of species on these lists should be made available to primary and secondary schools, museums, zoos, botanic gardens, and other institutions that could publicize it. Individual zoos or botanic gardens could focus fundraising campaigns on such species, using the proceeds to support conservation activities by the institution or donating them to other organizations.

Action 64

Improve and expand legal mechanisms to protect species.

An appropriate legal framework can make the difference between success and failure in species conservation. Species designated as endangered by a competent authority (such as a ministry of environment) and species for which the country has a particular responsibility (such as those protected under international conventions) should be protected by law. Endangered species legislation should cover plants, animals, and fungi and should prohibit the taking, possession, and trade of listed species. Crit-

ical habitats of endangered or vitally important species should also be protected. Recovery programs for species or habitats listed as endangered should be mandated by national legislation.

One of the benefits of the anticipatory, "upstream" approach to biodiversity conservation presented in this *Strategy* is the opportunity to avoid letting species reach the brink of extinction before acting. This can eliminate many conflicts between specific development projects and a species' survival, conflicts that often seem irreconcilable because the issues are only taken up when few options are left. Nevertheless, strong laws to protect endangered species and their habitats are a necessary component of biodiversity conservation.

Internationally, the most important legal agreement which has focused on single-species conservation needs is The Convention on International Trade in Endangered Species of Wild Fauna and Flora (CITES). *(See Box 15.)* CITES has already helped control trade in endangered species, but stricter enforcement, new parties, and more information on how trade affects threatened species are needed. CITES should also begin to monitor significant trade in species not yet declared endangered. The extra funds required should be provided to the international and national institutions that monitor species trade to ensure enforcement of CITES provisions—among them, the Wildlife Trade Monitoring Unit at the World Conservation Monitoring Centre, TRAFFIC offices in many countries, and the IUCN/SSC Trade Specialist Group.

Since many important populations of globally threatened species—especially birds, fish, and reptiles—are held privately in captivity, private collections should be required to take full part in the regional and international agreements governing captive populations in zoos and botanic gardens. Countries should adopt laws that prevent private parties from acquiring internationally threatened species unless it can be demonstrated that their specimens are "surplus"—that is, not needed for off-site conservation, captive breeding programs, and reintroductions to the wild—or have been obtained through certified sources.

Objective:

Strengthen the capacity of off-site conservation facilities to conserve biodiversity, educate the public, and contribute to sustainable development

Off-site biodiversity conservation centers—arboreta, aquaria, botanic gardens, seedbanks, captive breeding units, clonal collections, culture collections, field genebanks, forest nurseries, propagation units, tissue and cell cultures, and zoological gardens—are important components of a comprehensive, integrated conservation program. In various combinations, they can conserve stocks of both wild and domesticated animals, plants, fungi, and microorganisms.

Although most older arboreta, botanic gardens, and zoos were not established specifically with conservation in mind, the objectives of many have changed. Since the 1970s, *ex situ* facilities have emerged as an important element of biodiversity-conservation networks. Zoos, botanic gardens, and arboreta now maintain populations of a wide range of rare and endangered wild species and can supply them to reintroduction or restocking programs. For instance, botanists from the Rio de Janeiro Botanic Garden are collecting, cultivating, studying, and conserving plants from the relict Atlantic coastal forests of Brazil, while zoo curators are rearing golden-lion tamarin monkeys in captivity in Brazil and the United States for re-introduction into the same forest to help the natural population increase faster.

Many off-site facilities—notably botanic gardens, zoological gardens, and aquaria—also heighten public awareness of biodiversity and provide material for basic and applied scientific research in such areas as plant propagation, genetics, and systematics. At such institutions as the Cambridge Botanic Garden and the Jardín Botánico "Viera y Clavijo" in the Canary Islands, for instance, studies of the propagation of endangered species are contributing to efforts to restore wild populations without using materials from the endangered populations themselves.[120]

In step with their changing role in conservation, the institutional structure of zoos, botanic gardens, and aquaria is changing as well. The traditional physical separation of plants, animals, and fish is breaking down as environmental educators increasingly try to show people how species interact and function in natural systems. Some zoos are thus becoming "biological parks" or "Biodiversity Conservation Centers" that maintain plant and animal species from both marine and terrestrial habitats. *(See Figure 35.)*

One final transformation that may soon occur in off-site conservation will reflect growing recognition of the importance of property rights over resources held off-site. In the 1990s, the extension of property-rights regimes to cover what has traditionally been considered "raw" genetic material may affect the management and legal responsibilities of off-site conservation centers. For example, to ensure an equitable sharing of any profits that may later arise from the use of the material, representatives of botanic gardens or zoos may in the future need to negotiate agreements with both the countries where they are collecting and with private firms wishing to utilize their collections. Collecting permits may need to include statements that any future development of products is subject to royalty arrangements. *(See Chapters 4 and 6.)*

Some conservationists fear that giving greater emphasis to off-site conservation could cause governments to see it as a substitute rather than a complement to conservation in the wild. But many species and populations will slip through the cracks and be lost if off-site facilities are not strengthened, and the opportunities that off-site conservation provides for

FIGURE 35

Evolution of Zoos

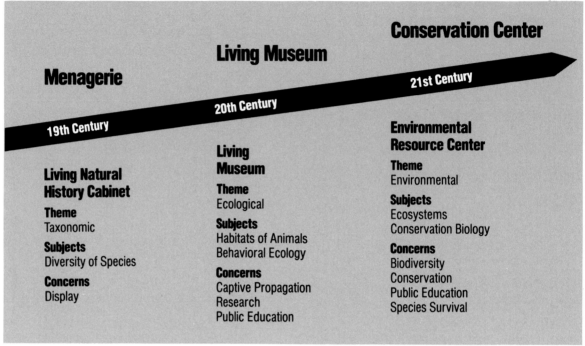

Source: Adapted from G. Rabb, unpublished figure

increasing awareness of and discovering new uses for biodiversity help provide the incentive needed to save biodiversity in the wild. Both on-site and off-site conservation actions are needed, and the two must be coordinated as parts of unified programs.

Action 65

Strengthen crop and livestock genetic resource conservation, and implement the Global Initiative for the Security and Sustainable Use of Plant Genetic Resources.

For millennia, farmers have selected and bred crop and livestock varieties for their own use. But during the past century, both public and private off-site collections that maintain plant germplasm for use by breeders were established. In the past three decades, international germplasm-conservation cen-

ters have been strengthened—work coordinated largely by the International Board for Plant Genetic Resources (IBPGR) and carried out mostly by genebanks in International Agricultural Research Centers. At the national level, genebanks have been established to complement this international network. Grassroots seed and livestock conservation networks also play an important role. *(See Chapter 6.)* Worldwide, more than 40 base seed collections, over 20 field genebanks, and several hundred other germplasm collections have been established, mostly within national programs.

Has this network performed well? Yes and no. The potentially catastrophic loss of genetic diversity caused by the spread of Green Revolution varieties in the 1960s and 1970s was averted through the quick international response to the problem. But the recent Keystone International Dialogue Series on Plant Genetic Resources identified six areas requiring improvement or expansion.[121]

- *ex situ* conservation, including collection, storage and regeneration, documentation and information systems, germplasm evaluation and enhancement, and exchange;
- on-farm community conservation and utilization;
- *in situ* conservation;
- monitoring and early warning of genetic erosion in specific locations;
- development of techniques for sustainable advances in agricultural productivity; and,
- research training and public education.

Besides identifying these areas needing support, the Keystone group called for a *Global Initiative for the Security and Sustainable Use of Plant Genetic Resources* to address them. Enhanced off-site conservation figures prominently in the group's idea of what is required to conserve plant genetic resources. Of the roughly $300 million that the group calculates will be needed annually to sustain agricultural genetic resource conservation, 43 percent would be devoted to national seedbank programs, 6 percent to field genebanks and *in-vitro* collections, 6 percent to on-farm conservation, 10 percent to supporting activities through the international community, 17 percent for research, 4 percent for training, 8 percent for public awareness, and 6 percent for building new facilities. (Costs of *in situ* conservation were not included in the Keystone estimate of financial needs.)

The Keystone group did not address needs for conserving germplasm of wild or semi-domesticated species, including thousands of species used by local communities for food and medicines. Nor did it address livestock genetic resources, which are even less well covered than crop genetic resources. *(See Box 32.)* As meat and milk have come to play larger dietary roles in much of the world during this century, new livestock breeds have been introduced to meet burgeoning demands. The result has been a rapid loss of indigenous breeds of domestic animals that are environmentally well adapted and often ensconced in regional culture. Cooperation is needed to establish regionally-based programs for conserving

FIGURE 36

Wild Cassava (left) is the Source of Resistance to Two of the Most Serious Cassava Diseases in Africa. Transfer of Genes to Cultivated Cassava (right) Increased Yields by a Factor of 18.

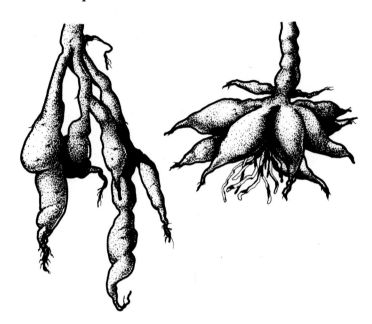

Source: Prescott-Allen and Prescott-Allen 1983

domesticates through captive breeding, through the storage of ova, semen and embryos, through collaboration with institutes that captively-breed wild relatives, and with regional breeding programs. Emphasis should focus on endangered or obsolete breeds or on breeds uniquely adapted to specific ecological conditions and uses.

Surprisingly, little information is available on livestock breeds, even though there are far fewer of them than crop varieties. Accordingly, one priority is to characterize and evaluate the conservation status of domestic species and their wild relatives. In some regions, such non-governmental organizations as the American Minor Breeds Conservancy are already doing this work, but most are seriously underfunded, and public germplasm-conservation organizations often fail to integrate them into the conservation network.

The costs of both genebanks and living collections for domesticated animals range much higher than those for conserving plants. For example, if eight regional centers were established to conserve ten domesticated species, with approximately 1,000 breeds per species, each center would need some $200,000 annually for operating costs, salaries, and maintenance. In comparison, recurring costs for maintaining a single accession (which could be one variety) of a crop in a seedbank run about $50 per sample—less than 5 percent of the cost for animals. Money aside, considerable strategic research is still needed on gene-bank storage techniques. So far, priorities and proposals have been developed, but there is no truly global system. Time is of the essence, particularly given the many years needed to produce mature animals from cryo-preserved genetic materials.

Backed by a strengthened crop and livestock germplasm-conservation system, public research institutions should increase their capacity to assess patterns of genetic diversity. Rapid screening techniques now make it easier to collect target samples, to establish the limits of variation in the collections, and to monitor genetic diversity in the field. With these new techniques, costly and often hit-or-miss fieldwork can be kept to a minimum and the extensive duplication of limited ranges of diversity in germplasm banks avoided.

Given the long-term responsibility of genebanks, stable sources of funding are essential. Endowments or trust funds should be established for significant germplasm collections, particularly those held in developing countries. Donors should also allocate funds from development assistance projects to national programs to collect and conserve plant germplasm that would otherwise be destroyed by the projects they fund.

Action 66

*Develop the world's collections of cultures of microorganisms as an **ex situ** network.*

Culture collections of microorganisms, including algae, bacteria, fungi, protozoa, and viruses, are becoming increasingly important tools for conservation and the development of sustainable agriculture, as well as increasingly important sources of material in biotechnology development. To fulfill these roles, collections must be expanded in scope and number, and information on the strains held must be documented and disseminated.

The world's collections of microorganisms currently preserve in a living state only about 20 percent of known species and less than 5 percent of the estimated undocumented total. Since many microorganisms are difficult to find and isolate, maintaining such strains in culture collections is the only practical way to ensure access to them for screening for beneficial properties and to check identifications.

The 19-country network of 23 Microbiological Resources Centers (MIRCENs) that was developed through UNESCO preserves, identifies, and

---

BOX 32

Targets for Genebank Coverage

	Current number	Target number in 5 years[1]
Crop genepools	2 million	3.0 million
Forest species	few thousands	1.5 million
Domesticated animals	few thousands	0.5 million?
Medicinal plants	±0	0.5 million
Ecosystem rehabilitation	±0	0.5 million
Locally important plants	few hundred	1.0 million
Microorganisms	500,000	1.0 million

1.Assumes the elimination of excessive duplication in existing collections. Targets are rough estimates; specific targets should be linked to national inventory and collecting activities.

distributes microbial germplasm. With its emphasis on the needs of developing countries, this network's role in both microbial conservation and in building capacity in biotechnology should be expanded. For this reason, the MIRCENs' work on conservation and technology transfer deserves increased support as biotechnology advances. *(See Figure 37.)*

More than 320 culture collections are registered with the World Federation of Culture Collections' World Data Center, and many more informal research collections are linked through the Microbial Strain Data Network. Along with such regional initiatives as the "Microbial Information Network Europe" sponsored by the European Community, these organizations form an effective network that is nevertheless vulnerable to national policy changes and competition for scarce resources. If commitments to long-term support do not come soon, past investments in microbial conservation and expertise

will be lost. By the same token, the databases and information networks now operating need increased funding to cover recurrent costs and to allow entry of existing data and expansion as the knowledge base grows. Finally, more funding is needed for research on methods for detecting, isolating, and preserving microbial diversity in culture collections.

Action 67

Fill major gaps in the protection of plant genetic resources.

Over the past 25 years, major advances have been made in the conservation of genepools of globally important crops. But, comparatively, forest trees, medicinal plants, ornamentals, and so-called "minor" crops of local or regional importance have

FIGURE 37

Microbiological Resources Centers (MIRCENs)

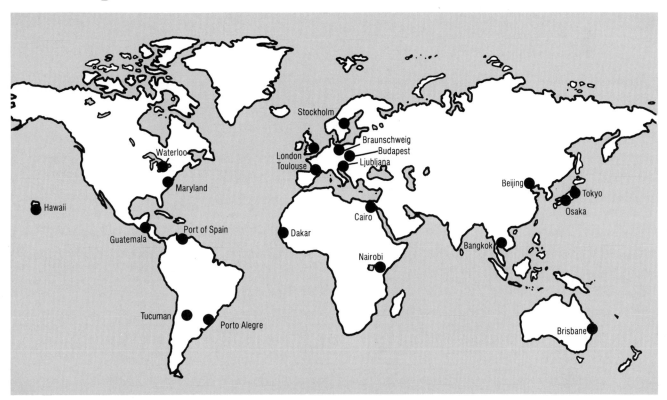

been neglected. International and national action has concentrated on major crops and forages, trees used in plantation forestry and agroforestry, and major breeds of animals. Currently, only a few tree genepools are targeted for *ex situ* conservation—among them, economically important temperate species, tropical pines, *Eucalyptus*, and nitrogen-fixing trees of use in fuelwood production, reforestation, and agroforestry. This focus must now be broadened to include wider genepools of local and global value. With only 250,000 species of plants in the world, it is well within the realm of global economic and technical capacity to conserve all of these species, but key groups particularly deserving increased attention include:

Tree species. Tree-seed genebanks and specially-designed living collections can complement *in situ* conservation and provide sources of genetic resources for breeding. New biotechnologies have opened up new possibilities for screening, for accelerating targeted collecting, and for putting diversity to use faster. For instance, rapid screening for storage characteristics makes it possible to conserve threatened tree genepools that might otherwise be passed over because their seeds are too "recalcitrant" to withstand storage. Additionally, *ex situ* materials can be used in ecosystem rehabilitation projects to avoid over-reliance on exotic materials, to establish plantation and social forestry projects, and to strengthen agroforestry programs.

Priority needs for conserving tree species' genetic diversity include:
■ new national and regional tree nurseries and germplasm banks, in most cases affiliated with crop genebanks, especially at the national level;
■ accelerated provenance trials and the development of scientific guidelines that governments can use to create or fortify networks of conservation genebanks for tree species;
■ screening programs to identify easily stored species;
■ revision of *ex situ* collecting and conservation priorities to include species important for ecosys-

tem rehabilitation and species of value as non-timber forest products;
■ the use of biochemical and molecular techniques to enhance knowledge of diversity of tree species genepools; and,
■ continued funding for international coordination.

Medicinal plants. Numerous medicinal plant species are facing serious threats of extinction or loss of genetic variation in the wild. As these plants die out, local communities lose cornerstones of traditional medicine and humankind more generally loses the stuff of which new pharmaceuticals are made. Many medicinal plants are kept in botanic gardens and associated nurseries, but nations need to accord the conservation of these plants higher priority and to carefully consider both how to structure property rights over these resources and how to compensate the individuals or communities who discovered their medicinal value.

For conserving and developing medicinal plants, botanic gardens are a natural institutional base. The cultivation of medicinal plants not only ensures continuity of supply but also provides a source of income. To relieve pressure on wild sources by helping to establish sources of cultivated medicinal plants, botanic gardens in China, India, Sri Lanka, Indonesia, and elsewhere are studying cultivation requirements and providing seed sources.[122]

Crops of local and regional importance. Several thousand species of fruits, nuts, vegetables, root and tuber crops, oil and fiber plants, herbs and spices, and beverage and forage plants are grown throughout the world as exclusively local crops. Few of these so-called minor crops have figured in any focused breeding program, though some have been bred on farms. Many are mainstays of the local market economy (even though they do not show up in trade statistics) and culture. Unfortunately, changes in land-use and the introduction of exotic germplasm threatens the survival of many of these undervalued species. The status of these crops needs to be assessed, surveys undertaken, and crops at risk of loss should either be collected or incorporated into new *in situ* conservation programs. Moreover, agricultural research institutions should devote more resources to improving the agricultural production of these regionally important crops instead of attempting to introduce more widespread crops as substitutes.

Ornamental species. Tens of thousands of species—among them orchids, bromeliads, bulbs, cacti, and succulents—are cultivated in parks, gardens, and homes. A flourishing horticultural industry and nursery trade exists in many countries, but these plants—many endangered in the wild—are generally ignored in germplasm conservation programs. Conservation organizations, collaborating closely with botanic gardens, should identify priorities for the conservation of ornamental species threatened in the wild and work with local *ex situ* facilities to ensure their conservation.

Action 68

Develop the world's botanic gardens as a major off-site network for conserving wild plant resources.

Together, the world's 1500 botanic gardens, arboreta, and national plant collections maintain the largest array of plant diversity outside of nature, and they have major, if often overlooked, potential as resource centers for conservation, education, and development. If the infrastructure and technical facilities of most of these institutions can be strengthened, they could conserve *ex situ* stocks of most of the world's endangered plant species. Already, individuals of an estimated 12,000 to 15,000 threatened species are being cultivated in botanic gardens and arboreta.

The cost of maintaining an adequate collection of a species depends on whether the species is a tree, shrub, or herb and whether it is maintained as

a desiccated or refrigerated seed sample in a seed bank or a field genebank, as a clonal collection, or in tissue or cell culture. Also, capital, maintenance, and labor costs differ from country to country. As a rule of thumb, $1,000 to $2,000 is needed annually to keep an adequate sample of a species. Accordingly, maintenance for 20,000 plant species would cost between $20 million and $40 million per year.

A strategy for improving the conservation role of botanic gardens was developed by the Botanic Gardens Conservation Secretariat (BGCS) in 1989. The BGCS, established by IUCN in 1987 and recently renamed Botanic Gardens Conservation International (BGCI), links nearly 400 botanic gardens committed to conservation.[123]

Among the priorities identified in the Botanic Gardens Conservation Strategy is expanding the number of botanic gardens in tropical countries. Botanic gardens are distributed unevenly in the world, reflecting history and politics, not the distribution of plant diversity. *(See Figure 38.)* Europe has 540 botanic gardens and the United States and Canada have 290, and together these regions contain 28,000 native plant species. In sharp contrast, Latin America boasts just under 100 gardens while the region contains some 90,000 species.

An encouraging development in the last decade has been the creation of new botanic gardens and arboreta in tropical countries. These include the Jardin Botánico de Brasilia, specializing in the flora of the cerradáo (transitional forests and open savannas), and the Conservataire et Jardin Botanique du Mascarin, Réunion, which maintains collections of many endangered species from Indian Ocean islands. Such gardens are ideally suited for local conservation in areas of high diversity. But the continued development of many will depend on substantial external support. This could come in part from botanic gardens in temperate countries, though they themselves face serious financial constraints. At the same time, northern counterpart gardens could "twin" themselves, providing technical assistance or supporting staff exchanges.

Also necessary to strengthen botanic gardens are new systems to provide local and global information on *ex situ* holdings of wild species in botanic gardens, arboreta, and crop genebanks. Most germplasm surveys exclude the holdings of botanic gardens. So do agricultural genetic-resource databases, though these at least contain data on some wild species. To fill this gap, a comprehensive database is needed that covers holdings of all wild species (especially those of economic importance) in seed banks, botanic gardens, or other institutions. Details of 60,000 accessions of threatened plants, representing 8,000 species in over 300 botanic gardens, are already held in BGCI databases. Linked with other databases on threatened and endangered plant species held by the World Conservation Monitoring Centre, these can form the core of an expanded information network.

Finally, national and regional botanic garden networks should be developed to coordinate and stimulate conservation activities. National networks

have already been created in Australia, China, Mexico, and many other countries. For example, the Center for Plant Conservation in the United States is an interactive network of about 25 botanic gardens that together possess a national collection of nearly 500 species (with genetically viable populations) of threatened and endangered plants on a cooperative, but centrally managed, basis. Regional networks or associations—such as the Latin American-Caribbean and the Ibero-Macronesian Associations of botanic gardens—may work better for clusters of countries with only a few botanic gardens each, though political constraints might impede some operations.

Action 69

Strengthen the conservation role of zoological parks.

Pére David's deer, European and American bison, the Przewalski horse, the Arabian oryx, and the nene goose, along with many other species, would be extinct today except for efforts by zoos and animal reserves. Such successes will multiply thanks to the cooperative management programs developed in the last decade by associations of zoos. The advantages of cooperation are clear. A single zoo may house too few animals of a species to ensure the species' long-term survival, but cooperative breeding programs involving many zoos increase the odds. Some 228 North American institutions are participating in cooperative breeding programs for 57 species, and collaborative efforts are planned for an additional 143 species programs by the year 2000. Similar programs are developing in the United Kingdom, Australia, New Zealand, and Japan.[124]

A conservation strategy should be developed to help set priorities and strengthen collaboration among zoos. The starting point would be identifying collective institutional strengths and weaknesses and evaluating national and international opportunities for further contributions to conservation.

FIGURE 38

Distribution of Botanic Gardens

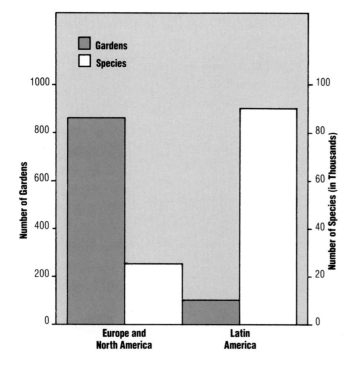

Such a strategy is likely to identify the need for a central information source or international conservation secretariat for zoological parks. Working with regional associations, this international secretariat could help strengthen zoo management, represent the interests and expertise of zoos in international forums, and help implement a global conservation strategy for zoos. The secretariat would build on already-existing networks:

■ the International Species Information System (ISIS)—a computer-based information system for wild animal species in captivity;

■ the IUCN/SSC Captive Breeding Specialist Group (CBSG)—a worldwide network of zoo staff who collect, analyze, and disseminate information about captive breeding; and,

■ the International Zoo Yearbook—An international forum for the exchange of information among zoos.

Some of these networks have already developed action plans and strategies. The CBSG's captive action planning program, for instance, aims to reduce the number of common species in captivity and to use that space for species requiring *ex situ* conservation.

As it is with botanic gardens, information management is key to strengthening zoos' role in conservation. Some 378 institutions in 36 countries comprise the ISIS network, and the database encompasses information on over 100,000 vertebrates. But to maximize its effectiveness, ISIS needs to add more zoos to its international network and to supplement its data sets with those of use to managers (including taxonomic lists and life-history information).

Finally, international and national regulations inhibiting movements of animals and cryo-preserved materials among zoos must be evaluated and safe regulations for animal exchange established. Complying with the formal requirements of conventions, treaties, and national laws governing movement of animals requires great energy and expense. As important as agricultural quarantine, the safe transport of threatened species, the need to protect captive populations from disease, and animal welfare more generally are, in many cases restrictions levied in their name needlessly hinder the safe and legitimate exchange of species and genetic material.

Action 70

Strengthen the role of public aquaria in the conservation of biodiversity.

Compared to zoos and botanic gardens, public aquaria are relative newcomers to conservation, even though they have always played key roles in raising public awareness about the diversity of aquatic organisms. The conservation role of aquaria is likely to expand in the coming decade, however, particularly in the case of freshwater aquaria. Many freshwater aquatic organisms have extremely circumscribed ranges, so their habitats are highly susceptible to degradation or loss, and the organisms themselves are particularly vulnerable to translocated competitors, predators, and introduced pathogens. Freshwater aquaria can minimize this problem by establishing captive breeding programs for threatened species. Over the longer term, these aquaria can also help ensure the survival of such taxa by joining in efforts to preserve or restore their habitats.

As for their educational function, some public aquaria have pioneered programs that present the organisms they display as integral components of complex communities and explain how these species can survive in healthy and naturally productive environments. Australia's Great Barrier Reef Aquarium, which includes a complete coral reef ecosystem, was designed and is managed by the Great Barrier Reef Marine Park Authority specifically to educate the public and thus help conserve the world's largest marine protected area. Such programs should be replicated and expanded.

To deepen public understanding of biodiversity's value, public aquaria must resist the temptation to showcase charismatic or unusual species and instead devote more attention to ecologically important organisms, threatened aquatic ecosystems (such as coastal marshes and desert springs), and the impact of human activities on aquatic biodiversity. Specifically, aquarium-goers should know about the high ecological costs of translocating exotic species, over-exploiting commercial fish stocks, using environmentally destructive fishing methods, impounding rivers, allowing chemical and thermal pollution, and pumping ground water without restraint.

Aquaria should also allocate more resources to scientific research. Public aquaria have long recognized that applied research is essential to the successful maintenance and breeding of aquatic organisms in captivity. However, they have not universally accorded a high priority to the basic research upon which such efforts rest. The immediate payoff of increased research of both types will be better-designed artificial environments for captive organisms. In the long run, *in situ* research may also shed light on the determinants of aquatic organisms' survival in nature and thus help scientists design more successful *in situ* conservation programs.

Action 71

Strengthen collaboration among off-site and on-site conservation institutions, partly to enlarge the role of off-site facilities in species reintroduction, habitat restoration, and habitat rehabilitation.

Despite the clear need for an integrated conservation strategy, off-site conservation centers are often institutionally isolated from each other and from organizations responsible for conservation in natural habitats. Breaking these barriers will require both individual and institutional action. Planning mechanisms such as those described in Chapters 3 and 7 can open up a dialogue among these different groups, as can the proposed International Panel on Biodiversity Conservation *(Chapter 3)*. At the same time, each institution should increasingly seek opportunities to collaborate bilaterally with others.

These various institutions have much to offer each other. For instance, the Center for Plant Conservation (CPC) facilitates cooperative work between botanic gardens growing rare flora and U.S. agencies managing wild populations and their habitats. Botanic gardens in the CPC network collect and propagate seed from rare populations that can then be used to bolster or restore populations in the wild.

Zoos also continue to play an important role in reestablishing naturally extinct species in the wild. In North America, off-site conservation is a basic part of the restoration of populations of the swift fox, whooping crane, California condor, and black-footed ferret.

Botanic gardens and arboreta can also cooperate with forestry agencies in the selection of indigenous species for reforestation, fuel-wood plantations, and other uses. The Royal Botanic Garden Peradeniya in Sri Lanka and associated nurseries are already involved in reforestation work. In Honduras, the Lancetilla Botanic Garden and Experimental Station is working with neighboring local communities to make fruit-tree germplasm available through jointly-run nurseries.

Aquaria are increasingly becoming involved in on-site conservation as well. Marine biologists studying sea otters at the Monterey Bay Aquarium, and at Sea World/Hubbs Research Institute, worked to save sea otters and other marine mammals following the EXXON-Valdez oil spill in Alaska. Similarly, the Boston Aquarium's Edgerton Laboratory directs a breeding program network to help maintain the diversity of African chichlid fish in Lake Victoria.

X

Expanding Human Capacity To Conserve Biodiversity

A greening of the human mind must precede the greening of our Earth.
A green mind is one that cares, saves, and shares.
These are qualities essential for conserving biological diversity now and forever.

M.S. SWAMINATHAN, FORMER PRESIDENT, THE WORLD CONSERVATION UNION (IUCN)

Research, training, and information management all help expand the human capacity to conserve genes, species, and ecosystems. But even more important is expanding people's awareness of biodiversity and appreciation of its significance. As the German philosopher Goethe observed, "Every man is given only enough strength to complete those assignments of whose importance he is fully convinced."

Conservation can succeed only if people understand biodiversity's distribution and value, see how it figures into their own lives and aspirations, and know how to manage bioregions to meet human needs without damage. This capacity is woefully inadequate today: resource managers are not trained to conserve biodiversity; the number of tax-onomists specializing in tropical species needs to be quintupled; no country has a complete listing of its species; and for most ecosystems little information exists on indicator and keystone species.

As noted in Chapter III, these gaps result from chronic under-investment in human capacity-building, which in turn reflects a lack of appreciation by governments of biodiversity's potential contribution to national development and human needs. Taxonomic research needs to be stimulated because it is an essential tool for managing biodiversity and mobilizing its benefits. Research on plant cultivation techniques is important because it can be applied not only to improve a botanic garden's collection but also to reforesting millions of hectares of degraded land.

Objective:

Increase appreciation and awareness of biodiversity's values and importance

Since policy-makers, activists, and scientists cannot slow biodiversity loss without wider public support, a multi-faceted effort is required to expand public awareness about biodiversity's importance and to strengthen the public's will and ability to act. While the avenues for strengthening awareness vary with place and culture, every society has numerous communication tools at its disposal.

Action 72

Build awareness of the importance and values of biodiversity into popular culture.

Since most people learn about important public issues through popular culture, biodiversity conservation will not attract public support unless it too is conveyed through entertainment, advertising, popular arts, and the print media. The recent popularization of rainforest conservation in industrialized countries illustrates the power of popular culture to incite government and consumer action. Now such concepts as human stewardship of Earth's life systems, mass extinction, biodiversity's contribution to people's livelihoods, and biodiversity's potential as security against future change should be debated within the popular media as urgent issues that touch on all people's lives and aspirations.

Public awareness campaigns waged by either non-governmental organizations or governments can shape public opinion. The key is cultivating interest among trendsetters. In all societies, "opinion leaders" expose and popularize new issues, as well as

catalyze action to address them. These leaders—village elders, television commentators, newspaper editors, popular entertainers, athletes, religious leaders, and corporate executives—can make the biodiversity message compelling.

Reaching out to these leaders is the responsibility of biodiversity specialists—scientists, activists, resource managers, and others. Some opinion leaders need only new information or ideas to galvanize their commitment to biodiversity conservation. Others may know little about the issue. In either case, biodiversity specialists need to provide information in such popular forms as articles, films, fact sheets, displays, and public awareness workshops.

Action 73

Use the formal education system to increase awareness about biodiversity and the need for its conservation.

Schools can become powerful vehicles for increasing public awareness about biodiversity. Primary and secondary schools are particularly important since they shape young people's perceptions and attitudes and reach far more people than universities, particularly in developing countries. Of course, nothing will happen in the classroom if educators themselves are not enthusiastic and informed about the topic, so classroom instructors as much as students themselves must be viewed as the in-school audience for the biodiversity message.

At the national level, ecological literacy belongs alongside other basic skills. National curricula on biodiversity should be developed by teachers' associations, other non-governmental organizations, and national education and environment ministries. These curricula should emphasize biodiversity's contributions to community health and welfare, as well as to ecosystems, and should tie ecological, economic, and social themes together. *(See Box 33.)*

But national curricula on biodiversity must be supplemented by locally developed curricula that bring biodiversity issues close to home. Ultimately, it is far more important for people to understand the importance of the species in their pastures or backyards, and the importance of healthy local ecosystems, than it is for educators to champion a few ecosystems of global importance or extraordinary beauty.

Action 74

Integrate biodiversity concerns into education outside of the classroom.

Many educational experiences take place outside of formal institutions and processes. Particularly in rural communities in developing countries, agricultural extension, primary health-care clinics, literacy campaigns, and many other institutions and activities convey important information and ideas.

These same channels can become vehicles for practical education on biodiversity conservation and use. Indeed, biodiversity conservation ideas are more likely to be accepted in rural communities if they answer immediate and tangible needs. Appeals for saving species and genetic diversity may be futile where bare survival is a daily issue. But if those aspects of biodiversity that help maintain or enhance local agricultural production are promoted, for instance, even destitute people will see the reasons to conserve it. Similarly, efforts to safeguard medicinal plants are more likely to be effective where traditional medicines are advanced as a part of an integrated primary health-care strategy. Along with carrying the right message, extension workers must also be the right messengers. For example, where women are the primary farmers and resource managers, most agricultural extension workers should be women too.

Extension workers and other educators outside of the classroom must respect and mobilize local knowledge of biodiversity, as well as bring new

---

BOX 33

Building Biodiversity Awareness in Primary and Secondary Schools

The awareness and commitment of teachers is the key in building biodiversity awareness among primary and secondary school students. Good teachers know best how to get the message across to their students, but some suggestions follow:

1. Explain that all "things that live" are encompassed by "biodiversity," including those too small to see with the naked eye. Point out that people and their cultures are part of the diversity of life. As an out-of-class assignment, ask students to describe the biodiversity of an area near their home.

2. Point out the importance of biodiversity's components mentioning medicines, industrial products, foods, and the contributions of breeding programs to agriculture. Stress the role that biodiversity and biological resources play in shaping human cultures, for example, citing the relationships between nomads and migratory species. Ask students to describe life without one aspect of biodiversity of importance to them, to identify examples of biodiversity use, or to assess how using various biological resources influences local economies and local environments.

3. Emphasize biodiversity conservation efforts close to home, acquainting students with any nearby protected areas, offsite conservation centers, and local management techniques that foster biodiversity conservation. Point out the importance of using resources sustainably. Arrange for the students to visit and tour a local conservation facility. Discuss respect for nature, self-preservation, and other components of a conservation ethic. Stage a biodiversity management meeting, assigning each student a different group interest to represent.

4. Ask students to design posters or write essays about the historic contributions of biodiversity, to recommend management plans for resource areas, to list ways that individuals can contribute to conservation, and to develop a board game demonstrating the obstacles to and rewards of sound biodiversity management.

5. Get the children out of the classroom and into the fields and forests, and let them experience and study the diversity of life directly.

information and ideas into the community. The most effective "education" about biodiversity often is not transmitting new information, but rather fostering appreciation of what is already known—practical knowledge about biodiversity, its local uses, and ways to manage resources sustainably. The knowledge elders possess of the value of certain species, the location or habitat needs of rare species, or the history of local ecological change, for example, may be far more valuable for biodiversity conservation than any imported expert knowledge.

Objective:

Help institutions disseminate the information needed to conserve biodiversity and mobilize its benefits

Just as the flow of biodiversity information invigorates protected areas, off-site facilities, research and development centers, and the people who need and depend upon biotic resources for their livelihood, a lack of relevant and accessible information impedes biodiversity conservation. *(See Figure 39.)* The people most interested in this information—those who formulate conservation policies, design and implement management plans, educate schoolchildren and the public about the values of biodiversity, and foster sustainable uses—often either fail to get information at all or find themselves stuck with reams of data, maps, and tables that they cannot use. Resolving their predicament requires attention to three basic issues:

First is structural ignorance—ignorance caused by poor access to existing information. The people who most need information on biodiversity often have no access to costly, unpublished, or classified publications. They may also find reports' terminol-

ogy obscure, and the bureaucratic procedures for obtaining them imposing. On the other hand, universities and governmental agencies may not let people know what information they have in the public domain. Many of these barriers exist because they are in certain individuals'—or the government's—self-interest; opening information flow thus may require concerted political pressure from potential users, as well as institutional changes.

Second, information too rarely meets users' needs. Those who prepare and publish information must systematically survey the user communities to determine what is needed and how best to present it.

Finally, much information is either too political or not scientifically credible. The solution is to gather and analyze data using methods approved by leading local and international experts and to make sure that the criteria for decisions on the status of biodiversity and priorities for action are spelled out plainly in all reports.

A number of actions are needed to increase information on biodiversity and to make it more readily available. Development-assistance funding should be provided for journals, published reports, conferences, newsletters, translations, and bibliographies, for example, and funders should not assume that the need to disseminate information is any less pressing than the need to generate it. But more important than piecemeal support for elements of an information network, donors should support the institutional development of the network itself in the following ways.

Action 75

Establish or strengthen national or subnational institutions providing information on the conservation and potential values of biodiversity.

Biodiversity information and monitoring centers should be established or strengthened in each country to facilitate the free flow of qualitative and

FIGURE 39

Biodiversity Information Flow

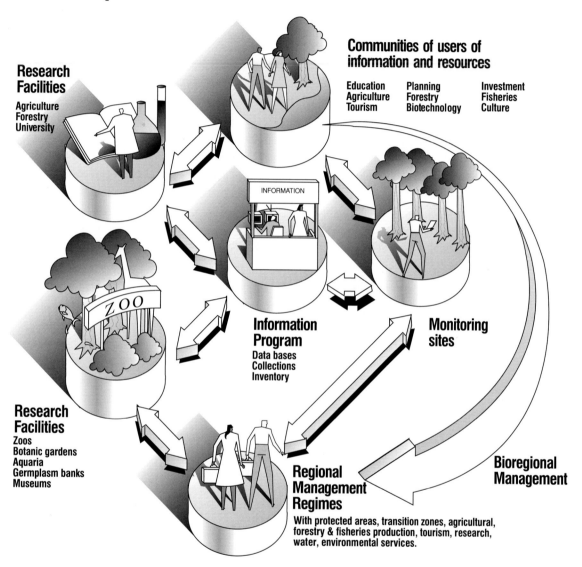

Research Facilities

Agriculture
Forestry
University

Communities of users of information and resources

Education	Planning	Investment
Agriculture	Forestry	Fisheries
Tourism	Biotechnology	Culture

INFORMATION

Information Program
Data bases
Collections
Inventory

Monitoring sites

Research Facilities
Zoos
Botanic gardens
Aquaria
Germplasm banks
Museums

Regional Management Regimes
With protected areas, transition zones, agricultural, forestry & fisheries production, tourism, research, water, environmental services.

Bioregional Management

---

quantitative information on biodiversity. *(See Box 34.)* Biodiversity Information and Monitoring Centers can form the heart of the information-flow system by performing these important functions:

■ *Coordinate collections.* In most places, specimens of the nation's species are scattered among university departments, various public and private facilities, and research institutes. A collection in each country

should be designated the national collection and given the financial resources needed to coordinate collecting efforts, serve as an official repository of voucher specimens, work with other collections to develop complementary collections policies, and store data from all collections within the country. Most university collections should be maintained since they play vital roles in training students and providing voucher material for local biodiversity

BOX 34

National Biodiversity Institute, Costa Rica

The Instituto Nacional de Biodiversidad (INBio) was established in 1989 as a private non-profit institution. Its goal is to promote the wise management and use of the nation's biotic wealth through the development and distribution of information on species, genes, and ecosystems. General operating funds come from a debt-for-nature swap, local and international grants, and development assistance. Funds for INBio's "parataxonomists" program are channeled through the national budget, international grants, and private foundations.

INBio is regarded by many scientists, conservationists, development-assistance experts, and local groups as a pioneering institution in biodiversity management. By promoting the study of biodiversity as a foundation of development, INBio has realized the synergy possible in the edict of "save, study, and use."

Located on the outskirts of San José, INBio's modest physical facility provides a climate-controlled environment for most of the country's formerly-scattered biological collections. Working agreements have been established with the national museum, the national universities, the Ministry of Natural Resources, Energy and Mines, the Ministry of Science and Technology, other public bureaus, and tropical research and education programs such as the Organization for Tropical Studies, Scouts of America, and Missouri Botanical Garden. Through these agreements, the institutions collaborate on the inventory of certain taxa, the housing and maintenance of collections, research on the chemical screening of natural products, and the promotion of the "intellectual" use of the information in museum displays, exhibits, and education programs.

INBio has launched an ambitious program to inventory all of the nation's species. It is concentrating on insects and plants initially—a choice guided by existing knowledge and expertise, the availability of funding, and information demand. The national team carrying out the inventory includes professional scientists as well as parataxonomists—local residents trained to collect and identify specimens. The national team draws on the expertise of such institutions as the University of Pennsylvania (USA), The Natural History Museum (United Kingdom), Missouri Botanical Garden (USA) and the United States Department of Agriculture/Smithsonian Institution (USA), through cooperative agreements.

INBio absorbed the country's Conservation Data Centre (CDC), integrating it into the National Biodiversity Data Base, and, collaborating with experts in information management, it has experimented with new biodiversity data-management techniques. It boasts one of the most advanced data capture-and-processing capabilities in the tropics.

The library of chemical substances being developed at INBio contains samples of materials of potential interest to biotechnology developers and industry. INBio basically brokers the nation's wild biotic wealth, liaising with organizations interested in using that wealth for profit. Under strict contractual arrangements, INBio collaborates with biotechnology concerns and industry to collect and evaluate materials from the wild. All income beyond costs will be placed in a special fund, managed in agreement with the Government and used to protect and manage the country's biological resources. In October 1991, Merck Pharmaceutical agreed to pay INBio $1 million for the opportunity to screen the samples that INBio is collecting. INBio will receive royalties on sales of any products developed from these samples. Even if INBio receives only 2 percent of royalties on pharmaceuticals developed from Costa Rica's biodiversity, it would take only 20 drugs for INBio to be able to earn more funds than Costa Rica currently gets from coffee and bananas—two major exports.

Through meetings with potential information users, INBio is now expanding its service capability to meet the data needs of governmental agencies, universities, educators, planners, scientists, and industry.

conservation efforts, but in some countries, it may be necessary to amalgamate some governmental and private collections to create a national repository.

■ *Inventory.* The challenge of making an inventory of a nation's biotic wealth is formidable. Not even 15 percent of the world's species have been named, patterns of genetic diversity are poorly documented, and few countries have classified their ecosystems at the fine-grained scale needed for proper management. Personnel must be trained, facilities developed to house expanding collections, and protocols on methods and procedures for inventory and collection established. Those who use this information must help set priorities for inventory and collection: Should the target be the most economically valuable species? The rarest? The most scientifically interesting? Those of greatest traditional value?

■ *Data bases.* So vast is the amount of data needed that its collection, organization, and analysis must be computerized, and the data collected tailored to individual national or regional needs. *(See Box 35.)* Video technologies, for example, are now being developed to help identify and document flora and fauna. At the National Biodiversity Institute in Costa Rica, basic information on taxonomy and species distribution is supplemented with information on the species' chemical and physical properties and on traditional uses—an aid in the Institute's search for potentially valuable chemical compounds. National information centers should be further strengthened through the application of Geographic Information Systems, which present data in geographic formats that can easily be integrated with other natural resource, demographic, and socio-economic information.

■ *Disseminate information.* The greatest weakness of the information centers now operating is their failure to get relevant information expeditiously to all who need it. National centers need to meet with user groups and offer them over-the-counter ser-

vices and negotiate new information programs. Pharmaceutical companies' growing interest in exploring fungi for potentially valuable chemicals, for example, should stimulate—and possibly fund—research by Biodiversity Information Centers on their identity and distribution.[125]

■ *Monitoring.* A network of stations, possibly linked to the UNESCO Biosphere Reserves and the International Geosphere-Biosphere Program, should be set up to monitor long-term trends and to calibrate and assess remote sensing information.

■ *Provide for policy needs.* Centers should support the formulation of national, regional, and local policies for development and resource management by making policy-relevant information available. Annual reports on the nation's biodiversity and biological resources, endangered species population trends, plants and animals of potential economic value, as well as maps on land use and the location of important endemic or threatened species, would help governmental administrators, community groups, and non-governmental organizations make rational land- or resource-management and conservation decisions.

■ *Network.* The degree of centralization of Biodiversity Information Centers should be determined by the size and biogeographic complexity of the country, by users' needs, and by the volume of information handled. The bioregional information centers discussed in Chapter 7, for example, can be linked to more centralized national and international institutions as warranted. In any case, protocols are needed for exchanging information among data centers and between national and international programs, including the World Conservation Monitoring Centre and the United Nations Environment Programme.

Local communities should play a central role in gathering information on biodiversity. Their knowledge of the location and use of species, as well as of their own domesticated varieties of plants and animals, are valuable resources. In addition, if local people are involved in the identification and classification of species in the field, the community can be kept better informed of its local resources and bio-

diversity. These workers can also be counted upon to pass on their interest in biodiversity to others in the community, including children.

Of course, such contributions should not go

BOX 35

The Conservation Data Center Network

Over the past twenty years, The Nature Conservancy (USA) has helped establish a network of 85 national and sub-national biodiversity information centers to help carry out conservation activities. These centers, known as Conservation Data Centers (CDCs) (in the United States, Natural Heritage Programs), provide a continually updated, computerized inventory of their regions' most significant biological and ecological features. The network covers the entire United States, portions of Canada, and much of Latin America and the Caribbean. Lay-naturalists, and representatives of natural history museums collectively provide much of the information for the databases.

Besides simply storing data, CDCs function as biodiversity information clearinghouses; each year, they answer more than 100,000 information requests from private conservation organizations, state and national government bureaus, and international development-assistance agencies. This information helps resource managers and conservation organizations identify high-priority natural areas in need of protection, manage wildlands sustainably, and identify potential conflicts between environmental protection and development needs.

Centers are partnerships between local institutions, which provide staffing and facilities, and the Conservancy. Latin American CDCs typically operate at a national level, run by such institutions as Costa Rica's National Biodiversity Institute *(see Box 34)* and the Paraguayan Ministry of Agriculture. Others—among them, the CDC of the Cauca Valley Corporation, a

Colombian watershed management agency—are regional. In the United States, Heritage Programs are typically part of state agencies, though several established recently by the National Parks Service cover specific protected areas. Elsewhere, host institutions include government agencies, universities, and nongovernmental organizations.

Because conservation and development decisions are most often made locally or nationally, the decentralized data center network helps develop in-country capabilities. At the heart of the network is a standardized database management system, the Biological and Conservation Data System, that can be tailored by individual centers to meet local needs, but that also provides a uniform basis for exchanging information. The databases and associated map files in this microcomputer-based system integrate information on species and habitats with information on land use, land tenure, and protected areas management. Information can be aggregated across political boundaries to define the conservation status of species and ecosystems at regional, national, and global levels, thus allowing decision-makers to set local conservation priorities within a global context.

As the network expands into developing tropical countries, high levels of biodiversity, weak information bases, and rapid rates of habitat destruction pose new challenges. The network is therefore developing new methods to quickly gather preliminary data that can be used to inventory critical areas in greater detail. CDCs increasingly use remote-sensing tech-

unrewarded. Any collection activities involving domesticated species or traditional knowledge should be coupled with educational campaigns to alert residents of their right to refuse access to local varieties

FIGURE 40

Distribution of Conservation Data Centers

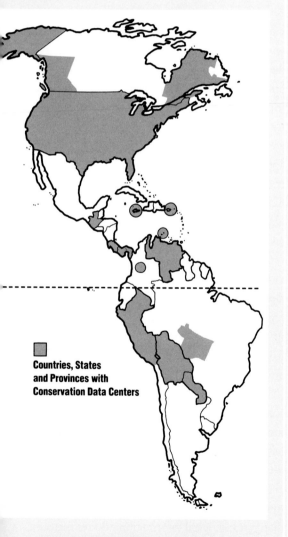

Countries, States and Provinces with Conservation Data Centers

nologies and geographic information systems to complete these rapid ecological assessments.

or traditional knowledge until they can negotiate equitable compensation for the commercial use of any such resources, including the initial testing stages of "chemical prospecting." *(See Chapter 6.)*

Governments must also ensure that their interests are protected in the operation and establishment of Biodiversity Information Centers, by establishing clear guidelines regarding the rights granted to such institutions and their access to public funds. All collectors should follow national collecting guidelines and should ensure that collections are maintained under the internationally accepted standards and that professional ethics are respected. Species collected from public lands by commercial firms should be subject to a collection fee or tax, and at least some of the ensuing revenues should support conservation activities.

Both public and private non-profit institutions should also be required to make available information gathered on the identity and distribution of species, genes, and ecosystems to public resource managers and to the public (except where the release of information may increase threats to the species or ecosystem). Specimens collected in the course of documenting a country's biota should be deposited in a recognized repository dedicated to maintain collections in perpetuity, and public or private funds for such collections should cover long-term maintenance. Public and private non-profit institutions should channel the profits from the exploitation of biodiversity into biodiversity conservation and should try to minimize any restrictions on research funds received from business. Similarly, commercial firms' role in determining research priorities should be limited, even if they purchase specific inventory or screening work.

Action 76

Undertake national biodiversity inventories and produce periodic national biodiversity assessments.

All countries need to know how their genes, species, and ecosystems are distributed and how they are faring. Biological inventories can provide them with essential data for managing biodiversity and biological resources, suggest possibilities for local or regional development, and help build a cadre of trained national scientists. Inventories also provide the baseline for evaluating biodiversity trends.

Biological inventories and taxonomic assessments should be conducted by local scientists working in the country's herbaria, museums, zoos, arboreta,

FIGURE 41

Species Remaining to be Described

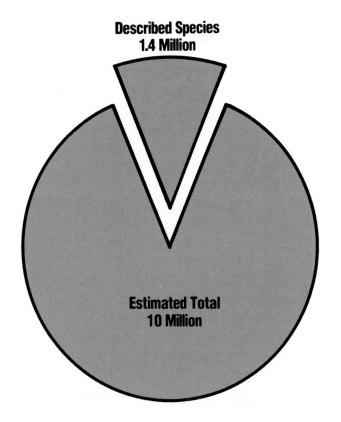

**Described Species
1.4 Million**

**Estimated Total
10 Million**

and universities. Indeed, strengthening these institutions should be an explicit objective of national inventories, and the chief role of specialists from other countries should be to help train local workers.

The inventory should be coordinated with a National Biodiversity Information Center; and, like the center, it should be user-driven. At the outset, the Flora of North America Project used this model and held a workshop with professionals from a wide range of existing and potential user groups to determine how information on flora is being used, and how it could be made more useful.[126]

Short-cuts and streamlined assessment techniques should be used where time and money are severely limited. Rapid regional assessments conducted by local scientists can often provide critical information for decision-makers. Soil, climate, and topographical information alone can be used to roughly delimit regions of probable value for biodiversity conservation. Such "quick-and-dirty" approaches, however, are not substitutes for more complete inventories and assessments. Since the margin of error is high with rapid assessment techniques, they should be used for planning only when an extreme risk to biodiversity is imminent.

Development assistance donors should provide significant new funds for inventories in *all* developing countries, according highest priority to regions with the least existing information. The cost of such inventories is not high. Costa Rica's plan to inventory its estimated 500,000 species will cost an estimated $50 million over the next decade.

Adequate inventories of a nation's genetic, species, and ecosystem diversity must be complemented by periodic assessments of their status. All nations should adopt indicators of the status of biodiversity and publish data enabling policy-makers and managers to respond to the trends these indicators reveal. These indicators should encompass more than just biological information. Better measures of private and government expenditures on biodiversity activities, public opinion, conservation programs, management capacity, and utilization of biodiversity are all needed.

Action 77

Establish a global biodiversity information network to speed the flow of data for local, national, regional, and global assessments.

An international information network can support national information programs by enabling a country to readily obtain data on biodiversity in adjacent countries, making possible the aggregation of data to reveal global trends, and providing channels for exchanging technical assistance and training among countries.

Although an effective network does not need a single "center," several international institutions already play important roles in biodiversity information exchange. The FAO Commission on Plant Genetic Resources plans to publish a periodic status report on crop-genetic diversity—an effort deserving increased international financial support. The International Board for Plant Genetic Resources (IBPGR) maintains a database of crop-genetic resources collections worldwide. And the World Conservation Monitoring Centre (WCMC) serves as a clearinghouse for information on biodiversity. Along with other services, WCMC publishes Red Data Lists of threatened species and reports on the status of specific ecosystems (coral reefs, wetlands, etc.) and taxonomic groups. WCMC's role as an international biodiversity information center will expand as it begins publication of the biennial *Global Biodiversity Status Report*, the first volume of which is a companion to the *Global Biodiversity Strategy*. This new report will be a compilation of indicators of the status and trends of biodiversity, biodiversity management and use, and the legal, financial, and institutional bases for conservation.

As important as these ongoing international information programs are, they are not enough. The single most important need for strengthening the international data network is to build national data-management capacity. *(See Action 75.)* But several steps must also be taken to facilitate the international exchange of data. First, a network linking national and international information and monitoring centers needs uniform computer protocols and definitions of data fields. A central coordinating body comprised of representatives of participating national and international data centers and agencies is needed to prepare these shared guidelines and to facilitate information exchange. Such an International Forum for Biodiversity Data could be organized under the umbrella of the proposed International Panel on Biodiversity Conservation *(See Action 3)* or by a consortium of the major international biodiversity information centers. It should be linked to the Early Warning System proposed in Action 4. After initial meetings to develop guidelines and help set priorities for action, the Forum would meet when computer technologies or information needs change.

A major gap in international databases relates to the *ex situ* holdings of wild species. No centralized data on wild species held by botanic gardens, arboreta, genebanks, and zoos exists. The International Species Inventory System (ISIS) should thus be expanded to cover more of the world's zoos, and its links to *in situ* resource managers should be strengthened by providing information tailored to their needs, such as information on numbers and locations of *ex situ* breeding populations where reintroduction into the wild could take place.

Within the international network, a central directory of who holds what information on biodiversity should be established by WCMC or FAO. To the extent practicable, all the data available through the network should be in the public domain and exempt from copyright restrictions when used for conservation, education, and research. Members of the network should exchange data without charge. Network data should be sold or used for commercial purposes only with the permission of the copyright holder (the original source) which could involve payment of a fee.

Provide all citizens with legal and institutional guarantees of access to information on development projects and other activities with potential impacts on biodiversity.

Information on biodiversity encompasses not only species distributions and potential economic uses, but also information on threats to diversity. Often, local communities receive no information until the officials or tractors arrive to build a dam, cut a forest, or settle a group of migrants. But with good information and advance warning of radical and imminent alterations in their local ecosystems, local communities can form the front line of resistance to ecologically and socially destructive development projects.

Such information should be freely accessible, and access should be guaranteed by law. Freedom of information should be a condition for funding by international development aid agencies. Key documents should be translated into local languages, and government agencies and project proponents should inform affected communities about both the process of project planning and the project's potential. Currently, the Bank Information Center (BIC), a non-governmental organization in Washington, D.C., helps notify local groups of planned World Bank-funded projects around the world, but providing such information routinely should be the duty and responsibility of both governments and donor agencies.

Objective:

Promote basic and applied research on biodiversity conservation

So much remains unknown about the diversity of life on Earth that proposed research agendas outstrip current research capacity. The absolute amount of funding for research on biodiversity clearly needs to be greatly increased. At the same time, countries must prioritize research options, striking a balance between applied research and the basic research on which it rests. Particularly important is long-term, site-specific, multidisciplinary research on the links among biodiversity, sustainable economic development, and conservation.

Promoting biodiversity research means much more than just setting research agendas. It requires improving skills and institutional capacity, and it must include increased work in the social sciences and humanities, as well as the natural sciences. At the same time, awareness of the rights of local people and the responsibilities of researchers must be heightened. In Panama, for example, non-Kuna scientists recently working on Kuna lands were required to secure permission from local communities and to leave copies of reports, photographic materials, and plant and animal specimens. The Kuna also produced a report detailing how researchers are to apply for permission to work on their land, which areas are off limits, and which research activities (plant gathering, animal marking, etc.) are allowed.

Action 79

Systematically assess national biodiversity research priorities.

Biodiversity inventories should be a priority for all countries. *(See Action 76.)* But beyond inventories, each country must set research priorities that reflect its own peculiar characteristics, needs, and resources. Thailand provides one example of how this can be done.

In 1989, the Science Society of Thailand held a conference called "Biodiversity in Thailand: Inventory and Values," which resulted in the publication of a widely distributed report summarizing general knowledge about Thai ecosystems, flora, and fauna. At four smaller workshops later, basic priorities and needs for biodiversity research were elaborated. The final report, *Biodiversity in Thailand: Research Priorities for Sustainable Development*, published in both Thai and English, identifies priorities for biological, social, and ethical research, along with needs for training, information systems, and institutional development. This report now serves as a common point of reference for government, the scientific community, and international aid donors as they try to strengthen biodiversity research. The Thai experience shows that a relatively wide consensus on research priorities can be developed quickly and that clearly defined priorities can draw attention to research needs and make fundraising easier.

Action 80

Promote basic and applied natural sciences research on biodiversity conservation.

Scientists now know enough about the distribution of biological diversity, the threats that it faces, and the conservation techniques available to maintain it, to expand conservation efforts considerably without fear of wasting effort or money. But remaining gaps in knowledge will continue to hinder conservation and limit the benefits that biological resources can provide to humanity unless research programs are greatly strengthened.

Advancing this research agenda *(detailed in Box 36)* will require intensified cooperation between developed and developing countries. Some of the highest-ranking research needs focus on tropical ecosystems, but developing tropical countries lack the funds and trained personnel to address them.

Currently, developed countries' financial commitment to advancing biodiversity research in developing countries is extremely weak. Only an estimated $24 million was spent, for example, by U.S.-based governmental and non-governmental organizations (including universities and museums) on biological diversity research activities in developing countries in 1989.[127] This amounts to less than one-half of one percent of all foreign assistance provided by the U.S. Agency for International Development that year. Clearly, a substantial increase in funding is needed from governments, donors, and scientific institutions in the North—particularly for training scientists. But sharing skills and technologies and developing collaborative research relationships between Northern and Southern scientific institutions are also very important. "Twinning" research scientists from industrialized and developing countries can be one effective means for technology transfer. Pairing women researchers with international scientists can be a particularly effective means of strengthening women's roles in developing countries.

Although building biodiversity research capacity within nations is the highest research priority, international scientific institutions and networks have an important role to play too. In particular, the planned research of the International Union of Biological Sciences (IUBS), the Scientific Committee on Problems of the Environment (SCOPE), and UNESCO on biodiversity could provide the scientific guidance needed for reaching international agreements on conservation, and deserves government support. These organizations are planning a

BOX 36

Key Biodiversity Research Topics for the Natural Sciences

■ Determine the impacts of land- and water-use changes on species diversity and ecological processes.

■ Elucidate the role of biodiversity in ecological processes, including water and nutrient cycling, energy flow in ecosystems, ecosystem stability, and soil formation.

■ Determine the consequences of anthropogenic and other environmental changes on the evolution of species.

■ Expand systematics research to provide a stable nomenclature and to enhance the ability to use inferential techniques to mobilize biodiversity's benefits.

■ Inventory genetic, species, habitat, and ecosystem diversity. Determine how fast biological diversity is changing and how change will affect community structure and ecosystem processes. Accelerate research on the determinants of diversity.

■ Accelerate research on the biology of rare and declining species and develop the scientific information needed to sustain populations, and determine the value and viability of these species.

■ Determine patterns and indicators of ecological responses to stress so that the technologies needed to assess the status of ecological systems, to forecast and assess stress, and to monitor the recovery of damaged ecological systems can be developed.

■ Develop and test principles of restoration ecology.

■ Advance, test, and apply ecological principles for the design and use of sustainable, managed ecological systems at the bioregional scale.

■ Deepen the understanding of how ecosystem fragmentation affects biological diversity and ecological processes.

■ Investigate the potential impacts of climate change on ecological systems and explore means of mitigating damages.

■ Expand and improve the monitoring of biodiversity and ecological processes.

■ Intensify research in population ecology.

■ Screen species for features of potential value to humanity.

■ Support long-term ecological research at selected sites to advance scientists' understanding of ecosystem composition, structure, and function.

Source: Lubchenco, et al., 1991; Reid and Miller, 1989.

program to deepen understanding of how biodiversity functions in ecosystems, focussing specifically on problems requiring international cooperation. This program will assess the adequacy of existing global databases on species loss or modification, compare the roles of species and systems on a global scale, sponsor studies in global comparative biogeography, and monitor biodiversity as an indicator of global change.[128]

Action 81

Strengthen social science research on the connections between biological and social processes.

The causes of biodiversity loss lie in the interactions among social and ecological processes. The perspectives of economics, sociology, anthropology, law, and political science are therefore needed to slow this loss. Accordingly, the biodiversity research agenda must also focus largely on people and their institutions, from the community to the international arena.

Most of this research should focus on local needs, constraints, and opportunities. How is production organized? How do changes in land and resources ownership affect conservation incentives? What do local biodiversity knowledge and biological resource-management systems have to offer? How does social stratification influence people's resource use? How can community organizations be strengthened? One of the most notable gaps in research relates to women and biodiversity. In many countries, women are much more directly involved in the use, study, and conservation of biodiversity than men, yet information detailing these differences is lacking—a serious obstacle to effective local and national planning and decision-making.

At the national level, research on how large organizations deal with biodiversity is particularly important. The failures of centralized government bureaucracies to adequately protect biodiversity—

even when this is their manifest aim—are well known and frequently lamented, but the reasons for these failures are less well understood. And relatively little can be confidently said about designing alternative institutions or getting political backing for them.

Laws and legal institutions affecting biodiversity also require study at the national level. Are the Environmental Impact Assessment laws and procedures in force in many countries effective tools for conserving biodiversity? If not, how could they be made more effective? Why are forestry laws affecting biodiversity conservation changing so slowly? Why are common property management systems—potentially valuable tools for biodiversity conservation—so poorly understood and so rarely recognized legally? And how can impediments to the marketing of non-timber forest products be scaled? Policy-makers need answers to these questions.

Research in environmental economics also needs to be strengthened. Uncertainty over the local, national, and international economic value of biological resources and biodiversity invites policy-makers to discount both and to skip conservation investments when other budget priorities offer more quantifiable benefits. If the costs of resource degradation and the benefits of saving and using biodiversity were better understood, better conservation incentives for resource users could be designed. More research is also required on how trade, Third World debt, and the activities of transnational corporations affect biodiversity—as well as on how commodity prices, inflation, exchange rates, and market instability influence biological resource management.

At the international level, research is needed on the efficacy of international law and the institutions covering biodiversity conservation. Many proposals for new international agreements and institutions have emerged, but little analysis has been done of legal precedents, the success of past international environmental mechanisms, and the impact of transnational corporations on biodiversity.[129]

Action 82

Strengthen research on ethical, cultural, and religious concerns related to conserving biodiversity.

The world's many cultures, faiths, and ethical traditions give people their basic orientation toward the natural world, and guide their actions. Often these values are so deeply ingrained that their importance is overlooked. For this reason, national research programs, as well as international donors, should fund systematic research on how ethical norms, culture, and religion condition human behavior toward nature.

People's commitment to conserving biodiversity springs from their "sense of place," and the most effective citizen action has been that of people who are intimately acquainted with a region, identify with it, wrest their livelihood from it, take pride in it, and ultimately take responsibility for it. For this reason, work on environmental ethics should take place primarily at the bioregional level, led by inter-disciplinary teams and community representatives from the region. This initiative should be incorporated within the wider campaign to develop, promote, and apply the world ethic for living sustainably called for in *Caring for the Earth*.

This action could be given practical expression by the creation of an expert group on ethical aspects of biodiversity conservation and use, working closely with a revitalized IUCN Ethics Working Group and the WWF Network on Conservation and Religion. Such a group should draw on cultural, ethical and religious traditions throughout the world, and might be linked to national-level coalitions or groups of experts in environment and development ethics, religion, social sciences and humanities, the arts, and communications.[130]

Objective:

Develop human resources capacity for biodiversity conservation

Committed and skilled people are key to the success of the actions called for in this *Strategy*. Increased funding, international conventions, expanded protected areas systems—all will be ineffective unless the pool of trained human talent for biodiversity conservation expands rapidly. More people need to be trained in biodiversity conservation, and financial and intellectual incentives are needed to insure that they work where they are needed—primarily in the field.

Action 83

Increase support for training biodiversity professionals, particularly in developing countries.

Biodiversity conservation in the coming decade will require a large cadre of "biodiversity professionals"—the people who will manage protected areas, conduct biodiversity inventories, develop and safeguard *ex situ* collections, and manage such biological resources as forests, fisheries, and agricultural lands. The need to train these people is particularly acute in developing countries. *(See Figure 42.)*

Just as protected areas lie at the heart of biodiversity conservation, protected-area managers form the core of a country's biodiversity professionals. In most countries, however, there are just too few of them to adequately manage the large areas entrusted to their care. In addition, most are poorly trained, poorly equipped, and poorly paid. Training centers therefore need to be established or expanded, curricula updated, and international

cooperation and support increased.

To help build this network of trained professionals, the IUCN Commission on National Parks and Protected Areas should recommend the establishment of regional associations of protected-area managers and provide start-up funding and institutional support to these associations. A professional association could provide opportunities for increased status, professional advancement and rewards that help keep professionals from leaving for higher levels of government. It would also set standards of practice, provide opportunities for collegial interaction among protected area managers, and enhance international cooperation in protected area management.

This new professional network should involve government agencies responsible for protected-area management, universities, and the private sector. International organizations—FAO, UNESCO, UNEP, IUCN, WWF, and others—should support such networks through technical and financial contributions and should be active members of the associations, bringing international perspectives and information to bear.

Since biodiversity cannot be adequately conserved unless the loss of habitat outside protected areas is slowed, and unless resources are managed with biodiversity conservation as an objective, resource managers who deal with forestry, fishery, and agricultural production must also become "biodiversity specialists." The Commonwealth Science Council's (CSC) Biological Diversity and Genetic Resources Project exemplifies such a broad-based training program. Since 1985, CSC has directly trained 725 professionals (with more than 2,000 other individuals benefiting from the training indirectly), established seven networks of biodiversity professionals, and developed five curricula and two training manuals.

While the absolute numbers of professional resource managers needs to be increased in many countries, the reorientation of current training programs is perhaps more important. Forestry schools, for example, tend to perpetuate traditional models

FIGURE 42

Environmental Educational Material Based on the Buddhist Scriptures from a WWF Conservation Education Campaign

Source: Tree of Life *by Ollie Dwiggins, for Buddhist Perception of Nature*

FIGURE 43

Distribution of Professional Ecologists in Relation to the Distribution of Plant Species Richness

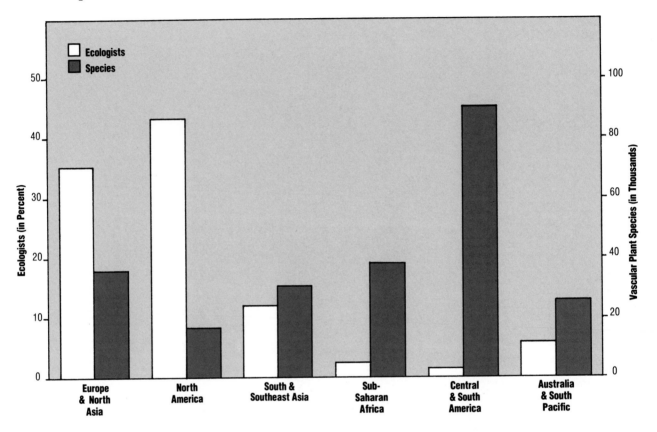

Source: Department of Environment 1991; P. Raven Pers. comm.

of timber production and custodial control of access to the forest. Until these schools incorporate biodiversity concerns into timber production, take full account of the importance of non-timber forest products, and better prepare forest managers to work with local communities, recent forestry graduates will not be motivated or equipped to take biodiversity effectively into account.[131] Similar changes are also needed in the training of agronomists, fisheries managers, and extension agents.

To optimize germplasm conservation, far more individuals must be trained in *ex situ* conservation and its integration with wider genepool conservation. Thanks largely to the work of the International Board for Plant Genetic Resources,

the number of *ex situ* scientists has grown impressively. But few of these scientists have been educated to carry out interdisciplinary conservation work. Additionally, research funding has not kept pace with growth in the field, so specialists too often lack the operating funds needed to perform effectively. Universities in both developed and developing countries, along with the International Agricultural Research Centers, could help training centers build personnel capacity for germplasm conservation. A particularly promising approach is pairing universities in industrialized nations with those in developing countries.

Greatly expanded training is also required for both professional and paraprofessional taxonomists.

In 1980, no more than an estimated 1,500 or so professional systematists worldwide were trained to carry out research on the taxonomy of tropical species, and the lack is believed to be just as glaring today.[132] Worldwide, the gaps in taxonomic research are astounding. Of the estimated one million free-living nematodes, only 13,000 have been described, and efforts to determine how many might exist have only recently begun. The U.S. National Research Council has estimated that at least 7500 systematists specializing in tropical organisms are urgently needed to provide the basic information on biodiversity necessary for wise decision-making.[133]

The parataxonomist program developed by INBio in Costa Rica *(See Box 34)* represents an innovative response to the gap in taxonomic expertise: parataxonomists are trained quickly, during five-month courses, and collaborate closely with professional taxonomists. But the need for professionals remains. National governments and international donors should support taxonomic research in universities—as well as such programs as the Biodiversity Information Centers and the North-South pairing of research institutes and universities described above.

Most training needs are best addressed through local and regional training programs. Learning new resource-management techniques for ecosystems unlike those in which a professional will ultimately work has little or no value. Training programs should thus use professionals or institutions within the region whenever possible.

Action 84

Revise career incentives provided by governments to increase the attractiveness of work in the field.

The worldwide need for trained biodiversity professionals must not overshadow the need to ensure that skilled workers end up in the places and positions where they can do the most good. All too often, those best trained for hands-on biodiversity conservation work end up in capital cities as administrators and bureaucrats; as long as financial, promotion, and other incentives point in this direction, this brain drain from the field is likely to continue.

Governments need to provide irresistible incentives for biodiversity professionals to spend years working in the field as protected area managers, taxonomists, or resource managers. They must provide a career ladder that will attract highly qualified individuals into resource management fields and other incentives—training, equipment, health care, education allowances, salaries, performance bonuses—that will bring out the best in the field staff. Along with financial incentives and fringe benefits, the decentralization of decision-making power would help tremendously since people tend to gravitate to the center of power in their professions.

Action 85

Strengthen the influence and capacity of non-governmental conservation and development organizations to promote biodiversity conservation.

The roles of non-governmental organizations (NGOs) in biodiversity conservation have grown and diversified greatly over the past decade. From grassroots community organization and assistance to policy research and advocacy at national and international levels, NGOs are increasingly important actors in promoting efforts to save, study, and use biodiversity sustainably and equitably. The roles of NGOs have expanded faster, however, than their capacity to carry them out. Rapid expansion and diversification of functions and objectives have also engendered strains and tensions.

Four key areas of action are required in the 1990s to realize the promise that NGOs hold in the struggle to conserve biodiversity. First and most important, the capacities of developing country NGOs—and grassroots NGOs everywhere—need to be strengthened. In particular, they need help with data management and analysis, policy research and writing, advocacy skills, media liaison, accounting, publications development, and public outreach. Donor organizations, governmental or private, can help by supporting well-considered projects and

---

BOX 37

The Philippine Development Forum:
An Emerging Model for North-South NGO Cooperation

The Philippine Development Forum (PDF) is a network of U.S. -based individuals and organizations from the environmental, development, religious, and human rights communities. PDF works in partnership with a broad range of Philippine NGOs to promote awareness and facilitate dialogue on equitable and sustainable development in the Philippines.

The genesis of PDF was a 1989 forum held in Washington with a delegation of ten leaders of Philippine non-governmental organizations (NGOs). The Philippine group shared their experiences in grassroots development and environmental activism and presented an integrated vision for community-based, environmentally sound, equitable, democratic development. The NGO leaders urged forum participants to form a network with which they could work on policy issues. Energized by this encounter, a group of 17 U.S. NGO representatives continued to meet monthly to share information and engage in joint advocacy work. By late 1991—when another Philippine NGO delegation came to Washington for PDF's first membership meeting—PDF had more than 40 U.S. members in five cities.

PDF's three goals are: to raise public awareness about equitable and sustainable development in the Philippines, to promote cooperation and linkages among NGOs working on environmental and development issues in the United States and the Philippines, and to educate policy-makers in the U.S. government and the multilateral development assistance community on Philippine NGOs' experiences and views of development. To achieve these goals, PDF works to improve the flow of public information between U.S. and Philippine NGOs, provide venues for sharing ideas and developing analyses, develop educational materials and briefing papers for policy-makers, write advocacy letters to policy-makers, and organize public education forums.

PDF's Philippine partners contribute ideas, information, and analysis from their field programs and advocacy campaigns, and their priorities for action influence PDF's program. PDF also maintains close relations with three large NGO coalitions in the Philippines and a host of smaller coalitions and individual NGOs.

The PDF is innovative in several respects. First, the NGOs from the North and the South are participating as true equals. Second, it works across sectors, linking environmental, economic, social, religious, and human rights organizations and issues. Third, PDF neither raises nor disburses funds for NGO projects in the Philippines, giving it unusual credibility and objectivity.

programs addressing these needs. NGOs can also help each other by sharing skills and expertise.

Second, governments and inter-governmental agencies need to be more receptive to the participation of NGOs in national and international policy and planning dialogues on biodiversity issues. Internationally, progress has already been great. NGOs contributed more to the preparations for the 1992 "Earth Summit" conference (UNCED) than to any previous UN conference. Many are registered observers at the meetings of the International Tropical Timber Organization (ITTO), and some are represented in official government delegations. NGOs have also played an important role in evaluating and reforming the Tropical Forestry Action Plan (TFAP). The World Bank increasingly consults with non-governmental organizations on policies and projects. Overall, this increased interaction has broadened the perspectives of officials involved in inter-governmental processes and spurred them to action.

NGOs' international effectiveness is constrained by several factors. First, many NGOs still encounter official suspicion, denials of access to information, and a lack of funds needed to attend international meetings. To remedy this, officials should support formal observer or participant status for non-governmental organizations in negotiations and meetings, and welcome these groups collegially. Governments should also revise the many rules that restrict non-governmental organizations' timely access to the information required for informed participation. Governments and international agencies should also increase financial support for NGO participation in key negotiations and meetings: an invitation to the table without the means to get there is not enough.

At the national level, government agencies and legislators in many industrialized countries depend on NGOs for information and policy advice. In many developing countries, however, NGOs are still restricted, if not suppressed. Donor organizations are well situated to foster dialogue between government agencies and NGOs, make their own information available to NGOs, and insist that governments value and expand the NGO role

in the development projects they support.

Third, NGOs' accountability to their own constituencies is sometimes tenuous and should be strengthened. Many international non-governmental organizations involved in biodiversity conservation are urban-based organizations working on behalf of rural peoples and communities, often located on different continents. The inherent risk is that the rural poor or other constituencies can become an abstraction, rather than genuine people with strong convictions and positions on the issues at hand. Compromise may be the lifeblood of negotiation, but nobody elected environmentalists in Washington, Geneva, Nairobi, or any other capital city to compromise on behalf of rural communities without consulting with them first. Similar questions arise in relationships between NGOs in the North and South. Resultant misunderstandings increasingly color NGO-led biodiversity initiatives and cloud the legitimacy of these initiatives in the eyes of both governments and those constituencies they try to serve. NGOs must therefore redouble their efforts to remain accountable to those whose interests they claim to champion. The Philippine Development Forum is one innovative example of efforts to do so. *(See Box 37.)*

Since NGOs play an increasingly important role in both raising and resolving biodiversity-related issues, they must recognize that their own diversity is one of their greatest strengths. Some groups are equipped to seize increasing opportunities for formal participation in governmental and inter-governmental processes. Others are best suited to work at the community level, helping communities find their own path to sustainable development. Still others find their niche as watchdogs, calling the bluff of empty rhetoric, advocating for those without a voice, and holding governments accountable for their actions and their promises. The latter path will often involve confrontation, but not all independent NGO activities need be confrontational. For example, the Keystone International Dialogue Series on Plant Genetic Resources, conducted under wholly independent NGO auspices, built consensus among all concerned parties.[134]

Notes

1. Prescott-Allen and Prescott-Allen, 1986.

2. FAO, 1988.

3. World Bank, 1991.

4. FAO, 1989.

5. Farnsworth, 1988.

6. Schultes, 1979. IUCN/WHO/ WWF, manuscript.

7. IUCN, 1991.

8. Miller and Brewer, 1991. The role of natural products includes direct use, serving as a model for a synthetic compound, and use to help understand the pharmacology of therapeutic classes of compounds

9. Filion et. al., 1985.

10. Lindberg, 1991.

11. Dahanayake, 1991.

12. Hoyt, 1988.

13. OTA, 1987.

14. The rationale for nature conservation is summarized in the World Charter for Nature of the United Nations General Assembly, reprinted in McNeely et al., 1990.

15. FAO, 1991.

16. Reid, 1992; Ehrlich and Wilson, 1991.

17. Raven, 1988.

18. Beebe, 1991.

19. Trexler, 1991.

20. Jaenike, 1991.

21. Ministry of Agiculture, Nature Management, and Fisheries, 1991; Synge, H., IUCN, Personal Communication.

22. Glynn and de Weerdt, 1991.

23. CEQ 1990, p. 137.

24. Reid and Miller, 1989.

25. NRC, 1991.

26. Knickerbocker, 1991.

27. Ministry of Population and Environment of the Government of Indonesia, 1989.

28. Griffith, 1991.

29. Plucknett et al. 1987.

30. Fowler and Mooney, 1990.

31. Council for Tropical and Subtropical Agricultural Research, 1991.

32. Clay, 1991.

33. Holdren, 1991.

34. Vitousek, et al., 1986.

35. EESI, 1991.

36. Government of Indonesia, 1991.

37. Carr et. al., 1988.

38. CEC, 1992.

39. Repetto, 1988.

40. Thorne-Miller and Catena, 1991.

41. IUCN, UNEP, WWF, 1991.

42. Barton, 1991.

43. Zaret and Paine, 1973.

44. Johnson, 1991.

45. Claiborne, 1991.

46. Palca, 1990.

47. Kloppenburg and Kleinman, 1987. Juma, 1989.

48. IUCN, UNEP, WWF, 1991.

49. EESI, 1991.

50. IUCN, UNEP, WWF, 1991.

51. IUCN, UNEP, WWF, 1991.

52. Postel and Ryan, 1991.

53. California Department of Forestry, 1988. USDA, 1991.

54. EESI, 1991. ODC and WWF, 1991.

55. EESI, 1991.

56. Cohen, 1991.

57. Interim Report No. 4 Vol. 1, p.85, Commission of Inquiry into Aspects of the Timber Industry in Papua New Guinea, 1989.

58. Pearson, 1987.

59. Dankelman and Davidson, 1988.

60. Repetto and van Bolhuis, 1989.

61. Keystone Center, 1991.

62. McNeely, et al., 1990.

63. Colchester, 1991.

64. Spears and Ayensu, 1985; Westoby, 1984.

65. IUCN, UNEP, WWF, 1991.

66. Berkes, et. al., 1991.

67. Shingi, 1990; Ford Foundation, 1990; Ljungman et al., 1987; Cornista and Escueta, 1990.

68. Schwartzman, 1989.

69. Poole, 1989.

70. Zerner, 1991.

71. Peters et al., 1989.

72. de Beer and McDermott, 1989.

73. Kaur, 1990.

74. Caldecott, 1988.

75. Salazar, 1991.

76. Montecinos and Altieri, 1991.

77. Dahl and Nabhan, 1991.

78. Dahl and Nabhan, 1991; Salazar, 1991.

79. Salazar, 1991.

80. Weniger and Robineau, 1988.

81. For descriptions of bioregionalism, and bioregional management, see: Bridgewater, 1988, Lang, 1986, and Sale, 1985.

82. In subsequent versions of the model, the buffer zone and transition areas were renamed the inner and outer buffer zones, respectively, although their functions remain essentially unchanged.

83. WCMC, 1992.

84. Wells, 1991.

85. Montaña, 1988.

86. Elfring, 1989.

87. Spaid, 1991.

88. Elfring, 1989.

89. Lewis et al., 1987.

90. IUCN, UNEP, WWF, 1991.

91. Poore et al., 1989.

92. Sayer, 1991.

93. Hartshorn, 1990.

94. Byerlee and Heisey, 1990.

95. WRI and IIED, 1988.

96. National Wastelands Development Board, Government of India, 1986.

97. Oldeman, et al., 1990.

98. WRI and IIED, 1988.

99. WRI and IIED, 1988.

100. Uhl et al., In press.

101. Ministry of Natural Resources, Energy, and Mines of the Government of Costa Rica, 1991.

102. WCMC, unpublished data. Includes marine and terrestrial protected areas of at least 1000 ha in size.

103. Lindberg, 1991.

104. Lucas, In Press.

105. McNeely and Thorsell, 1991.

106. Miller, 1980; McNeely and Thorsell, 1991.

107. IUCN and UNEP, 1986a; 1986b; 1986c.

108. The Commission on National Parks and Protected Areas (CNPPA) was established by IUCN in 1959 under a mandate issued by the Economic and Social Council of the United Nations (# 713).

109. The Network is based at the FAO Regional Office for Latin America and the Caribbean, Santiago, Chile. *See,* for example: Ormazabal, 1988.

110. World Heritage In Danger List of the Convention on the World's Cultural and Natural Heritage, Unesco; prepared by CNPPA under contract to Unesco and the World Heritage Committee of the Convention.

111. Hales, 1989.

112. McNeely, 1988.

113. Kelleher, unpublished manuscript.

114. Husey, et. al., 1991; Wells, et. al., 1990.

115. Wells, et. al., 1990; Oldfield, 1988.

116. Wells, et. al., 1990.

117. Wells, et. al., 1990.

118. Stuart et al., 1990.

119. Guzmán and Iltis, 1991.

120. Raven, 1981.

121. Keystone Center, 1991.

122. Akerele et al., 1991.

123. IUCN, WWF. 1989.

124. American Association of Zoological Parks and Arboreta (AAZPA): Conservation Center, 1991.

125. Eisner, 1989.

126. Morin, et. al., 1989.

127. Abramovitz, 1991.

128. Solbrig, O.T. 1991.

129. International Environmental Law Conference, 1991.

130. IUCN, UNEP, WWF, 1991.

131. Poffenberger, 1990.

132. NRC, 1980.

133. NRC, 1980.

134. Keystone Center, 1990; 1991.

Bibliography

The following publications include several important references not cited in the text.

Abramovitz, Janet N. 1991. *Investing in Biological Diversity: U.S. Research and Conservation Efforts in Developing Countries.* World Resources Institute, Washington, D.C.

Akerele, O., V. Heywood, H. Synge (eds.). 1991. *Conservation of Medicinal Plants.* Cambridge University Press, Cambridge, UK.

Alameda, F. and C.M. Pringle (eds.). 1988. *Tropical Rainforest: Diversity and Conservation.* California Academy of Sciences, and Pacific Division, American Association for the Advancement of Science, San Francisco, California, USA.

American Association of Zoological Parks and Arboreta (AAZPA): Conservation Center. 1991. *Species Survival Plan Overview 1991.* AAZPA, USA. Mimeo.

Arbhabhirama, Anat, Dhira Phantumvanit, John Elkington, and Phaitoon Ingkasuwan. 1987. *Thailand Natural Resources Profile.* Thailand Development Research Institute. Bangkok, Thailand.

Barton, J.H. 1991. *Relating the scientific and the commercial worlds in genetic resources negotiations.* Paper presented at the Workshop on Property Rights, Biotechnology, and Genetic Resources; Nairobi, Kenya.

Beebe, Spencer B. 1991. Conservation in temperate and tropical rain forests: the search for an ecosystem approach to sustainability. Paper presented at the 56th Annual North American Wildlife and Natural Resources Conferences. March Edmonton, Alberta, Canada.

Berkes, F., P. George, and R.J. Preston. 1991. Co-Management. *Alternatives* 18(2): 12-18.

Bridgewater, Peter. 1988. Biodiversity and landscape. *Earth-Science Reviews* 25:486-491.

Byerlee, Derek, and Paul W. Heisey. 1990. Wheat varietal diversification over time and space as factors in yield gains and rust resistance in the Punjab. Pp. 5-24 In: P.W. Heisey (ed.) *Accelerating the Transfer of Wheat Breeding Gains to Farmers: A Study of the Dynamics of Varietal Replacement in Pakistan.* CIMMYT Research Report No. 1. Mexico, D.F. Mexico.

Cabarle, B. 1990. *Ecofarming in the Peruvian Amazon: An Indigenous Response.* World Resources Institute. Washington, D.C., USA. Mimeo.

Caldecott, Julian. 1988. Climbing towards extinction. *New Scientist* 118(1616):62-66.

California Department of Forestry. 1988. California's forests and rangelands: growing conflicts over changing uses. California Dept. of Forestry, Sacramento, CA, USA.

Carr, A.B., W.H. Meyers, T.T. Phipps, and G.E. Rossmiller. 1988. *Decoupling Farm Programs.* National Center for Food and Agricultural Policy, Resources for the Future, Washington, D.C., USA.

CEC [Commission of the European Communities]. 1992. Report of the Commission of the European Communities to the United Nations Conference on Environment and Development. Draft.

CEQ [Council for Environmental Quality of the United States]. 1990. State of the Environment. U.S. Government Printing Office, Washington, D.C., USA.

Chaney, W.R., and M. Basbous. 1978. The cedars of Lebanon, witnesses of history. *Economic Botany.* 32:118-123.

Claiborne, W. 1991. Mollusks overwhelm great lakes. *Washington Post,* USA. August 12.

Clay, Jason. 1991. *Building and supplying markets for non-wood forest products.* Paper presented at the American Association for the Advancement of Science Annual Meeting, Washington, D.C., USA.

Cohen, J.I. 1991. *Conserving Biodiversity by Ensuring its Utility.* Paper presented at the International Workshop on Property Rights, Biotechnology, and Genetic Resources; African Centre for Technology Studies, Nairobi, Kenya.

Colchester, M. 1991. Guatemala: the clamour for land and the fate of the forests. *The Ecologist* 21 (No. 4): 177-185.

Collinson M.P., and K.L. Wright. 1991. *Biotechnology and the International Agricultural Research Centers of the CGIAR.* Paper presented at the 21st Conference of the International Association of Agricultural Economists, Tokyo, Japan, August 22-29, 1991.

Commission of Inquiry into Aspects of the Timber Industry in Papua New Guinea. 1989. *Interim Report No. 4 Vol. 1.* Government of Papua New Guinea, Port Moresby, Papua New Guinea.

Cornista, L. B., and E.F. Escueta. 1990. Communal forest leases as a tenurial option in the Philippine uplands. Pp. 134-144 In: M. Poffenberger (Ed.). *Keepers of the Forest. Land Management Alternatives in Southeast Asia.* Kumarian Press. Connecticut, USA.

Council for Tropical and Subtropical Agricultural Research (ASTAF). 1991. *ASTAF Circular* 28:17.

Cultural Survival. 1991. Paper presented at the Symposium on "Alternativas Economicas para las Reservas Extractivistas", Institute of Amazonian Studies, 22-28 February, 1991.

Dahanayake, Chula. 1991. *The legal framework for environmental protection and conservation.* Paper presented at the Workshop on Property Rights, Biotechnology, and Genetic Resources. African Centre for Technology Studies, Nairobi, Kenya.

Dahl, K., and G.P. Nabhan. 1991. *Genetic resource conservation by grassroots organizations in North America: A southwestern case study.* Background paper prepared for the WRI/IUCN/UNEP Biodiversity Conservation Strategy Program, World Resources Institute, Washington, D.C., USA.

Dankelman, I. and J. Davidson. 1988. *Women and The Environment in the Third World.* IUCN and Earthscan Publications Limited. London.

de Beer, J.H., and M.J. McDermott. 1989. *The Economic Value of Non-Timber Forest Products in Southeast Asia.* Netherlands Committee for IUCN, Amsterdam, Netherlands.

Department of Environment. 1991. Conserving the World's Biological Diversity: How Can Britain Contribute? Proceedings of a seminar presented by the U.K. Department of the Environment in association with the Natural History Museum, London, U.K.

Diamond, J.M. 1989. The present, past and future of human-caused extinctions. *Phil. Trans. R. Soc. Lond.* B 325:469-477.

Dogsé, Peter and Bernd von Droste. 1990. Debt-for-Nature Exchanges and Biosphere Reserves: Experiences and Potential. MAB Digest 6. Unesco, Paris, France.

EESI [Environmental and Energy Study Institute]. 1991. *Partnership for Sustainable Development.* EESI, Washington, D.C., USA.

Ehrlich, Paul R., and Edward O. Wilson. 1991. Biodiversity studies: science and policy. *Science* 253:758-762.

Eisner, Thomas. 1989. Prospecting for nature's chemical riches. *Issues in Science and Technology.* 5(2):31-34.

Elfring, C. 1989. Preserving land through local land trusts. *Bioscience* 39 (2): 71-74.

FAO [Food and Agriculture Organization of the United Nations]. 1988. *Current Fisheries Statistics.* FAO, Rome.

FAO. 1989. *Trade Yearbook, vol. 43.* FAO, Rome.

FAO. 1991. *Second interim report on the state of tropical forests.* Paper presented at the 10th World Forestry Congress, Paris, France.

Farnsworth, Norman R. 1988. Screening plants for new medicines. Pp. 83-97 In: E.O. Wilson and F.M. Peter (eds.). *Biodiversity.* National Academy Press, Washington, D.C., USA.

Filion, F.L., A. Jacquemot, and R. Reid. 1985. *The importance of wildlife to Canadians.* Canadian Wildlife Services, Ottawa, Canada.

Ford Foundation, 1990. *Joint Management of Forest Lands: Experiences from South Asia.* Ford Foundation, New Delhi, India.

Fowler C., and P. Mooney. 1990. *Shattering: Food, Politics, and the Loss of Genetic Diversity.* University of Arizona Press, Tucson, AZ.

Frankel, O.H., and M.E. Soule. 1981. *Conservation and Evolution.* Cambridge University Press, Cambridge, U.K.

Galli, Luiz Fernando, and Janio Carlos Goncalves. 1991. *Recuperacão de Areas Degradadas atraves do Reflorestamento com Especies Nativas—A Experiencia da Companhia Energetica de São Paulo (CESP).* Mimeo (July 1991).

Glynn P.W. and W.H. de Weerdt. 1991. Elimination of two reef-building hydrocorals following the 1982-1983 El Niño warming event. *Science* 253: 69-71.

Government of Indonesia. 1991. *Biodiversity Action Plan For Indonesia.* Unpublished draft. Bappenas-Ministry of Population and Environment and The World Bank, in cooperation with Department of Natural Resources Conservation Faculty of Forestry, Bogor Agricultural University.

Grassle, J.F. 1989. Species diversity in deep-sea communities. *Trends in Ecology and Evolution* 4(1):12-15.

Grassle, J.F., N.J. Maciolek, and J.A. Blake. 1990. Are deep sea communities resilient? Pp. 385-393 in: G.M. Woodwell (ed.), *The Earth in Transition: Patterns and Process of Biotic Impoverishment.* Cambridge University Press, Cambridge, U.K.

Griffith, Victoria. 1991. Diseases Put Brazil's Oranges at Risk, *Financial Times,* June 14, p. 34. London, U.K.

Grossman, Lawrence S. 1984. *Peasants, Subsistence Ecology, and Development in the Highlands of Papua New Guinea.* Princeton University Press, Princeton, New Jersey, USA.

Guzmán Rafael and Hugh H. Iltis. 1991. *Biosphere reserve established in Mexico to protect rare maize relative. Diversity* 7:82-84.

Hales, David. 1989. Changing Concepts of National Parks. Pp. 139-144 in: D. Western and M. Pearl (eds.), *Conservation for the Twenty-First Century*. Oxford University Press, N.Y., New York, USA.

Hartshorn, Gary. 1990. Natural Forest Management by the Yanesha Forestry Cooperative in the Peruvian Amazon. Pp. 128-138 in: A. Anderson (ed.), *Steps Toward Sustainable Use of the Amazon Rain Forest*. Columbia University Press, New York, New York, USA.

Hedberg, I. (ed.) 1988. Systemic Botany—a Key Service for Tropical Research and Documentation. *Symbolae Botanicae Upsaliences* 28(3). Alunquist and Wiksell International, Stockholm, Sweden.

Holdren, Constance. 1991. Endangered languages. *Science* 251:159.

Hoyt, E. 1988. *Conserving the wild relatives of crops*. International Board for Plant Genetic Resources, World Conservation Union (IUCN), and World Wide Fund for Nature, Rome, Italy and Gland, Switzerland.

Husey, B.M.J., R.J. Hobbs, and D.A. Saunders. 1991. Guidelines for Bush Corridors. In: Saunders, D.A. and Hobbs, R.J. (eds.) *Nature Conservation 2: The Role of Corridors*. Surrey Beatty and Sons, Chipping Norton, NSW, Australia.

International Environmental Law Conference. 1991. *The Hague Recommendations on International Environmental Law*. The Hague, The Netherlands. Mimeo.

IPCC [Intergovernmental Panel on Climate Change]. 1990. Climate Change: The IPCC Scientific Assessment. Houghton, J.T., G.J. Jenkins, and J.J. Ephraums (eds.). Cambridge University Press, Cambridge, U.K.

IUCN [World Conservation Union]. 1983. *The IUCN Invertebrate Red Data Book*. IUCN, Gland, Switzerland.

IUCN. 1987. *Translocations of living organisms*. IUCN, Gland, Switzerland.

IUCN. 1991. *Environmental Status Reports 1990; Volume 3: USSR*. IUCN, Gland Switzerland

IUCN and CNPPA, 1990. *United Nations List of Parks and Protected Areas*. World Conservation Monitoring Centre, Cambridge, United Kingdom. December.

IUCN and UNEP. 1986a. Review of the Protected Areas System in the Indo-Malayan Realm. IUCN, Gland, Switzerland.

IUCN and UNEP. 1986b. Review of the Protected Areas System in the Afrotropical Realm. IUCN, Gland, Switzerland.

IUCN and UNEP. 1986c. Review of the Protected Areas System in Oceania. IUCN, Gland, Switzerland.

IUCN, UNEP, and WWF. 1980. *World Conservation Strategy: Living Resource Conservation for Sustainable Development*. IUCN, Gland, Switzerland.

IUCN, UNEP, and WWF. 1991. *Caring for the Earth: A Strategy for Sustainable Living*. IUCN, Gland, Switzerland.

IUCN, WHO, and WWF [World Conservation Union, World Health Organization, World Wide Fund for Nature]. 1991. Guidelines on the Conservation of Medicinal Plants. Unpublished manuscript. IUCN, Gland, Switzerland.

IUCN and WWF. 1989. *The Botanic Gardens Conservation Strategy*. IUCN, Gland, Switzerland.

Jaenike, John. 1991. Mass extinction of European fungi. *Trends in Ecology and Evolutionary Biology* 6 (6): 174-175.

Janzen, D.H. 1988. Tropical dry forests: the most endangered major tropical ecosystem. Pp. 130-137 in: E.O. Wilson and F.M. Peter (eds.), *Biodiversity*. National Academy Press, Washington, D.C., USA.

Johnson, J. 1991. Biologists plot revenge in war of the snails. *New Scientist.* 24 August: 14.

Juma, C. 1989. *The Gene Hunters: Biotechnology and the Scramble for Seeds.* Princeton University Press, Princeton, NJ, USA.

Kapoor, Promila. 1988. *Biological Diversity and Genetic Resources: Status Report.* CSC Technical Series No. 258. Commonwealth Science Council, London, U.K.

Kaur, Ravinder. 1990. *Women in Forestry in India.* Unpublished manuscript. World Bank, Washington, D.C.

Kelleher, Graeme. Unpublished manuscript. Sustainable development of the Great Barrier Reef Marine Park. Great Barrier Reef Marine Park Authority, Australia.

Keystone Center. 1990. *Final Consensus Report of the Keystone International Dialogue Series on Plant Genetic Resources: Madras Plenary Session.* The Keystone Center, Keystone, Colorado, USA.

Keystone Center. 1991. *Final Consensus Report: Global Initiative for the Security and Sustainable Use of Plant Genetic Resources. Oslo Plenary Session.* The Keystone Center, Keystone, Colorado, USA.

Kloppenburg, J.R., and D.L. Kleinman. 1987. The plant germplasm controversy. *BioScience* 37(3):190-198.

Knickerbocker, B. 1991. The Clock is Running on Salmon Survival. *Christian Science Monitor,* USA. 3 May.

Knutson, L. and A.K. Stoner (eds.). 1989. *(13) Biotic Diversity and Germplasm Preservation, Global Imperatives.* Klower Academic Publishers, The Netherlands.

Lang, R. (ed). 1986. *Integrated Approaches to Resource Planning and Management.* University of Calgary Press. Calgary, Alberta, Canada.

Lean, Geoffrey, Don Hinrichsen, and Adam Markham. 1990. Atlas of the Environment. Prentice Hall Press, New York, N.Y.

Lewis, D.M., G.B. Kaweche, and A. Mwenya. 1987. *Wildlife conservation outside protected areas: lessons from an experiment in Zambia.* Lupande Research Project, National Parks and Wildlife Service, Publication #4, Zambia.

Lindberg, K. 1991. *Policies for maximizing nature tourism's ecological and economic benefits.* World Resources Institute, Washington, D.C., USA.

Ljungman, L., Douglas McGuire, Augusta Molnar. 1987. *Social Forestry in India: World Bank Experience.* mimeo.

Lubchenco, J. et al. 1991. The sustainable biosphere initiative: an ecological research agenda. *Ecology:* 72(2):371-412.

Lucas, P.H.C. In Press. *Conserving biological diversity through protected areas: from a world perspective to New Zealand as a case study.* Proceedings of the Pacific Science Congress, Honolulu, Hawaii, USA.

MacKenzie, Deborah. 1986. Crayfish pesticide decimates Spanish birds. *New Scientist* October 16:24.

MacKinnon, K. 1990. *Biological Diversity in Indonesia: A Resource Inventory.* World Wide Fund for Nature, Bogor, Indonesia.

McNeely, J.A. 1988. *Economics and Biological Diversity: Developing and Using Economic Incentives to Conserve Biological Diversity.* IUCN, Gland, Switzerland.

McNeely, J.A., K.R. Miller, W.V. Reid, R.A. Mittermeier, and T.B. Werner. 1991. *Conserving the World's Biological Diversity.* World Resources Institute, World Conservation Union, World Bank, World Wildlife Fund, Conservation International, Washington, D.C. and Gland, Switzerland.

McNeely, J.A., and J. Thorsell. 1991. *Guidelines for Pre-paring Protected Area System Plans.* Unpublished manuscript. IUCN, Gland, Switzerland.

Miller, J.S., and S.J. Brewer. 1991. The discovery of medicines and forest conservation. Unpublished manuscript, Missouri Botanical Garden and Monsanto Company, St. Louis, Missouri, USA.

Miller, K.R. 1980. *Planificación de Parques Nacionales: Ejemplos y Casos de América Latina.* FEPMA, Madrid.

Miller, R.R., J.D. Williams, and J.E. Williams. 1989. Extinctions of North American fishes during the past century. *Fisheries* 14(6):22-38.

Ministry of Agriculture, Nature Management, and Fisheries. 1991. *Nature Policy Plan of the Netherlands.* Ministry of Agriculture, Nature Management, and Fisheries, The Hague, Netherlands.

Ministry of Natural Resources, Energy, and Mines of the Government of Costa Rica; National System of Conservation Areas. 1991. *Conserving Biodiversity through the Sustainable Use of Conservation Wildlands: The Guanacaste Conservation Area.* Proposal to the Government of Denmark. San José, Costa Rica.

Ministry of Natural Resources, Energy, and Mines of the Government of Costa Rica (MIRENAM), Ministry of Planning and Economic Policy of the Government of Costa Rica (MIDEPLAN), Organization of American States (OAS), and Conservation International (CI). 1990. Summary Description, *Strategy for the Institutional Development of La Amistad Biosphere Reserve.* CI, OAS, and the Government of Costa Rica; San José, Costa Rica.

Ministry of Population and Environment of the Government of Indonesia (KLH). 1989. *National Strategy for the Management of Biodiversity.* KLH, Jakarta, Indonesia.

Mohsin, A.K.M., M.A. Ambak. 1983. *Freshwater Fishes of Peninsular Malaysia.* University Pertanian Malaysia Press, Kuala Lumpur, Malaysia.

Montaña, C. (ed.) 1988. *Estudio Integrado de Los Recursos Vegetación, Suelo y Agua en la Reserva de la Biosfera de Mapimí.* Instituto de Ecologia, Mexico D.F., Mexico.

Montecinos, C. and M. Altieri. 1991. *Status and trends in grass-roots crop genetic resource conservation efforts in Latin America.* Consortio Latino Americano sobre Agroecologica y Desarrollo (CLADES), Santiago, Chile.

Morin, N.R., R.D. Whetstone, D. Wilken, and K.L. Tomlinson. 1989. *Floristics for the 21st Century.* Proceedings of the workshop 4-7 May, 1988, Alexandria, VA. Missouri Botanical Garden, St. Louis, MO., USA.

National Wastelands Development Board, Government of India. 1986. *Discussion Papers, Minutes and Decisions.* First Meeting of the National Land Use and Wastelands Development Council. February 6, 1986. New Delhi, India.

Nations, J.D. and D.I. Comer. 1982. Indians, immigrants, and beef exports: deforestation in Central America. *Cultural Survival Quarterly* 6:8-12.

Nectoux, Francis and Yoichi Kuroda. 1989. *Timber From the South Seas: An Analysis of Japan's Tropical Timber Trade and its Environmental Impact.* WWF International, Gland, Switzerland.

Netherlands National Committee for IUCN/Steering Group for World Conservation Strategy. 1988. *The Netherlands and the World Ecology: Towards a National Conservation Strategy in and by the Netherlands.* Netherlands National Committee, Amsterdam.

Norgaard, Richard. 1987. *Economics as Mechanics and the Demise of Biological Diversity.* Ecological Modelling 38: 107-121.

Norwegian Institute for Nature Research (NINA). 1991. *Recommendations of The International Conference on Conservation of Genetic Resources for Sustainable Development.* Roros, Norway. 10-14 September 1990, NINA, Trondheim, Norway.

NRC [National Research Council]. 1980. *Research Priorities in Tropical Biology.* National Academy of Sciences, Washington, D.C., USA.

NRC. 1991. *Managing Global Genetic Resources: Forest Trees.* National Academy Press, Washington, D.C., USA.

ODC and WWF [Overseas Development Council and World Wildlife Fund]. 1991. *Environmental Challenges to Trade Policy.* Conference Report, ODC, Washington, D.C., USA.

Oldeman, L.R., Hakkeling, R.T.A., and Sombroek, W.G. 1990. *World Map of the Status of Human Induced Soil Degradation: An Explanatory Note.* International Soil Reference and Information Center, Wagegingen, and UNEP, Nairobi, Kenya.

Oldfield, S. 1988. *Buffer zone management in tropical moist forests: case studies and guidelines.* IUCN, Gland, Switzerland.

Ormazabal, C. 1988. *Sistemas Nacionales de Areas Silvestres Protegidas en America Latina.* FAO/UNEP, Santiago, Chile.

OTA [Office of Technology Assessment of the U.S. Congress]. 1987. *Technologies to Maintain Biological Diversity.* OTA-F-330. U.S. Government Printing Office, Washington, D.C., USA.

Palca, J. 1990. Libya gets unwelcome visitor from the west. *Science 249:* 117-118.

Pardey, Philip G., and Johannes Roseboom. 1989. ISNAR Agricultural Research Indicators Series: A Global Data Base on National Agricultural Research Systems. Cambridge University Press, New York, N.Y., USA.

Pearson, C.S. 1987. *Environmental Standards, Industrial Relocation, and Pollution Havens. Multinational Corporations, Environment, and The Third World: Business Matters.* World Resources Institute, Washington, D.C., USA.

Peters, C.M., A.H. Gentry, and R. Mendelsohn. 1989. Valuation of a tropical forest in Peruvian Amazonia. *Nature 339:* 655.

Petocz, R., and G.P. Raspado. 1989. *Conservation and Development in Irian Jaya.* E.J. Brill, Netherlands.

Plucknett, D.L., N.J.H. Smith, J.T. Williams, N.M. Anishetty. 1987. *Gene Banks and the World's Food.* Princeton University Press, Princeton, N.J., USA.

Poffenberger, M. (Ed.). 1990. *Keepers of the Forest.* Kumarian, West Hartford, Connecticut, USA.

Poole, P. 1989. *Developing a Partnership of Indigenous Peoples, Conservationists, and Land Use Planners in Latin America.* Environment Working Paper, World Bank, Washington, D.C., USA.

Poore, D., P. Burgess, J. Palmer, S. Rietbergen, and T. Synnott. 1989. *No Timber Without Trees: Sustainability in the Tropical Forest.* Earthscan Publications Limited. London, U.K.

Postel, S. and J. Ryan. 1991. Reforming Forestry. In: L.R. Brown, A. Durning, C.Flavin, H. French, J. Jacobson, N. Lenssen, M. Lowe, S. Postel, M. Renner, J. Ryan, L. Starke, and J. Young. *State of the World 1991.* W.W. Norton and Co., N.Y., USA.

Prance, G.T. 1987. The Amazon: Paradise Lost? Pp. 63-106 In: L. Kaufman and K. Mallory (eds.), *The Last Extinction.* The MIT Press, Cambridge, Mass. USA.

Prescott-Allen, C, and R. Prescott-Allen. 1986. *The First Resource.* Yale University Press, New Haven, Connecticut, USA.

Prescott-Allen, Robert, and Christine Prescott-Allen. 1983. Genes from the Wild. Earthscan, London, U.K.

Propst, L. and S.W. Carothers. 1991. Urban Land. June: 15-19.

Raven, P.H. 1981. Research in botanical gardens. *Bot. Jahrb. Syst. 102*: 53-74.

Raven, P.H. 1988. Biological resources and global stability. Pp. 3-27 In: S. Kawano, J.H. Connell, and T. Hidaka (eds.), *Evolution and Coadaptation in Biotic Communities.* University of Tokyo Press, Tokyo, Japan.

Reid, W.V. 1992. How many species will there be? In: T. Whitmore and J. Sayer (eds.), *Tropical Deforestation and Species Extinction.* Chapman and Hall, London, U.K.

Reid, W.V., and K.R. Miller. 1989. *Keeping Options Alive: The Scientific Basis for Conserving Biodiversity.* World Resources Institute, Washington, D.C., USA.

Reid, W.V., and M.C. Trexler. 1991. *Drowning the National Heritage: Climate Change and U.S. Coastal Biodiversity.* World Resources Institute, Washington, D.C., USA.

Repetto, R. 1988. *The Forest for the Trees? Government Policies and the Misuse of Forest Resources.* World Resources Institute, Washington, D.C., USA.

Repetto, R., and F. van Bolhuis. 1989. *Natural Endowments: Financing Resource Conservation for Development. International Conservation Financing Project Report.* World Resources Institute, Washington, D.C.

Repetto, R., W. Cruz, R. Solórzano, R. de Camino, R. Woodward, J. Tosi, V. Watson, A. Vásquez, C. Villa Lobos, J. Jiménez. 1991. *Accounts Overdue: Natural Resource Depreciation in Costa Rica.* World Resources Institute, Washington, D.C., USA.

Ryan, J.C. In Press. Conserving biological diversity. In: L. Brown, et. al. *State of the World 1992.* W.W. Norton and Co., N.Y., USA.

Salazar, R. 1991. The community plant genetic resources system: Options and Potentials. Background paper prepared for the WRI/IUCN/ UNEP Biodiversity Conservation Strategy Program, World Resources Institute, Washington, D.C., USA.

Sale, K. 1985. *Dwellers in the Land: The Bioregional Vision.* Sierra Club Books. San Francisco, California, USA.

Salm, R.V., and M. Halim. 1984. *Marine Conservation Data Atlas, Indonesia.* World Wildlife Fund, Bogor, Indonesia.

Sastrapradja, D., S. Adisoemarto, K. Kartawinata, M. Rifai, and S. Sastrapradja. 1990. *Membangun negeri dengan Keanekaragaman Hayati.* LIPI, Bogor, Indonesia.

Sayer, J.A. 1991. Biological conservation issues in forest management. In IUCN/ITTO, *Conserving Biological Diversity in Managed Tropical Forests.* Draft.

Schneider, S.H. 1989. The greenhouse effect: science and policy. *Science* 243:771-781.

Schultes, R.E. 1979. The Amazonia as a source of new economic plants. *Economic Botany* 33: 259-266.

Schwartzman, S. 1989. "Extractive reserves: distribution of wealth and the social costs of frontier development in the Amazon." Paper presented at the Symposium on Extractive Economies in Tropical Forests: A Course of Action. Washington, D.C., USA. November 30-December 1.

Shingi, Prakash, M. (ed.) 1990. *Studies on Social Forestry in India. Management Perspectives.* FAO, Bangkok, and Indian Institute of Management, Ahmedabad.

Silvius, M., E. Djuharsa, A. Taufik, A. Steeman, and E. Berczy. 1987. *The Indonesian Wetland Inventory.* PHPA-AWB/Interwader & Edwin.

Solbrig, O.T. 1991. Biodiversity: Scientific Issues and Collaborative Research Proposals. *MAB Digest #9.* UNESCO.

Soulé, M.E. and B.A. Wilcox (eds.). 1980. *Conservation Biology: An Evolutionary Ecological Perspective.* Sinauer Associates, Sunderland, Massachusetts, USA.

Spaid, E.L. 1991. *Christian Science Monitor.* USA. August 5.

Spears, J., and E. Ayensu. 1985. Resources, development, and the new century: Forestry. In: R. Repetto *(ed.) The Global Possible.* Yale University Press, New Haven, CT, USA.

Stuart, S.N., R. J. Adams, with a contribution from M.D. Jenkins. 1990. *Biodiversity Conservation in Sub-Saharan Africa and its Islands.* IUCN, Gland, Switzerland.

Thomas, C.D. 1990. Fewer species. *Nature* 347:237.

Thorne-Miller, B., and J. Catena. 1991. *The Living Ocean: Understanding and Protecting Marine Biodiversity.* Island Press, Covelo, California, USA.

Thorsell, J. 1990. The IUCN register of threatened protected areas of the world. Paper presented to the 34th Working Session of the IUCN Commission on National Parks and Protected Areas, Perth, Australia, November 26-27, 1990.

Trexler, M.C. 1991. *Minding the Carbon Store: Weighing U.S. Forestry Strategies to Slow Global Warming.* World Resources Institute, Washington, D.C., USA.

Turner, B.L., William Clark, Robert Kates, John Richards, Jessica T. Mathews, and William Meyer, Eds. 1990. *The Earth as Transformed by Human Action.* Cambridge University Press, Cambridge, U.K.

Uhl, C., A. Verissimo, M. M. Mattos, P. Barreto, and R. Tarifa. In press. Aging of the Amazon frontier: opportunities for genuine development. In Kim, K.C., ed. *Biodiversity and Landscapes: A Paradox of Humanity.*

United Nations Department of Public Information. 1989. *World Economic Survey 1989.* United Nations, N.Y., USA.

U.S. Bureau of the Census. 1990. *Statistical Abstract of the United States.* U.S. Government Printing Office, Washington, D.C., USA.

USDA [United States Department of Agriculture]. 1991. Timber harvest and supply projections. USDA Forest Service, Pacific Southwest Region, Berkeley, CA, USA.

Usher, A.D. 1991. Inhabitants of the Mool River. *The Nation,* March 31. Bangkok, Thailand.

Vitousek, P.M., P.R. Ehrlich, A.H. Ehrlich and P.M. Matson. 1986. Human Appropriation of the Products of Photosynthesis. *Bioscience* 36(6): 368-373.

Vitousek, P.M., L.R. Walker, L.D. Whiteaker, D. Mueller-Dombois, and P.A. Matson. 1987. Biological invasion by *Myrica faya* alters ecosystem development in Hawaii. *Science* 238:802-804.

WCMC [World Conservation Monitoring Centre]. 1992. *Global Biodiversity 1992. Status of the Earth's Living Resources,* WCMC, Cambridge, U.K.

Wells, M., K. Brandon, and L. Hannah. 1990. People and Parks: Linking Protected Area Management with Local Communities. World Bank, World Wildlife Fund/US, and USAID, Washington DC. Unpublished manuscript.

Wells, Michael. 1991. Trust Funds and Endowments as a Biodiversity Conservation Tool. *Policy and Research Divisional Working Paper No. 1991-26*, Environment Department, World Bank, Washington, D.C.

Weniger, B. and L. Robineau. 1988. *Elements of a Caribbean Pharmacopeia.* Enda-Caribe; Ministerio de Salud Publica, Cuba.

Westoby, J. 1984. *Halting Tropical Deforestation: The Role of Technology.* U.S. Congress, Office of Technology Assessment, Washington, D.C., USA.

Whitmore T., and J. Sayer (eds.). 1992. *Tropical Deforestation and Species Extinction.* Chapman and Hall, London, U.K.

Whitten, A.J., S. Damanik, J. Anwar, and N. Hisyam. 1984. *The Ecology of Sumatra.* GAMA Press, Yogyakarta, Indonesia.

Whitten, M.J., M. Mustafa, and G. Henderson. 1987. *The Ecology of Sulawesi.* GAMA Press, Yogyakarta, Indonesia.

Williams, J.E., J.E. Johnson, D.A. Hendrickson, S. Contreras-Balderas, J.D. Williams, M. Navarro-Mendoza, D.E. McCallister, and J.E. Deacon. 1989. Fishes of North America: endangered, threatened or of special concern. *Fisheries* 14(6):2-20.

Wilson, E.O., and F.M. Peter (eds.). 1988. *Biodiversity.* National Academy Press, Washington, D.C.

Worede, M. 1991. Crop genetic resource conservation and utilization: an Ethiopian perspective. Unpublished manuscript. Plant Genetic Resources Center, Addis Ababa, Ethiopia.

World Bank. 1991. *World Development Report.* Oxford University Press, London, U.K.

World Commission on Environment and Development. 1987. *Our Common Future.* Oxford University Press, Oxford, U.K.

WRI and IIED [World Resources Institute and International Institute for Environment and Development]. 1988. *World Resources 1988-89.* Basic Books, New York, USA.

WRI and USAID [World Resources Institute and US Agency for International Development]. 1991. *Environmental Strategy Options for Latin America and the Caribbean.* Washington, D.C., Draft.

WWF, IUCN, and BGCS. 1989. *The Botanic Gardens Conservation Strategy.* World Wide Fund for Nature, World Conservation Union (IUCN), Botanic Gardens Conservation Secretariat, Gland, Switzerland, and Richmond, U.K.

Zaret, T.M., and R.T. Paine. 1973. Species introduction in a tropical lake. *Science 182*: 449-455.

Zerner, C. 1991. *Turning the Tide: Community Management of Coastal Resources in Southeast Asia and the Pacific.* Unpublished manuscript. World Resources Institute, Washington, D.C., USA.

User's Guide to the
Global Biodiversity Strategy

User's Guide to the
Global Biodiversity Strategy

I The Nature and Value of Biodiversity..1

II Losses of Biodiversity and Their Causes...7

III The Strategy For Biodiversity Conservation..............................19

The Goal of Biodiversity Conservation...19

The Approach of the Strategy 22

The Strategy: Contents and Catalysts 26

Catalysts for Action 29

Action 1

Adopt, in 1992, the international Convention on Biological Diversity 29

Action 2

Adopt, in the General Assembly of the United Nations, a resolution designating 1994-2003 the International Biodiversity Decade..*30*

Action 3

Establish a mechanism such as an International Panel on Biodiversity Conservation (preferably within the Convention on Biological Diversity), including scientists, non-governmental organizations, and policy-makers to provide guidance on priorities for the protection, understanding, and sustainable and equitable use of biodiversity..*30*

Action 4

Establish an Early Warning Network, linked to the Convention on Biological Diversity, to monitor potential threats to biodiversity and mobilize action against them..*33*

Action 5

Integrate biodiversity conservation into national planning processes...*34*

Implementing the Strategy.. **34**

IV   Establishing a National Policy Framework For Biodiversity Conservation 37

Objective:

Reform existing public policies that invite the waste or misuse of biodiversity.......................38

Action 6

Abandon forestry policies that encourage resource degradation and the conversion of forest ecosystems to other less valuable uses..*38*

Action 7

Reform policies that result in the degradation and loss of biodiversity in coastal and marine ecosystems.....*39*

Action 8

Reform policies that hasten loss of biodiversity in freshwater ecosystems.......................................*41*

Action 9

Eliminate agricultural policies that promote excessive uniformity of crops and crop varieties or that encourage the overuse of chemical fertilizers and pesticides...41

Objective:

Adopt new public policies and accounting methods that promote conservation and the equitable use of biodiversity 43

Action 10

Assert national sovereignty over genetic resources and regulate their collection 43

Action 11

Strictly regulate the transfer of species and genetic resources and their release into the wild.........................45

Action 12

Establish incentives for effective and equitable private-sector plant breeding and research 47

Action 13

Modify national income accounts to make them reflect the economic loss that results when biological resources are degraded and biodiversity is lost...48

Objective:

Reduce demand for biological resources...49

Action 14

Provide universal access to family planning services and increase funding to support their adoption............50

Action 15

Reduce resource consumption through recycling and conservation 51

Action 16

Audit the consumption of biological resources to raise awareness of the balance between local consumption and production..52

V Creating An International Policy Environment That Supports National Biodiversity Conservation..............55

Objective:

Integrate biodiversity conservation into international economic policy....................................56

Action 17

Develop a principle and policy of "national ecological security" to ensure that international trade policies do not intensify biodiversity loss...56

Action 18

Establish an International Debt Management Authority to purchase debt on the secondary market............57

Action 19

Facilitate the exchange and development of technologies for conserving and using biodiversity sustainably 58

Action 20

Ensure that the activities of transnational corporations (TNCs) that destroy biodiversity are curbed in the countries where they are based and where they operate, and that compensation for, or restoration of, damages is sought where applicable...59

Action 21

Ensure that countries are free to decide whether to adopt intellectual property rights protection for genetic resources and how strong that protection should be 60

Objective:

Strengthen the international legal framework for conservation to complement the Convention on Biological Diversity...62

Action 22

Strengthen the effectiveness of existing international conventions and treaties covering the conservation of ecosystems, species, and genes. 62

Action 23

Ensure that international agreements on climate change and forests are compatible with the Convention on Biological Diversity and that they support biodiversity conservation. 65

Objective:

Make the development assistance process a force for biodiversity conservation......................67

Action 24

Incorporate biodiversity values into the criteria for choosing, designing, and evaluating development assistance loans and projects, and for assessing developing countries' economic performance. 67

Action 25

Open the development-assistance process—the design, implementation, and evaluation of projects and the policies that guide them—to public scrutiny, participation, and accountability. 69

Action 26

Ensure that development assistance strengthens the role of women in the sustainable use of biological resources 70

Objective:

Increase funding for biodiversity conservation, and develop innovative, decentralized, and accountable ways to raise funds and spend them effectively......................................71

Action 27

Involve governments, multilateral development agencies, and non-governmental organizations jointly in establishing new biodiversity conservation funding sources and mechanisms, initially totalling at least $1 billion per year..72

Action 28

Improve debt-for-nature swaps as a means of protecting biodiversity 74

Action 29

Promote the use of trust funds or endowments for biodiversity conservation 75

Action 30

Develop mechanisms to fund grassroots organizations and initiatives 76

VI Creating Conditions and Incentives For Local Biodiversity Conservation

VI Creating Conditions and Incentives For Local Biodiversity Conservation 79

Objective:

Correct imbalances in the control of land and resources that cause biodiversity loss and develop new resource management partnerships between government and local communities 80

Action 31

Reduce pressure on fragile ecosystems and wildlands by using land already under cultivation more efficiently and equitably 81

Action 32

Increase incentives for local stewardship of public lands and waters 82

Action 33

Recognize the ancestral domains of tribal and indigenous peoples and support their efforts to maintain traditional practices and adapt them to modern pressures and conditions 83

Action 34

Compensate individuals and local communities who own or depend on land or resources taken for public purposes. 83

Action 35

Manage living resources on public lands through new forms of community-state partnership and cooperation 84

Objective:

Expand and encourage the sustainable use of products and services from the wild for local benefits 86

Action 36

Recognize and quantify the local economic value of wild products in development and land-use planning...86

Action 37

Encourage local communities to explore opportunities for developing a larger market share for wild products harvested sustainably...88

Action 38

Increase the local benefits of tourism in natural areas—"ecotourism"—and ensure that tourism development does not result in biodiversity loss or cultural conflict 89

Action 39

Strengthen local capacity for maintaining and benefiting from crop and varietal diversity..........................90

Action 40

Develop the role of traditional medicines and ensure their appropriate and sustainable use 92

Objective:

Ensure that those who possess local knowledge related to genetic resources benefit appropriately when it is used...93

Action 41

Promote recognition of the value of local knowledge and genetic resources and affirm local peoples' rights...94

Action 42

Base the collection of genetic resources on contractual or other agreements ensuring equitable returns........94

VII Managing Biodiversity Throughout the Human Environment 97

Objective:

Create the institutional conditions for bioregional conservation and development...............101

Action 43

Develop new methods and mechanisms at the bioregional level for dialogue, planning, and conflict resolution. 101

Action 44

Give weak and disenfranchised groups the means to influence how the bioregion's resources should be managed and distributed..104

Action 45

Establish intersectoral and interagency task forces to facilitate bioregional planning and action 104

Action 46

Establish bioregional information centers to heighten public awareness and support biodiversity conservation..105

Objective:

Support biodiversity conservation initiatives in the private sector 105

Action 47

Establish tax incentives for conservation..106

Action 48

Support the establishment of private Biodiversity Conservation Trusts...106

Objective:

Incorporate biodiversity conservation into the management of biological resources.............107

Action 49

Incorporate biodiversity conservation practices into the management of all forests...................108

Action 50

Promote agricultural practices that conserve biodiversity...109

Action 51

Restore degraded lands in ways that enhance their productivity and biodiversity......................110

VIII Strengthening Protected Areas................117

Objective:

Identify national and international priorities for strengthening protected areas and enhancing their role in biodiversity conservation..119

Action 52

Conduct national reviews of protected area systems..119

Action 53

Propose immediate and long-term action to establish and strengthen protected areas................121

Action 54

Undertake an international assessment of present and future protected area needs.....................121

Action 55

Provide incentives for establishing private protected areas...125

Action 56

Promote international cooperation on protected area management.....................................125

Objective:

Ensure the sustainability of protected areas and their contribution to biodiversity conservation..126

Action 57

Broaden participation in the design of protected area management plans and expand the range of issues addressed by those plans..126

Action 58

Expand the management objectives of protected areas to include the full scope of biodiversity conservation...128

Action 59

Enhance the ecological and social value of protected areas through land purchase and zoning outside the protected area and by providing financial incentives for conservation on adjacent private lands.....................128

Action 60

Enhance the ecological and social value of protected areas by increasing the benefits to people in and around them..131

Action 61

Restore degraded lands within protected areas and in adjacent lands and corridors.....................................132

IX   Conserving Species, Populations, and Genetic Diversity 133

Objective:

Strengthen capacity to conserve species, populations, and genetic diversity in natural habitats 134

Action 62

Integrate the conservation of species, populations, and genetic resources into regional management and protected area reviews..134

Action 63

Use flagship species to increase support for conservation............136

Action 64

Improve and expand legal mechanisms to protect species............136

Objective:

Strengthen the capacity of off-site conservation facilities to conserve biodiversity, educate the public, and contribute to sustainable development 137

Action 65

Strengthen crop and livestock genetic resource conservation, and implement the Global Initiative for the Security and Sustainable Use of Plant Genetic Resources...........138

Action 66

*Develop the world's collections of cultures of microorganisms as an **ex situ** network*...........140

Action 67

Fill major gaps in the protection of plant genetic resources...........141

Action 68

Develop the world's botanic gardens as a major off-site network for conserving wild plant resources...........143

Action 69

Strengthen the conservation role of zoological parks...........144

Action 70

Strengthen the role of public aquaria in the conservation of biodiversity...........145

Action 71

Strengthen collaboration among off-site and on-site conservation institutions, partly to enlarge the role of off-site facilities in species reintroduction, habitat restoration, and habitat rehabilitation...........146

X Expanding Human Capacity to Conserve Biodiversity

X Expanding Human Capacity to Conserve Biodiversity 147

Objective:

Increase appreciation and awareness of biodiversity's values and importance 148

Action 72

Build awareness of the importance and values of biodiversity into popular culture 148

Action 73

Use the formal education system to increase awareness about biodiversity and the need for its conservation 148

Action 74

Integrate biodiversity concerns into education outside of the classroom 149

Objective:

Help institutions disseminate the information needed to conserve biodiversity and mobilize its benefits 150

Action 75

Establish or strengthen national or sub-national institutions providing information on the conservation and potential values of biodiversity 150

Action 76

Undertake national biodiversity inventories and produce periodic national biodiversity assessments 156

Action 77

Establish a global biodiversity information network to speed the flow of data for local, national, regional, and global assessments 157

Action 78

Provide all citizens with legal and institutional guarantees of access to information on development projects and other activities with potential impacts on biodiversity 158

Objective:

Promote basic and applied research on biodiversity conservation 158

Action 79

Systematically assess national biodiversity research priorities. 159

Action 80

Promote basic and applied natural sciences research on biodiversity conservation. 159

Action 81

Strengthen social science research on the connections between biological and social processes 160

Action 82

Strengthen research on ethical, cultural, and religious concerns related to conserving biodiversity..............161

Objective:

Develop human resources capacity for biodiversity conservation 162

Action 83

Increase support for training biodiversity professionals, particularly in developing countries......................162

Action 84

Revise career incentives provided by governments to increase the attractiveness of work in the field..........165

Action 85

Strengthen the influence and capacity of non-governmental conservation and development organizations to promote biodiversity conservation. 165

Contributors to the Global Biodiversity Strategy

Partner Organizations

The following organizations have asked to be listed as partner organizations in the Biodiversity Strategy Program:

African Centre for Technology Studies, Kenya

Asian Development Bank, Philippines

Association of Systematics Collections, USA

Australian Department of the Arts, Sport, Environment, Tourism, and Territories, Australia

Australian National Parks and Wildlife Center, Australia

Botanic Gardens Conservation International, U.K.

Caribbean Natural Resources Institute, U.S. Virgin Islands

Center for Marine Conservation, USA

Commonwealth Science Council, U.K.

Conservation International, USA

Defenders of Wildlife, USA

Endangered Species Scientific Commission, China

The George Wright Society, USA

Indigenous Food Plants Programme, Kenya

Indonesian Environmental Forum (WALHI), Indonesia

Institute of Nature Conservation and Reserves, Russia

International Board for Plant Genetic Resources, Rome, Italy

International Council for Bird Preservation, U.K.

International Council for Research in Agroforestry, Kenya

Kenya Institute for Organic Farms, Kenya

The Keystone Center, USA

Linnean Society of London, U.K.

London Environmental Economics Centre, U.K.

Missouri Botanical Garden, USA

National Biodiversity Institute (INBio), Costa Rica

National Museums of Kenya, Kenya

National Parks Foundation, Costa Rica

The Natural History Museum, U.K.

The Nature Conservancy, USA

Nature Foundation, Ecuador

Neotropica Foundation, Costa Rica

Plant Conservation Office (IUCN), U.K.

Plant Genetic Resources Centre, Ethiopia

Pro-Nature Foundation (FUNATURA), Brazil

Pro-Sierra Nevada Foundation of Santa Marta, Colombia

Ramsar Conservation Secretariat, Switzerland

Rare Breeds International, Italy

Smithsonian Institution, USA

Society for Conservation Biology, USA

Venezuelan Foundation for Conservation of Biological Diversity (BIOMA), Venezuela

Western Hemisphere Shorebird Reserve Network, USA

Woods Hole Research Center, USA

World Bank, USA

World Conservation Monitoring Centre, U.K.

World Wide Fund for Nature, Switzerland

World Wildlife Fund, USA

Regional Consultations— Organizers, Steering Committees, and Sponsors

AFRICA

10-14 JUNE 1991, NAIROBI, KENYA

CALESTOUS JUMA, AFRICAN CENTRE FOR TECHNOLOGY STUDIES, KENYA

Steering Committee:

Kihika Kiambi, Kenya Energy and Environment Organization, Kenya

R.R.N. Kigame, Ministry of Environmental and Natural Resources, Kenya

Robert Malpas, Director, East Africa Regional Office, International Union for Conservation of Nature and Natural Resources, Kenya

W.K. Ngulo, Ministry of Research, Science and Technology, Kenya

Steven Njuguna, National Museums of Kenya, Kenya

J. Nyangeri, National Council for Science and Technology, Kenya

Reuben Olembo, United Nations Environment Programme, Kenya

Fred Owino, International Council for Research in Agroforestry, Kenya

Permanent Secretary, Ministry of Foreign Affairs, Kenya

G. Thitai, National Council for Science and Technology, Kenya

Sponsors:

The Danish International Development Agency

International Development Research Centre

Stockholm Environment Institute

Swedish International Development Authority

Swedish Society for Conservation of Nature

United Nations Development Programme

United Nations Environment Programme

World Conservation Union (IUCN)

World Resources Institute

CENTRAL AMERICA

23-26 JUNE, 1991, SAN JOSE, COSTA RICA

RODRIGO GAMEZ, NATIONAL BIODIVERSITY INSTITUTE (INBIO), COSTA RICA

Sponsors:

Canadian International Development Agency

The Heinz Charitable Trust

United Nations Development Programme

World Conservation Union (IUCN)

World Resources Institute

NORTH AMERICA

14-17 JULY, 1991, KEYSTONE, COLORADO
MICHAEL LESNICK, THE KEYSTONE CENTER, USA
CONNIE LEWIS, THE KEYSTONE CENTER, USA

Steering Committee:

D. Dean Bibles, Bureau of Land Management, USA

Fernando Blackgoat, Exxon Company, USA

William Bourgeois, MacMillan Bloedel, Ltd., Canada

James Broadus, Woods Hole Oceanographic Institution, USA

Connie Brooks, Davis, Wright and Tremaine, USA

Faith Campbell, Natural Resources Defense Council, USA

Arthur Campeau, Department of Environment, Canada

Craig Ferguson, Environment Canada, Canada

Arlin Hackman, World Wildlife Fund Canada, Canada

John Heissenbuttel, National Forest Products Association, USA

John Humke, The Nature Conservancy, USA

Peter Jutro, Environmental Protection Agency, USA

Reg Kucey, Agriculture Canada, Canada

Thomas Lovejoy, Smithsonian Institution, USA

Donald McAllister, Canadian Centre for Biodiversity, Canada

David Miller, Freeport-McMoran, USA

Kenton Miller, World Resources Institute, USA

Laurie Montour, Assembly of First Nations, Canada

Pat Mooney, Rural Advancement Fund International, Canada

John Morrison, Department of External Affairs, Canada

Ted Mosquin, Mosquin Bio-Information Ltd., Canada

David Neave, Wildlife Habitat Canada, Canada

Christopher Peters, Seventh Generation Fund for Indian Development, USA

Peter Raven, Missouri Botanical Gardens, USA

David Runnalls, Institute for Research on Public Policy, Canada

Henry Shands, U.S. Department of Agriculture, USA

Robert Szaro, U.S. Forest Service, USA

John Whiting, Canadian Wildlife Service, Canada

Sponsors:

American Forest Council

Chevron Corporation

Environment Canada

Freeport-McMoran Inc.

Noranda Forest Products Inc.

Pew Charitable Trusts

Robert Birks of the Panicaro Foundation

U.S. Department of Agriculture (Bureau of Land Management)

U.S. Department of Agriculture (Agricultural Research Service)

U.S. Department of Defense

U.S. Environmental Protection Agency

U.S. National Park Service

SOUTHEAST ASIA

17-19 JULY, 1991, WEST JAVA, INDONESIA

SURAYA AFIFF, INDONESIAN ENVIRONMENTAL FORUM (WALHI), INDONESIA

ACA SUGANDHY, ASSISTANT MINISTER OF STATE FOR POPULATION AND ENVIRONMENT, INDONESIA

CHARLES BARBER, WORLD RESOURCES INSTITUTE, USA

Organizing Committee:

Euis Ekawati, Ministry of State for Population and Environment

Susi Fauziah, WALHI

Siti Nissa Mardiah, Ministry of State for Population and Environment

Akhmad Saikhu, WALHI

Lori Scarpa, World Resources Institute

Karlina Sutaprawira, WALHI

Sponsors:

United Nations Development Programme

World Resources Institute

SOUTH AMERICA

JULY 8-10, 1991, BRASILIA, BRAZIL

MARIA TEREZA JORGE PADUA, FUNDACAO PRO-NATUREZA

(FUNATURA), BRAZIL

Steering Committee:

Fernando Antonio Thome Andrade, FUNATURA, Brazil

Fernando Antonio Barros, Journalist, Brazil

Lidio Coradin, Embrapa/Cenargen, Brazil

Maria Tereza Jorge Padua, FUNATURA, Brazil

Herbert O.R. Schubart, INPA, Brazil

Sponsors:

Canadian International Development Agency

The Heinz Charitable Trust

United Nations Development Programme

World Conservation Union (IUCN)

World Resources Institute

EUROPE

JULY 22-24, LONDON, U.K.

JACK HAWKES, LINNEAN SOCIETY, U.K.

VERNON HEYWOOD, IUCN PLANTS OFFICE, U.K.

Steering Committee:

Jan Cerovsky, World Conservation Union (IUCN), Czechoslovakia

Michael Claridge, University of Wales, United Kingdom

John Corkindale, Department of Environment, United Kingdom

Francoise Burhenne-Guilmin, Environmental Law Centre, Germany

Jack Hawkes, Linnean Society of London, United Kingdom

Vernon Heywood, World Conservation Union (IUCN), United Kingdom

Veit Koester, Ministry of Environment, Denmark

Jeff McNeely, World Conservation Union (IUCN), Switzerland

Robin Pellew, World Conservation Monitoring Centre, United Kingdom

Sponsors:

The Act on Environmental Assistance to East Europe, Danish Government

The European Economic Community

The Foreign and Commonwealth Office, U.K. Government

The Linnean Society of London

The Natural History Museum

Expert Workshops

Technical Consultation on Conserving Biological Diversity

SEPTEMBER 19-20, 1988, BOGOTA, COLOMBIA

ALEX COBO, ADVANCED EDUCATION FOUNDATION, COLOMBIA

Sponsors

Advanced Education Foundation

National Institute for Natural Resources

World Resources Institute

World Wildlife Fund/US

Conservation of Critical Ecosystems and Economic Development

OCTOBER 30 - 1 NOVEMBER, 1989, BANGKOK, THAILAND

COLIN REES, WORLD BANK, USA

NAI HTUN, UNITED NATIONS ENVIRONMENT PROGRAMME, THAILAND

KENTON MILLER, WORLD RESOURCES INSTITUTE, USA

WALTER REID, WORLD RESOURCES INSTITUTE, USA

Sponsors

Asian Development Bank

Economic and Social Commission for Asia and the Pacific

United Nations Environment Programme

U.S. Agency for International Development

World Bank

World Conservation Union (IUCN)

World Resources Institute

World Wildlife Fund—U.S.

Implementing the Biodiversity Conservation Strategy

NOVEMBER 30, 1990, PERTH, AUSTRALIA

(IUCN GENERAL ASSEMBLY)

JEFFREY MCNEELY, WORLD CONSERVATION UNION (IUCN), SWITZERLAND

KENTON MILLER, WORLD RESOURCES INSTITUTE, USA

Property Rights, Biotechnology and Genetic Resources

10-13 JUNE, 1991, NAIROBI, KENYA

CALESTOUS JUMA, AFRICAN CENTRE FOR TECHNOLOGY STUDIES, KENYA

WALTER REID, WORLD RESOURCES INSTITUTE, USA

BETTINA NG'WENO, AFRICAN CENTRE FOR TECHNOLOGY STUDIES, KENYA

Sponsors:

The Danish International Development Agency

International Development Research Centre

Stockholm Environment Institute

Swedish International Development Authority

Swedish Society for Conservation of Nature

United Nations Development Programme

United Nations Environment Programme

World Conservation Union (IUCN)

World Resources Institute

Information for Decision-Makers: How to Mobilize a Developing Nation's Biotic Wealth

JUNE 20-22, 1991, SAN JOSE, COSTA RICA

RODRIGO GAMEZ, NATIONAL BIODIVERSITY INSTITUTE (INBIO), COSTA RICA

KENTON MILLER, WORLD RESOURCES INSTITUTE, USA

Sponsors:

Canadian International Development Agency

The Heinz Charitable Trust

United Nations Development Programme

World Conservation Union (IUCN)

World Resources Institute

The Potential for Integration of Biodiversity Conservation Technologies

JULY 3-5, 1991, BRASILIA, BRAZIL

MARIA TEREZA JORGE PADUA, PRO-NATURE FOUNDATION (FUNATURA), BRAZIL

KENTON MILLER, WORLD RESOURCES INSTITUTE, USA

Sponsors:

Canadian International Development Agency

The Heinz Charitable Trust

Ministry of the Environment, Brazil

Secretary for Science and Technology, Brazil

United Nations Development Programme

World Conservation Union (IUCN)

World Resources Institute

International Conference on Women and Biodiversity

OCTOBER 4-6, 1991, CAMBRIDGE, MASSACHUSETTS

LEA BORKENHAGEN, HARVARD UNIVERSITY, USA

JULIA BOOMS, HARVARD UNIVERSITY, USA

JANET N. ABRAMOVITZ, WORLD RESOURCES INSTITUTE, USA

WALTER REID, WORLD RESOURCES INSTITUTE, USA

Sponsors:

Connie and Edward Bransilver

Edmund A. Stanley Jr.

Education for Action, Radcliffe College

Harvard College: Dean of Students

Harvard Institute of International Development

Radcliffe Union of Students

World Bank

World Resources Institute

Steering Committee:

Joan Martin-Brown, United Nations Environment Programme

Rosalie Huisinga Norem, U.S. Agency for International Development

Deborah Strauss, Diversity Magazine

Kenton Miller, World Resources Institute

Other Contributors

*The following individuals took part in consultations or workshops, prepared back- ground papers for the **Strategy**, contributed written comments, served on Steering Committees, or helped in the research and preparation of the manuscript.*

Janet N. Abramovitz, Associate, World Resources Institute, USA;

Abdulaziz Abuzinada, Secretary General, National Commission for Wildlife Conservation and Development, Saudi Arabia;

Rohini Acharya, MERIT, The Netherlands;

Soenartono Adisoemarto, Naturindo, Indonesia;

Suraya Afiff, Biodiversity Program Director, Indonesian Environmental Forum (WALHI), Indonesia;

Jorge Ahumedes, President, National Parks Foundation, Argentina;

Paul Aird, Professor, The Earth Sciences Center University of Toronto, Canada;

J. Akeroyd, United Kingdom;

Vickie Alaimo, Office of Voluntary & Humanitary Progs., USAID, Indonesia;

Rita Alfaro, Data Base Coordinator, National Institute of Biodiversity, Costa Rica;

Pablo Alfonso, University of the Philippines at Los Banos, the Philippines;

Cleber Alho, Brasilian Representative, WWF-WorldWide Fund for Nature, Brazil;

Hadi Alikodra, Deputy to the Assistant Minister for Natural Resources Conservation, Ministry of State for Population and Environment, Indonesia;

Porfirio Alino, Marine Science Institute, the Philippines;

Bob Allkin, Royal Botanical Gardens, United Kingdom;

Sergio Almeida, Forestry Engineer, Brasilian Institute for the Environment and Renewable Natural Resources (IBAMA), Brazil;

Mayra Altamirano C., Association of Biologists and Ecologists, Nicaragua;

Miguel Altieri, Associate Professor, University of California at Berkeley, USA;

Wdies Beves do Amaral, Professor, UNESP - Botucatu/SOS Mata Atlantica, Brazil;

C. Ambler, Globe Book Services, United Kingdom;

Rajo Ameresekere, Ministry of Environment, Sri Lanka;

Ira Amstadter, Madagascar Program Officer, World Wildlife Fund, USA;

James K. An, Curator and Chairman, Department of Zoology Taiwan Museum, Taiwan;

Germán Andrade, Nature Foundation, Colombia;

Martin Angel, Institute of Oceanographic Sciences, Deacon Laboratory, United Kingdom;

A. Aniol, Plant Breeding Institute, Poland;

Paulo de Tarso Zuquim Antas, Chief Biologist, CEMAVE/Brasilian Institute for the Environment and Renewable Natural Resources (IBAMA), Brazil;

Aldo Antonietti, Swiss Office on Environment, Forests, and Landscape, Switzerland;

Wilfredo Aragón, V. President, Coordinating Body - Indigenous Peoples' Organizations of the Amazon Basin (COICA), Peru;

Jorge Aranda B., National Association for Nature Conservation (ANCON), Panama;

Pedro Araya, Chief of the National Parks Section, National Corporation for Forestry (CONAF), Chile;

Guillermo Archibold, Director Pemasky, PEMASKY, Panama;

Oscar Arias, Agri-Biotechnology of Costa Rica, Costa Rica;

Khalid M.A. Arkanji, MEPA, Saudi Arabia;

Moacir Bueno Arruda, Brasilian Institute for the Environment and Renewable Natural Resources (IBAMA), Brazil;

Gilbert Arum, Indigenous Fruits Project Officer, Kenya Energy and Environment Organization, Kenya

Robert Arunga, Kenya Industrial Research Development Institute, Kenya

William Asigau, Department of Environment and Conservation, Papua New Guinea

Michael Atchia, EETU, United Nations Environment Programme, Kenya

Harris Surono Wardi Atmodjo, Chief of Directorate for Environmental Impact Analysis, Ministry of Forestry, Indonesia;

Ana Auer, Post-Graduate Student, Federal University of Paraná, Brazil;

Bruce Aylward, Research Associate, International Institute for Environment and Development (IIED), United Kingdom;

C.R. Babu, University of Delhi, India;

Danilo Balete, Haribon Foundation, Philippines;

Elisa Barahona, General Secretary for Environment, Spain;

James Barborack, Professor, Peace University, Costa Rica;

C. Barden, WWF, United Kingdom;

B.A. Barlow, CSIRO Division Plant Industry, Australia;

Ernesto Barriga B., Consultant, Colombia;

Jorge Eduardo Granja e Barros, FUNATURA, Brazil;

Mariluza Araujo Barros, Professor, Brazilian Botanical Society, Brazil;

John Barton, Stanford Law School, USA;

Valerie Barzetti, Panos Institute, United Kingdom;

Marjorie Beane, Development Director, World Resources Institute, USA;

Timothy Beatley, School of Architecture, USA;

Vitor Bechkek, Researcher, Brazilian Corporation for Agriculture Research - CPAC, Brazil;

Benjamin Beck, National Zoo, Smithsonian Institute, USA;

K. Beese, Commission of European Communities, Belgium;

Lekh Nath Belbase, National Planning Commission, Nepal;

G. Belchansky, Academy of Sciences of the USSR Institute of Ecology and Animal, USSR;

S. Beldescu, Romanian Academy, Romania;

J. Benfield, Natural History Museum, United Kingdom;

Bo Bengtsson, Director General, Swedish Agency for Research Cooperation with Developing Countries, Sweden;

Manuel Benitez, Programs Coordinator, IUCN Friedrich Ebert Foundation, El Salvador;

James Bennett, Aquatic Non-Game Specialist, Colorado Division of Wildlife, USA;

Peter Bennet, National Federation of Zoos, United Kingdom;

Woodraff Whitman Benson, Professor, UNICAMP, Brazil;

Wim Bergmans, Species Survival Commission, The Netherlands;

Angela Bernardes, USAID, Brazil

Dean Bibles, Director WA and OR Bureau of Land Management, USA;

Simone Bilderbeek, Netherlands National Committee for IUCN, The Netherlands;

Mona Bjorklund, Senior Program Officer, Environmental Management, United Nations Environment Programme (UNEP), Kenya;

Stephen Blackmore, Keeper of Botany, Natural History Museum, United Kingdom;

Delmar Blasco, Director of International Affairs, World Conservation Union (IUCN), Switzerland;

Mario S. Boiteux, Biologist, FUNATURA, Brazil;

Clovis Ricardo Scharape Borges, President, SPVS, Brazil;

Lea Borkenhagen, Harvard University, USA;

E. Boukvareva, Academy of Sciences of the USSR Institute of Ecology and Animal, USSR;

William Bourgeois, General Manager of Woodland Services, MacMillan Bloedel, Ltd., Canada;

Mario Boza, Vice Minister, Ministry of Natural Resources, Energy and Mines, Costa Rica;

David Brackett, Director General, Canadian Wildlife Service, Canada;

Maria Gorett Braga, Renewable Natural Resources Analyst, Nature Foundation of Tocantins (NATURATINS), Brazil;

Susan Bragdon, Consultant, United Nations Environment Programme (UNEP), Kenya;

Tore Brevik, Chief, IPA, UNEP, Nairobi, Kenya;

Alan Brewster, Vice President for Administration and Finance, World Resources Institute, USA;

Peter Bridgewater, Director, Australian National Parks and Wildlife Service, Australia;

Per Brinck, University of Lund, Sweden;

James Broadus, Director, Marine Policy Center, USA;

Warren Brockelman, Center for Conservation Biology, Mahidol University, Thailand;

Daniel Bromley, University of Wisconsin, USA;

Joyce Bromley, University of Wisconsin, USA;

Connie Brooks, Partner, Davis, Wright and Tremaine, USA;

S.J. Brooks, Natural History Museum, United Kingdom;

Mick Brown, Tasmanian Forestry Commission, Australia;

Rick Brown, Resource Specialist, National Wildlife Federation, USA;

William Brown, Waste Management, Inc., USA;

Stephen Brush, Associate Professor, University of California at Davis, USA;

Ludewig Buckup, Representative, AGAPAN, Brazil;

Gerardo Budowski, Director of Natural Resources, Peace University, Costa Rica;

Tamara Budowski, Horizontes, Costa Rica;

Bruce Bunting, Director, Asia Program, World Wildlife Fund, USA;

Jim Burbee, Chief Forester, Northwood Pulp and Timber Ltd, Canada;

Andrew Burbilge, Western Australian Dept. of Conservation and Land Management, Australia;

Francoise Burhenne-Guilmin, Environmental Law Centre, IUCN, Germany;

John Burke, Head, Communications Division, World Conservation Union (IUCN), Switzerland;

Sarah Burns, NGO Liaison, World Resources Institute, USA;

Rebecca Butterfield, North Carolina State University, USA;

Marie Bystrom, Environmental Program Officer, Agriculture Division, Swedish International Development Agency (SIDA), Sweden;

Milton Cabrera, Center for Conservation Studies (CECON), Guatemala;

Dulce Cacha, President, Foundation for Sustainable Development, Inc., Philippines

John Denys Cadman, Chief Environmental Coordinator, Eletronorte, Brazil;

Ibsen de Gusmao Camara, President, Brazilian Society for the Protection of the Environment, Brazil;

João Batista Drummond Camara, Chief of Protected Areas, Brasilian Institute for the Environment and Renewable Natural Resources (IBAMA), Brazil;

Faith Campbell, Senior Project Scientist, Natural Resources Defense Council, USA;

Arthur Campeau, Special Advisor for International Affairs to the Minister of Environment, Canada;

José Campoy, Biologist, Ecological Center of Sonora, Mexico;

Indra Candanedo, National Parks and Environment Foundation (PANAMA), Panama;

Vanderlei Canhos, Coordinator,Tropical Data Bases, Foundation "Andre Tosello", Brazil;

Joao Paulo Capobianco, Superintendent of Foundation SOS Mata Atlantica, Brazil;

Eric Cardich, Pachamama Society, Peru;

R.C.J. Carling, Chapmans & Hall, United Kingdom;

Gonzalo Castro, Program Manager, Western Hemisphere Shorebird Reserve Network, USA;

John Catena, Marine Policy Coordinator, Maine Coastal Program, USA

Henrique Cavalcanti, Brazilian Society for Environmental Technology, Brazil;

Roberto Cavalcanti, Professor, Brasilia University, Brazil;

Ana Isabel Cazemajou, University of Brasilia, Brazil;

Charles O. Cecil, U.S. Department of State, USA;

Flora Cerqueira, Consultant, UNDP, Brazil;

Paul Chabeda, Kenya Wildlife Service, Kenya;

Chris Chaney, U.S. Geological Survey, USA;

Maria Elfi Chavez, Nature Foundation, Colombia;

Ralph Cheesman, Chair, Mineral Industry Land Use Committee, Canada;

S. Chin, Western Australian Herbarium, Australia;

Mark Christensen, Russell McVeagh Solicitors, New Zealand;

M.F. Claridge, President, Linnean Society (London), United Kingdom;

H. A. Clark, Director General, Environment Canada, Canada;

Tim Clark, Yale University, USA;

David Cleveland, Research Associate, Native Seeds/SEARCH, USA;

Alex Cobo A., Division Director, Higher Education Foundation, Colombia;

Joel Cohen, Office of Agriculture, USAID, USA;

José Concepción Delgado, Biologist, INIFAP, Field Experiment Station, Zacatepec, Mexico;

David Cooper, Genetic Resources Action International, Spain;

Lidio Coradin, Brazilian Corporation for Farm and Agriculture Research (EMBRAPA), Brazil

Jane Corbett, Earthwatch Europe, United Kingdom;

John Cordell, Pacific Program Director, Cultural Survival, USA;

J. Corkindale, Department of Environment, United Kingdom;

Mireya Correa A., Smithsonian Researcher, Smithsonian Institution Tropical Research Center, Panama;

Cheryl Cort, World Resources Institute, USA;

Jorge Cortes, Biologist, University of Costa Rica, Costa Rica;

Judith Cortesão, Environmental Policy Advisor, SEMAM, Brazil;

José Pedro de Oliveira Costa, Consultant, World Conservation Union (IUCN), Brazil;

Sylvie Cote, Environment Canada, Canada;

Kathleen Courrier, Publications Director, World Resources Institute, USA;

Mauricio Coutinho, Amara dos Deputados, Legislative Advisor, Brazil

Gordon M. Cragg, National Cancer Institute, USA;

Wendy Craik, Assistant Executive Officer, Great Barrier Marine Park Authority, Planning and Management Section, Australia;

Doreen Crompton, World Bank, USA;

Debbie Crouse, Center for Marine Conservation, USA;

Gustavo Cruz, Department of Biology, National Autonomous University of Honduras, Honduras;

Marcos Cruz, Engineer, Associacão Pro-Fundacão Vespertina, Brazil;

Marios Antonio Cardoso Cruz, Associacão Pro-Fundacão Vespertina, Brazil;

Gustavo da Fonseca, Professor, University of Minas Gerais, Brazil;

Uttam Dabholkar, Chief, DPCU, United Nations Environment Programme, Kenya;

Chula Dahanayake, Law Department, University of Botswana, Botswana;

Kevin Dahl, Native Seeds/SEARCH, USA;

Kenneth Dahlberg, Department of Political Science, Western Michigan University, USA;

Lukito Daryadi, Assistant to the Minister of Forestry, Ministry of Forestry, Indonesia;

Bruce Davidson, Wildlife Society of Southern Africa, South Africa;

Peta Davies, Conservation Council of Western Australia, Australia;

Steven Davies, Landmark Consultancy, U.K.;

Gloria Davis, Chief, Division for Environment and Social Affairs, World Bank, USA;

S.D. Davis, World Conservation Union (IUCN), Switzerland;

Xue Dayuan, National Environmental Protection Agency, China;

Giovanni Carvalho de Amorim, Researcher, Brazil;

Eulalia A. Machado de Carbalho, Superintendent, Brasilian Institute for the Environment and Renewable Natural Resources (IBAMA), Brazil;

Eliani Alves de Carvalho, Assistant Coordinator, Rapporteur, UNCED 92, Brasilian Institute for the Environment and Renewable Natural Resources (IBAMA), Brazil;

Machado de Carvalho, Superintendent of Brasilian Institute for the Environment and Renewable Natural Resources (IBAMA), Brazil;

Gina de Ferrari, House of Representatives, USA;

Graciela de la Garza Garcia, General Director of Ecological Conservation, Secretariat of Urban Development and Ecology, Mexico;

Charles de Haes, Director General, Worldwide Fund for Nature, Switzerland;

Maria Pereira de Jarsioj, Second Secretary, Brazilian Embassy, Paraguay;

Marlen de Mendez, Secretariat, National Institute of Renewable Natural Resources and the Environment (INDERENA), Colombia;

Zulma Ricord de Mendoza, Director of National Patrimony, David J. Guzman Museum, El Salvador;

Carlos de Paco, Technical Director, National Parks Foundation, Costa Rica;

José de Ribamar Pereira, Chief Advisor, SEMATUR, Brazil;

Lalanath de Silva, Environmental Foundation, Sri Lanka;

Paulo de Torso Antas, Biologist, Head of the Center, Brasilian Institute for the Environment and Renewable Natural Resources (IBAMA), Brazil;

Matthijs de Vreede, Radio Nederland Training Centre, The Netherlands;

Daniel Debouck, Research Programme, IBPGR, Italy;

José Concepción Boyas Delgado, Researcher, Zacatepec Research Station, INIFAP-SARH, Zacatepec, Mexico;

Alonso Delgado, Consultant in Natural Resources, Costa Rica;

Tim Dendy, South Australian Dept. of Environment and Planning, Australia;

John Dennis, Supervisory Biologist, Wildlife & Vegetation Division, National Park Service, USA;

Robert Dennis, President, The Piedmont Environmental Council, USA;

Everett Deschenes, Manager of Forest Development, Fraser, INC., Canada;

Joe Dever, Consultant, USA;

Inés Dias, Information/Documentation Coordinator, SOS Mata Atlantica Foundation, Brazil;

Emma Díaz, National Commission on the Environment (CONAMA), Guatemala;

Elaine Dickinson, Program Assistant, Commission on Ecology, World Conservation Union (IUCN), Switzerland;

JoAnne DiSano, First Assistant Secretary, Australian Department of Arts, Sport, Environment, Tourism, Territories, Australia;

Akiko Domoto, Member, House of Councillors, Japan;

Eduardo Doryan, Costa Rica;

Eduardo Batista Dos Passos, Administrator of FUNATURA, Brazil;

L. Dotlacil, Research Institute of Crop Production, Czechoslovakia;

F. Doumen, Director, Oceanographic Museum of Monaco, Monaco;

Marc J. Dourojeanni, Chief, Environment Protection Division, Inter-American Development Bank, USA;

Paul Driver, Head, Conservation Services Division, World Conservation Union (IUCN), Switzerland;

Jack Dubois, Curator, Manitoba Museum of Man and Nature, Canada;

K.L. Duff, Chief Scientist, Nature Conservancy Council, U. K.;

Pat Dugan, Wetlands Programme, World Conservation Union (IUCN), Switzerland;

David Duthie, United Kingdom;

Donald Duvick, Affiliate Professor of Plant Breeding, Iowa State University, USA;

Mary Dyson, Environment Department, World Bank, USA;

Johannes Eck, Environment Secretary to the President of Brazil, Brazil;

William Eddy, President, Environmental Concerns International, USA;

Ione Egier, Consultant, SCT/PR, Brazil;

Thomas Eisner, Sherman Prof. of Biology, Cornell University, USA;

Mohamed El-Ashry, Director, Environment Department, World Bank, USA;

Daniel Elder, Marine Program, World Conservation Union (IUCN), Switzerland;

W.A. Ely, Clifton Park Museum, United Kingdom;

J. Ronald Engel, Professor of Social Ethics, Meadville/Lombard Theological School, USA;

Ron Erickson, Executive Director, British Columbia Nature Trust, Canada;

Kevin Erwin, Consulting Ecologist, USA;

Elsa Matilde Escobar, Research Coordinator, Fondo Fen Colombia, Colombia;

José Euceda, World Neighbors Office for Central America and the Caribbean, Honduras;

Ardith Eudey, International Primate Protection League, USA;

Dora H. Eudey, International Primate Protection League, USA;

Perry Fagan, Kenya Wildlife Service, Kenya;

Donald Falk, Director, Center for Plant Conservation, USA;

Helio Fallas, Minister, Ministry for Planning, Costa Rica;

Jorge Fallas, Director, Regional Program in Wildlife Management for Mesoamerica and the Caribbean, National University, Costa Rica;

L. Fandino, Natural History Museum, United Kingdom;

Henrik Faudel, United Nations Development Programme (UNDP), Costa Rica (PNUD), Costa Rica;

Jean-Marie Fayemi, Sustainable Agriculture Coordinator, Environmental Liaison Center International, Kenya;

Vitus Fernando, Coordinator for Asia and Pacific, World Conservation Union (IUCN), Switzerland;

Loumdis Maria Ferreira, Ecologist, FUNATURA, Brazil;

Alison Field-Juma, Initiatives Publishers, Kenya;

Netatua Fifita, Ministry of Lands Survey & Natural Resources, Tonga;

Adelmar Filho, Director, Rio Primatology Center, State Foundation of Environmental Engineering, Brazil

Aristides Filho, Environmental Reporter, Gazeta Mercantil S/A, Brazil;

Francisco Filho, Department Coordinator Cartography and Forests, Soils Institute, Brazil;

Michael Finley, Superintendent, U.S. Department of Interior, National Parks Service, Yosemite National Park, USA;

Nathan Flesness, International Species Information System, USA;

Wayne Fletcher, Australian Dept. of the Arts, Sport, Environment, Tourism and Territories, Australia;

Vladimir Flint, Institute for Nature Conservation, USSR;

Gustavo de Fonseca, Scientific Advisor, Biodiversity Foundation, and Professor, Conservation Biology, University of Minas Gerais, Brazil;

Linda Forbes, Zoological Society of London Institute of Zoology, United Kingdom;

M. Ford, Head of International Branch, Joint Nature Conservation Committee, United Kingdom;

Enrique Forero, Director of Research, Missouri Botanical Garden, USA;

P. Forey, Natural History Museum, United Kingdom;

Warwick Forge, Victorian Conservation Trust, Australia;

Rodrigo Fournier, Univision, Costa Rica;

Donald Fowler, Research Scientist, Forestry Canada, Canada;

Sarah Fowler, The Nature Conservation Bureau, United Kingdom;

Thomas Fox, Director, Center for International Development and Environment, World Resources Institute, USA;

George Francis, University of Waterloo, Canada;

Reinaldo Francisco Lourival, Pantanal Coordinator, Conservation International, Brazil;

Thomas Franklin, Wildlife Policy Dir., The Wildlife Society, USA;

Kigenyi Frederick, Ministry of Environmental Protection, Uganda;

Esbern Friis-Hansen, Centre for Development Research, Denmark;

Ian Fry, Wildlife Survival, Australia;

Marty Fujita, The Nature Conservancy, Indonesia;

Roy Funch, Brazil;

Madhav Gadgil, Director, Centre for Ecological Sciences, Indian Insitute of Science, India

Maria Galante, Geographer, Brasilian Institute for the Environment and Renewable Natural Resources (IBAMA), Brazil;

P. Galland, Swiss Commission of UNESCO, Switzerland;

Louis Gama, Executive Director, Bio Industry Assoc. (BIA), U. K.;

R. Gambell, International Whaling Commission, United Kingdom;

Rodrigo Gamez, Director, National Institute of Biodiversity (INBIO), Costa Rica;

Dutra Garcia, President, Naturatins Foundation, Brazil;

Lina Andrea Garcia, Executive Director, Foundation for Green Reserves in Colombia, Colombia;

Neil Gardiner, Kenya Wildlife Services, Kenya;

John Gardner, AGCOR of Australia, Australia;

Ian Gauld, Natural History Museum, United Kingdom;

John Gavitt, Enforcement Officer, CITES Secretariat, Switzerland;

H. Gee, *Nature*, United Kingdom;

Shirley Geer, Director of Communications, World Resources Institute, USA;

D. Geldman, Herbarium, Kamarov Botanical Institute, USSR;

Dalmo Giacometti, Brazilian Corporation for Farm and Agriculture Research (EMBRAPA), National Center of Genetic Resources and Biotechnology, Brazil;

Vinay Gidwani, University of California at Berkeley, USA;

Dow Given, Dept. Scientific and Industrial Research, United Kingdom;

Gerry Glezier, EMDI, Indonesia;

Bruce Goldstein, Consultant, USA;

Arturo Gomez-Pompa, Director, Department of Botany & Plant Sciences, University of California, USA;

Ada Goncalves, Technical Programs/Project Coordinator for the Environment, FINEP, Brazil;

Antonio Gonzales, Planning and Research Technician, Institute of Applied Economics (IPEA), Brazil;

Maria Gonzalez, National Council on Protected Areas (CONAP), Guatemala;

J.M. Gopo, Biological Sciences Dept., Univ. of Zimbabwe, Zimbabwe;

Gary Graham, Marine Fisheries Specialist, Sea Grant, USA;

Barry Greengrass, Vice Secretary-General, International Union for Protection of New Varieties of Plants, Switzerland;

Colin Groves, Australian National University, Australia;

Michael Gucovsky, Deputy Assistant Administrator and Director, United Nations Development Programme (UNDP), USA;

Estella Guier, UNEP, Costa Rica;

João Regis Guillamon, Research Scientist, Forestry Institute, Brazil;

Lothar Gundling, Environmental Law Centre, IUCN, Germany;

Anil Gupta, Chairman, Research and Publications, Indian Institute of Management, India;

Erich Haber, Associate Curator of Vascular Plants, Canadian Museum of Natural Resources, Canada;

Arlin Hackman, Director, Endangered Species Campaign, World Wildlife Fund Canada, Canada;

Herman Haeruman, National Development Planning Agency (Bappenas), Indonesia;

Sharon Haines, Forest Environment, International Paper, USA;

N.F. Halbertsma, WWF, The Netherlands;

Gonzalo Halffter, Director General, Instituto de Ecologia, Mexico;

Mark Halle, Director of Development, World Conservation Union (IUCN), Switzerland;

A. Hamilton, Plant Conservation Officer, WWF, United Kingdom;

Andrew Hamilton, Director, Special Projects, Rawson Academy of Aquatic Science, Canada;

Lawrence Hamilton, Research Associate, East-West Center, USA;

Allen Hammond, Director, Program in Resource and Environmental Information, World Resources Institute, USA;

P. Hammond, Natural History Museum, United Kingdom;

Maria Hanai, University of São Paulo, Brazil;

L.L. Hankla, Partner, Andrews & Kurth, USA;

D.J.L. Harding, School of Applied Sciences, United Kingdom;

J. Hardon, Dutch National Genebank, The Netherlands;

Barbara Hardy, WorldWide Fund for Nature (WWF), Australia;

Paulo Harkot, Executive Secretary, SUDEMA/State Management Commission, Tocoseiro, Brazil;

David Harmon, Deputy Exec. Dir., The George Wright Society, USA;

Jill Harris, Conservation Council of Western Australia, Australia;

Soedjadi Hartono, Secretary, Ministry of Forestry, Indonesia;

Gary Hartshorn, Vice President, Science, World Wildlife Fund, USA;

D. Harvey, University of Newcastle-Upon-Tyne, United Kingdom;

David Haskell, The George Wright Society, USA;

Doc Hatfield, Cattleman Association, Hatfield Ranch, USA;

J.G. Hawkes, University of Birmingham, United Kingdom;

D.L. Hawksworth, Director, International Mycological Inst., U. K.;

R. Hazell, The Nuffield Foundation, United Kingdom;

J. Hemming, Director/Secretary, Royal Geographical Society, U.K.;

Ole Hendrickson, Coordinator, Forestry Canada Science Directorate, Canada

Armando Hernández, Colombian Fund for Scientific Research and Special Projects Francisco José de Caldas, Colombia;

Jorge Hernández, Scientific Advisor, National Institute of Renewable Natural Resources and the Environment (INDERENA), Colombia;

Monica Herzig, RAMSAR, Switzerland;

Vernon Heywood, Chief Scientist, Plant Conservation, World Conservation Union (IUCN), United Kingdom;

Elaine Hoagland, Executive Director, Association of Systematics Collections, USA;

Sandra Hodge, Research Associate, University of Virginia, USA;

John Hodges, Rare Breeds International, Italy;

Marjorie Holland, Director, Ecological Society of America, USA;

M. Hollands, Environmental Management Unit, Otley College, U. K.;

L. Holly, Research Centre for Agrobotany, Hungary;

Elizabeth Honda, Environmental Program Supervisor, CNPq, Brazil;

Cao Hongfa, Director, The Institute of Ecology, China;

Sun Honglie, Vice President, Chinese Academy of Sciences, China;

S. Hopper, Western Australia Department of Conservation and Land Management, Australia;

Christiane Horowitz, Forestry Engineer, Brasilian Institute for the Environment and Renewable Natural Resources (IBAMA), Brazil;

Donna House, Tribal Lands Protection Planner, The Nature Conservancy, USA;

Eric Howard, Law & Policy Info. Officer, IUCN Law Centre, Germany;

Nay Htun, Director/Regional Representative for Asia and Pacific, United Nations Environment Programme (UNEP), Thailand;

Wendy Hudson, Duke University, USA;

D.G. Hughes, Zoological Society of Glasgow, Scotland;

John Humke, Vice President, The Nature Conservancy, USA;

C. Humphries, Natural History Museum, United Kingdom;

Guillermo Hurtado, Executive Director, Nature Foundation, Colombia;

J. Huyler, Keystone Center, USA;

Jorge Illueca, Coordinator of Environmental Mgt., Chief, Terrestrial Ecosystems Branch, UNEP, Nairobi, Kenya;

Christoph Imboden, Director, International Council for Bird Preservation, United Kingdom;

Hussein Isack, National Museums of Kenya, Kenya;

M.A. Isahakia, Director/Chief Executive, National Museums of Kenya;

Esko Jaarkoda, Ministry of Environment, Finland;

Paul Jahnige, Yale University, USA;

Richard Jakob-Hoff, Auckland Zoo, New Zealand;

Malcolm Jansen, World Bank, USA;

Daniel Janzen, Professor, University of Pennsylvania, USA;

Jon Jarvis, The George Wright Society, USA;

Hadley Jenner, Mennonite Central Committee, Kenya;

Jan Jenner, Mennonite Central Committee, Kenya;

Deborah Jensen, University of California at Berkeley, USA;

C. Jermy, Natural History Museum, United Kingdom;

Belkis Jiménez, National Association for Nature Conservation (ANCON), Panama;

Nels Johnson, Associate, World Resources Institute, USA;

Randall Johnson, International Society for Preservation of Tropical Forests, USA;

Timothy Johnson, ICBP, United Kingdom

Maria Carolina Lyra Jorge, University of Botucatu, Brazil;

Eugene Joubert, Ministry of Wildlife, Conservation and Tourism, Namibia;

Calestous Juma, Executive Director, African Centre for Technology Studies (ACTS), Kenya;

Peter Jutro, Senior Scientist, U.S. Environmental Protection Agency, USA;

Christine Kabuye, Botanist-in-Charge, E. African Herbarium, Kenya;

Maximo Kalaw, President, Haribon Foundation; President, Green Forum, the Philippines;

Tabitha Kanogo, Kenyatta University, Kenya;

Promila Kapoor, Project Officer, Commonwealth Science Council, U.K.;

Patrick Karani, African Centre for Technology Studies, Kenya;

Gakeri Kariuki, University of Nairobi, Kenya;

Z. Karpowicz, World Conservation Monitoring Centre, United Kingdom;

Peter Karsten, Director, Calgary Zoological Society, Canada;

Kuswata Kartawinata, UNESCO, Indonesia;

Masakazu Kashio, Regional Forest Officer, Food and Agriculture Organization, Thailand;

Ryosuke Kato, Reforestation and Training Project, Royal Forest Department, Thailand;

Ronald Kaufman, District Manager, Bureau of Land Management, Eugene District Office, USA;

R.W. J. Keay, United Kingdom;

Stjepan Keckes, UNEP, Switzerland;

Graeme Kelleher, Chairman, Great Barrier Reef Marine Authority, Australia

Stephen Kellert, School of Forestry, Yale University, USA;

Michael Kennedy, World Wide Fund for Nature, Australia;

M. Kent, Natural History Museum, England, United Kingdom;

Patrice Kent, University of Washington, USA;

Gene Kersey, Regional Coordinator for Biodiversity, Environmental Protection Agency, USA;

Mohamed Momin Khan, Dept. of Wildlife and National Parks, Malaysia;

Sergei Khromov, Communication Programme Officer, UNEP, Kenya;

Kihika Kiambi, Seed Project Officer, Kenya Energy and Environment Organization, Kenya

Jiro Kikkawa, The University of Queensland, Australia;

Lee Kimball, Senior Associate, Institutions, World Resources Institute (WRI), USA;

B. Kirsop, Cambridge University, United Kingdom;

Margaret Klinowska, University of Cambridge Research Group in Mammalian Ecology, United Kingdom;

S. Knees, Royal Botanic Garden, United Kingdom;

Dagoberto Koehntopp, Advisor, Ministry of Economy, Housing and Planning, Institute of Applied Economics (IPEA) - CMR, Brazil;

William Koemen, Co-Founder, Native Resource Coalition, USA;

Veit Koester, Ministry of the Environment, Denmark;

F. Krahulec, Institute of Botany, Czechoslovak Academy of Science, Czechoslovakia;

Royanne Kremer, The International Society for Preservation of the Tropical Rainforest, USA;

Hartmut Krugman, International Development Research Center, Kenya;

Z. Krzeminski, Ministry of Environmental Protection, Poland;

Gerald Kuchling, Dept. of Zoology, University of Western Australia, Australia;

Guy Kula, Dept. of Environment and Conservation, Papua New Guinea;

Elmer Kure, Agricultural Representative, Alberta Fish and Game Association, Canada;

Indah Dianti Kusuma, National Development Planning Agency, Indonesia;

Edward LaRoe, Director, Cooperative Research Units, U.S. Fish and Wildlife Service, USA;

Thor Larsen, Adviser, Norwegian Agency for Development Cooperation, Norway;

Abdul Latiff Mohd, Faculty of Life Sciences, National University of Malaysia, Malaysia;

Clark LeBlanc, Population Program, Audubon Society, USA;

Bruce Leighty, Biodiversity Support Program, WWF, USA;

J.M. Lenn'e, Natural Resources Institute, United Kingdom;

C. Leon, Royal Botanic Gardens, United Kingdom;

Pedro León, President, National Parks Foundation, Costa Rica;

Michael Lesnick, Vice President, The Keystone Center, USA;

Connie Lewis, The Keystone Center, USA;

Mpande Lewis, Ministry of Community and Cooperation, Kenya;

Steven Light, Special Assistant to the Exec. Director, South Florida Management District, USA;

Kreg Lindberg, Ecotourism Society, USA;

Scott Morrow Lindbergh, Researcher, Brazil;

Walter Lindley, Treasurer, Friends of Pronatura, Inc., USA;

Robert Linn, Executive Director, The George Wright Society, USA;

Yu Hu Liu, Institute of Botany, China;

Eduardo Lizano, Consejeros Economicos, Costa Rica;

Roberto Espinosa Llanos, Advisor, Coordinating Body for the Indigenous Peoples' Organizations of the Amazon Basin (COICA), Peru;

Bindu Lohani, Manager, Environment Division, Asian Development Bank, Philippines;

Larry Lohmann, The Ecologist, Editorial Dept., United Kingdom;

Paul Loiselle, Curator of Freshwater Fishes, New York Aquarium, New York Zoological Society, USA;

T. Long, WWF International, Belgium;

Sally Loomis, Yale University, USA;

Jose Claudio Lima Lopes, Accountant, FUNATURA, Brazil;

Carlos Lopez-Ocaña, Environmental Specialist, Inter-American Development Bank, USA;

Thomas Lovejoy, Assistant Secretary of External Affairs, Smithsonian Institute, USA;

David Lowe, Coordinator, Indigenous Food Plants Programme, Kenya;

P.H.C. Lucas, Chairman, Commission on National Parks and Protected Areas, IUCN, New Zealand;

Oscar Lucke, Central American Regional Office, IUCN, Costa Rica

Kuang-Yang Lue, National Taiwan University, Taiwan;

Evans Luseno, Kenya Times, Kenya;

Laurie MacDonald, Chair, Biodiversity Resource Group, Sierra Club United Nations NGO Representative, USA;

Kathy MacKinnon, World Wide Fund for Nature, Indonesia;

Don E. McAllister, Canadian Centre for Biodiversity, Canada;

Jerry McCormick-Ray, Research Coordinator, National Aquarium, USA;

Alison McCusker, Head of Research, IBPGR - Rome, Italy;

Janet McGowan, Attorney, Cultural Survival, USA;

Roger McManus, President, Center for Marine Conservation, USA;

Jeffrey McNeely, Chief Conservation Officer, IUCN, Switzerland;

Richard McNeil, Cornell University, USA;

R.C. Macer, Cherry Trees, United Kingdom;

Rajeshwari Mahalingam, M.S. Swaminathan Research Foundation, India;

P.J. Mahler, Special Adviser to the Director-General, United Nations Food and Agriculture Organization (FAO), Italy;

Johnathan Majer, School of Biology, Curtin University of Technology, Australia;

Boniface Makau, Office of the President, Kenya;

Silvanus Makhong'o, Insurance Marketer, Kenya;

Juan Mayr Maldonado, Executive Director, Foundation Pro-Sierra Nevada de Santa Marta, Colombia;

Edward Maltby, University of Exeter, United Kingdom;

Ted Manning, Chief, Conservation Strategies, Environment Canada, Canada;

Aldo Manos, Mediterranean Regional Seas Programme, UNEP, Kenya;

Albert Manville, Senior Staff Wildlife Biologist, Defenders of Wildlife, USA;

Jouve Marcel, Ministry of Environment, France;

Milton Mariani, Geografo, Associacão Pro-Vespertina, Brazil;

Jean-Pierre Martel, Director, Forest Environment, Canadian Pulp & Paper Association, Canada;

Roberto Martin, Consultant, USA;

Joan Martin-Brown, Chief of Washington Office, UNEP, USA;

Roderic Mast, V. President for Asia, Conservation International, USA;

Jessica Mathews, Vice President, World Resources Institute, USA;

Emmah Matias, Kenya Agricultural Research Institute, Kenya;

Sharon Matola, Director, Belize Zoo & Tropical Education Center, Belize;

S.C. Maudgal, Advisor, Ministry of Environment and Forestry, India;

Claudia Maria Maury, Biologist, FUNATURA, Brazil;

N. Maxted, University of Southampton, United Kingdom;

Valmira Mecenas, Technician, Secretary of Science and Technology, SEMATEC, Brazil;

S. Meer, Counselor for Scientific and Technical Affairs, U.S. Embassy, Mexico City, USA;

Chanpen Mekrati, Research Assistant in Science & Technology Education, UNESCO, Thailand;

Meng Xianlin, China Wildlife Conservation Association, China;

Gray Merriam, President, International Association for Landscape Ecology, Canada;

Judy Messer, Nature Conservation Council of New South Wales, Australia;

Jack Metzger, Arizona Cattle Growers, USA;

Miguel Milano, Professor, Federal University of Paraná, Brazil;

Kerrie Milburn-Clark, Business Council of Australia, Australia;

Connie Millar, Geneticist, Pacific Southwest Station, USDA Forest Service, USA;

Carlos Miller, Director, Victoria Amazonic Foundation, Brazil;

John Milton, President, Threshold, Inc., Colorado, USA;

Russ Mittermeier, President, Conservation International, USA;

Haruo Miyata, Program Officer, UNEP, Thailand;

John Monarch, Senior Ecologist, Chevron Corporation, USA;

Sandra Moniaga, Coordinator Environmental Law Program, Indonesian Environmental Forum (WALHI), Indonesia;

Camila Montecinos, Center of Education and Technology, Chile;

Nigel Moore, Deputy Director Development Assistance Division, Ministry of External Relations and Trade, New Zealand;

Mario Moraes, Advisor, Brasilian Institute for the Environment and Renewable Natural Resources (IBAMA), Brazil;

Monica Moraes, Herbario Nacional de Bolivia, Bolivia;

Hideyuki Mori, Environment Specialist, Asian Development Bank, the Philippines;

John Morris, Translator, ELECTRONORTE, Brazil;

John Morrison, Energy and Environment Division, Canada;

L. Mound, Natural History Museum, United Kingdom;

Rodger Lewis Mpande, Ministry of Community and Coop Development, Zimbabwe;

J.K. Muchae, Kenyas Industrial Property Office (KIPO), Kenya;

John Mugabe, Biopolicy Institute of the African Centre for Technology Studies, The Netherlands;

Namukolo Mukutu, Ministry of Water Lands and Natural Resources, Zambia;

Arnaldo Carlos Muller, Advisor to the Director, Itaipú Binacional, Puerto Rico;

Danny Wahyu Munggoro, Indonesian NGO Network for Forest Conservation (SKEPHI), Indonesia;

Kirk Munro, Chair, Clean Ocean Committee, Maritime Fisherman's Union, Canada;

Enrique Murgeuitio, Green Heritage Foundation, Colombia;

M.G. Murray, University of Cambridge, United Kingdom;

James Musis, Lecturer, Faculty of Law, Makerere University, Kampala, Uganda;

Wanjiku Mwagiru, UNCED Nairobi Liaison, Kenya;

Norman Myers, Consultant in Environment and Development, U. K.;

Gary Nabhan, Chairman, Native Seeds/SEARCH, USA;

Makoto Nakamura, Director of the Environment Department, Japan International Cooperation Agency, Japan;

Daniel Navid, Secretary General, RAMSAR Convention, Switzerland;

J. Ndeberi, University of Burundi, Burundi;

David Neave, Executive Director, Wildlife Habitat Canada, Canada;

G. Nechay, Ministry for Environment, Hungary;

Leo Neto, Biology Student, Brazil;

Timothy Richard New, Royal Zoological Soc. of London, U.K.;

Bettina Ng'weno, African Centre for Technology Studies (ACTS), Kenya;

Magnus Ngoile, Institute of Marine Science, Kenya;

E.M. Nicholson, Earthwatch - Europe, United Kingdom;

Ebbe S. Nielsen, Comonwealth Scientific And Research Organization CSIRO, Australia;

Anders Nilsson, Swedish Society for Nature Conservation, Sweden;

John Wanjau Njoroge, Director, Kenya Institute of Farms, Kenya;

Eliana Nogueira, President, Botanical Society of Brazil, Brazil;

Richard Norgaard, Professor, Univ. of California-Berkeley, USA;

David Norriss, Corporate Environmental/Safety Department, Freeport-McMoran, Inc., USA;

Elliot Norse, Chief Scientist, Center for Marine Conservation, USA;

Carlos Noton, National Forestry Corporation (CONAF), Chile;

John Ntambirweki, Lecturer in Public Law, University of Nairobi, Kenya;

J.O. Nyagua, Ministry of Research Science and Technology, Kenya;

Johnson Nyangeri, National Council for Science and Technology, Kenya;

Brian Nyberg, Manager, Wildlife Habitat Research, Canada;

F.B. O'Connor, Joint Nature Conservation Committee, United Kingdom;

Robin O'Malley, Associate Director, Council on Environmental Quality, USA;

H. Obara, WWF-Japan, Nature Conservation Society of Japan, Japan;

Argwings Odera, Nation Newspapers, Kenya;

Rispa Odongo, Ministry of Research, Science and Technology, Kenya;

Pietronella van den Oever, Head, Social Science Division, IUCN, Switzerland;

H.W.O. Okoth-Ogendo, Centre of African Family Studies, Kenya;

J.B. Ojwang, Professor of Law, University of Nairobi, Kenya;

Reuben Olembo, Deputy Assistant Executive Director, United Nations Environment Programme (UNEP), Kenya;

Perez Olindo, African Wildlife Foundation, Kenya;

Rosa de Oliveira, Junior Legislative Advisor, Brazil;

Silvio Olivieri, Conservation International, USA;

J.A. Omotola, Faculty of Law, University of Lagos, Nigeria;

Jorge Orejuela, Chief, Environment and Natural Resource Section, Higher Education Foundation, Colombia

Gordon Orians, Professor, University of Washington, USA;

Douglass Owen, Geologist, U.S. Geological Survey, USA;

Thomas Owen, Strategic Planning Advisor, EMDI Project, State Ministry for Population and Environment, Indonesia;

?. Owino, Senior Scientist, International Council for Research in Agroforestry, Kenya;

Maria Tereza Jorge Padua, President, FUNATURA, Brazil;

Suzana & Claudio Padua, Mico-Leao-Preto Project, USA;

William Paleck, Park Superint., Saguaro National Monument, USA;

Victor Pandjaitan, Program Specialist, United States Agency for International Development (USAID) Indonesia;

David Papps, National Parks and Wildlife Service, New South Wales, Australia;

Phil Paradine, Canadian International Development Agency (CIDA), Indonesia;

Federico Paredes, Advisor to the Minister, Ministry of Natural Resources, Energy and Mines, Costa Rica;

G.L.J. Paterson, Natural History Museum, United Kingdom;

G.A. Pattison, Horticultural Advisor, National Council for Conservation of Plants and Gardens, United Kingdom;

George Paul, Co-Chair, Synthesis Committee, The Foundation for BioDiversity, USA;

Bob Pegler, Assistant Secretary, Dept. of Arts, Sports, Environment, Tourism and Territories, Australia;

Egbert Pelinck, Environmental Advisor, Ministry of Foreign Affairs, The Netherlands;

Robin Pellew, Director, World Conservation Monitoring Centre, U.K.;

M. Pencic, Federal Secretariat for Development, Yugoslavia

Mike Penfold, Asistant Director of Land's Resources, Bureau of Land Management, USA;

Adriano Peracchi, President, Brazilian Zoological Society, Brazil;

Jose de Ribamar Rodrigues Pereira, Chief, SEMATUR, Brazil;

Ajith Perera, Landscape Ecologist, Ontario Ministry of Natural Resources, Canada;

Ramón Perezgil, Natural History Institute (FUNDAMAT), Chiapas, Mexico;

Chris Peters, Seventh Generation Fund for Indian Development, USA;

V. Petrosjan, Academy of Sciences of the USSR Institute of Ecology and Animal, USSR;

Allan Phillips, Denver Museum of Natural History, USA;

Barbara Pickersgill, Dept. of Agricultural Botany, University of Reading, United Kingdom;

Sun Qui Ping, China Center Television, China;

E. Phil Pister, Executive Secretary, Desert Fishes Council, USA;

Alfio Piva, Director of Biodiversity, National Biodiversity Institute, Costa Rica;

Mark Plotkin, World Wildlife Fund, USA;

V. Pomakov, Ministry of Environment, Bulgaria;

Ismael Ponciano, Center for Conservation Studies (CECON), Guatemala;

Duncan Poore, International Institute for Environment and Development, United Kingdom;

Darrell Posey, Museo Goeldi, Brazil;

Bill Posstel, The Nature Conservancy, Brazil;

Kathy Potter, Missouri Botanical Garden, USA;

Ghillean Prance, Director, Royal Botanical Gardens, England;

Robert Prescott-Allen, Senior Consultant, PADATA, Canada;

P.C.H. Pritchard, Florida Audubon Society, USA;

L. Profirov, Ministry of Environment, Bulgaria;

R.W. Purdie, Australian Heritage Commission, Australia;

Allen Putney, Director, Caribbean Natural Resources Institute (CANARI), U.S. Virgin Islands;

Kathy Quick, Indonesian Environmental Forum (WALHI), Indonesia;

Rosario Ortiz Quijano, Biodiversity Program Coordinator, Foundation Pro-Sierra Nevada de Santa Marta, Colombia;

Ayle Quintao, Marketing Advisor, Permanent Forum for Traditional Values and the Environment, Brazil;

George Rabb, Director, Brookfield Zoo, Chicago Zool. Park, and Chairman, Species Survival Commission, IUCN, USA;

Omar Abdul Rahman, Science Advisor to the Prime Minister, Malaysia;

M.A. Rai Madoya, Programme Officer, Canadian Embassy, Indonesia;

M.H. Ramos-Lopes, SNPRCN-Nucleo de Botanica, Portugal;

Mario Ramos, Program Officer for Mexico, World Wildlife Fund, USA;

M.S. Ranatunga, Forestry Advisor, Ministry of Lands, Irrigation, Forestry, and Mahaweli Development, Sri Lanka;

Y. S. Rao, Regional Forestry Officer, United Nations Food and Agriculture Organization (FAO), Thailand;

Barbara Rashbass, The Wolfson Foundation, United Kingdom;

Peter Raven, Director, Missouri Botanical Garden, USA;

Carlton Ray, Professor, University of Virginia, USA;

Ruben B. Rayalk, Protected Areas and Wildlife Bureau, the Philippines;

Michael Redclift, Professor, University of London, United Kingdom;

Colin Rees, Senior Ecologist, World Bank, USA;

Rodolfo Rendon, President, Nature Foundation, Ecuador;

Robert Repetto, Director, Program in Economics and Technology, World Resources Institute, USA;

Raj Ressarah, Friends of the Earth, India;

Maria Reyna de A., Director, La Laguna Botanical Gardens, El Salvador;

Deok-Gil Rhee, Director, Environmental Ecology Division, Ministry of Environment, Korea;

F. Ribeiro, Biologist, FUNATURA, Brazil

Richard Rice, Sr. Resource Economist, The Wilderness Society, USA;

V. Rich, New Scientist, United Kingdom;

Sonia Rigueira, Director, Conservation International, Brazil;

Herman Rijksen, Head of Dept. of International Cooperation, Ministry of Agriculture and Fisheries, The Netherlands;

Hidely Rizzo, Project Manager, SEMAM/PR, Brazil;

Jane Robertson, Division of Ecological Sciences, UNESCO, France;

Alejandro Robles, Technical Institute of Higher Education/Guaymas, Mexico;

Sergio Rocha, Agronomist, Brasilian Institute for the Environment and Renewable Natural Resources (IBAMA), Brazil;

Eric Rodenburg, Research Director, *World Resources Report*, World Resources Institute, USA;

Carlos Rodriguez, Environmental Lawyer, Costa Rica;

Miguel Angel Rodriguez, President, Legislative Assembly, Costa Rica;

J. Rodwell, Institute of Environment and Biology, United Kingdom;

Mario Rojas, La Amistad Conservation Area, National Park Service, Ministry of Natural Resources, Costa Rica;

Holmes Rolston, Colorado State Univ. Department of Philosophy, USA;

Aldemaro Romero, Executive Director, Venezuelan Foundation for Biodiversity Conservation (BIOMA), Venezuela;

Celso Roque, Undersecretary, Department of Natural Resources, Philippines;

G. Kristin Rosendal, Fridtjof Nansen Institute, Norway;

Pedro Ruestra, Peruvian Foundation for Nature Conservation (FPCN), Lima, Peru;

Iwona Rummel-Bulska, Chief, ELIU, United Nations Environment Programme, Switzerland;

John Ryan, Research Associate, Worldwatch Institute, USA;

Carlos Saavedra, Program Officer, World Wildlife Fund, USA;

Andres Sada, President, Pronatura, AC, Mexico;

Mark Sagoff, Director, Ctr. for Philosophy and Public Policy, USA;

Oscar Lopez Salaberry, Minister, Patagonia Development Commission, Presidency, Argentina;

Renato Salazar, Southeast Asia Regional Institute for Community Education, the Philippines;

Emil Salim, Minister of State for Population and Environment, Indonesia;

Anajulia Salles, Director, Botanical Gardens of Brazil, Brazil;

Hal Salwasser, Project Director, U.S. Forest Service, USA;

Mr. Sulayman S. Samba, Principal Secretary, Ministry of Natural Resources and the Environment, The Republic of Gambia;

Heliodoro Sanchez, Scientific Advisor, National Inst. for Renewable Natural Resources and the Environment (INDERENA), Colombia;

Vicente Sanchez, Ambassador of Chile to UNEP, Chair, Convention on Biodiversity, Kenya;

Roger W. Sant, Chairman of the Board and Chief Executive Officer, AES Corporation, USA;

Charles Santiapillai, WWF-Asia Programme, Indonesia;

Vitor do Espirito Santo, Forestry, FUNATURA, Brazil;

Setijati Sastrapradja, National Center for Research in Biotechnology, Indonesia;

Kathryn Saterson, Director, Biodiversity Support Program, USA;

Paul Sattler, Acting Assistant Director, Queensland National Parks and Wildlife Service, Australia;

Don Saunders, Dept. of Conservation and Environment, Australia;

Richard Saunier, Environmental Specialist, Organization of American States, USA;

Eleanor Savage, Director, Office of Ecology, Health and Conservation, Department of State, USA;

Melissa Savage, Department of Geography, University of California at Los Angeles, USA;

John Sawhill, President, The Nature Conservancy, USA;

Jeffrey Sayer, Senior Programme Advisor, Forest Conservation, Tropical Forests Program, World Conservation Union (IUCN), Switzerland;

Celso Schenkel, Ecosystems Director, Brasilian Institute for the Environment and Renewable Natural Resources (IBAMA), Brazil;

Manfred Schneider, Junior Program Officer, UNEP, Kenya;

Herbert Schubart, Researcher, National Institute for Investigations of the Amazon (INPA), Brazil;

Richard Schultes, Professor, Harvard University, USA;

Jeff Schweitzer, Senior Science Policy Advisor, USAID, USA;

Mats Segnestam, Senior Policy Advisor, Swedish International Development Authority (SIDA), Sweden;

Abu Y.M. Selim, Deputy Regional Representative, UNDP, Thailand;

Lester Seri, Dept. Environment and Conservation, Papua New Guinea;

Toshifumi Serizawa, Coordinator, Research and Training in Reforestation Project, Royal Forest Department, Thailand;

L.O. Sese, Kenya Industrial Property Office (KIPO), Kenya;

R.C. Sharma, Regional Adviser, UNESCO, Thailand;

E. Shaughnessy, Natural History Museum, United Kingdom;

Susan Shen, Ecologist, World Bank, USA;

John Shores, Consultant, USA;

M.G.C. Shouten, The Netherlands Foundation for International Nature Protection, The Netherlands;

Surendra Shrestha, Chief Administrator, International Centre for Integrated Mountain Development, Nepal;

Gerard Siero, Landmark Consultancy, U.K.;

Ana Christina M.F. Sigueira, Scientific Researcher, Forestry Institute, Brazil;

Danilo Silva, ECOCIENCIA, Ecuador;

Jose Guerra Silva, Assistant Manager, Electric Corporation of São Paulo (CESP), Brazil;

Maria Silva, UNDP, Costa Rica;

Ligia Silveira, Post-graduate student, UNICAMP, Brazil;

Ram Badan Singh, Regional Forest Resources Officer, United Nations Food and Agriculture Organization (FAO), Thailand;

Samar Singh, Additional Secretary, Ministry of Environment and Forests, India;

Ana Sittenfeld, Director of Research and Development, National Institute of Biodiversity, Costa Rica;

J. Skoupy, Senior Program Officer, UNEP, Kenya

Ralph Slatyer, Department of the Prime Minister's Cabinet, Australia;

Campbell Smith, Natural History Museum, United Kingdom;

Clifford Smith, National Park Service Cooperative Park Studies Unit, USA;

Michael Smith, Museum of Natural History, USA;

R.D. Smith, Royal Botanic Gardens, United Kingdom;

Stephen Smith, V. President/Manager, Weyerhaeuser Canada Ltd., Canada;

Nicholas Smythe, Smithsonian Tropical Research Institution, Panama;

Kasem Snidvongs, Director General, Department of Science Service, Ministry of Science, Technology, and Energy, Thailand;

Achmad Soedarsan, Chairman, National Commission on Conservation of Genetic Resources, Indonesia;

S.H. Sohmer, Biodiversity Specialist, USAID, USA;

Angel Solís, Entomologist, National Biodiversity Institute (INBIO), Costa Rica;

Vivienne Solís, Central America Regional Office, World Conservation Union (IUCN), Costa Rica;

Beni Sormin, Senior Lecturer, School of Environmental Conservation Management, Indonesia;

Michael Soulé, Chair, Environmental Studies, University of California at Santa Cruz, USA;

Patricia Souza, Brazil;

Creuza Souza, Brasilian Institute for the Environment and Renewable Natural Resources (IBAMA), Brazil;

Ken Spann, Y Bar Ranch, USA

Richard Spellenberg, Professor of Biology, New Mexico State University, USA;

Phillip Sponenberg, Technical Chair, The American Minor Breeds Conservancy, USA;

Bruce Stein, Director, Latin America Science Program, The Nature Conservancy, USA;

Alan Stoner, Research Leader - Germplasm Resources Laboratory, U.S. Department of Agriculture, USA;

N.E. Stork, Head, Biodiversity Division, The Natural History Museum Department of Entomology, United Kingdom;

D. Stoyanov, Director, IIPGRA, Bulgaria;

Stuart Strahl, New York Zoological Society, USA;

Peggy Strankman, Environmental Coordinator, Canadian Cattlemen's Association, Canada;

Simon Stuart, Executive Officer, Species Survival Commission, World Conservation Union (IUCN), Switzerland;

Roy Stubbs, Chief, Environment Section, Economic and Social Commission for Asia and the Pacific (ESCAP), Thailand;

Miguel Stutzen, National Committee for the Defense of Fauna and Flora, Chile;

Aca Sugandhy, Assistant Minister, Ministry of State for Population and Environment, Indonesia;

Mohammad Sulayem, National Commission for Wildlife Conservation and Development (NCWCD) Saudi Arabia;

Siwatibali Suliana, Pacific Union Project, Vanuatu;

Timothy Sullivan, School of Forestry and Environmental Studies, Yale University, USA;

Wang Sung, Executive Vice Chairman, Endangered Species Scientific Commission, Chinese Academy of Sciences, China;

Shannan Sunoto, Assistant Regional Representative, UNDP, Thailand;

Keith Suter, Wilderness Society, Australia;

Hanne Svarstad, University of Oslo, Norway;

Jonas Svensson, Junior Program Officer, Forestry, UNEP, Kenya;

M.S. Swaminathan, Director, Centre for Research on Sustainable Agriculture and Rural Development, India;

Byron Swift, Executive Director, IUCN-U.S., USA;

I. Swingland, Durrell Institute of Conservation and Ecology, University of Kent, United Kingdom;

Hugh Synge, Consultant, Surrey, United Kingdom;

Robert Szaro, Research Ecologist, USDA Forest Service, USA;

B.M. Taal, SPO/Forests and Ecosystems, UNEP, Nairobi, Kenya;

Frank Talbot, Director, National Museum of Natural History, USA;

Denise Tanaka, Researcher, Brazilian Research Association of Amazonia, Brazilian Corporation for Farm and Agriculture Research (EMBRAPA), Brazil;

Merv Tano, Senior Environmental Program Manager, Council of Energy Resource Tribes (CERT), USA;

Pedro Tarak, Deputy Director, Environment and Natural Resources Foundation (FARN), Argentina;

A.R.D. Taylor, Uganda Wetlands Programme, IUCN, Uganda;

Peter Thomas, Protected Areas Management Officer, South Pacific Regional Environment Programme (SPREP), New Caledonia;

Shaju Thomas, Senior Lecturer, Nirmala College, India;

Janice E. Thompson, CalBioMarine Technologies, Inc., USA;

Steven Thorne, Minnesota State Director, The Nature Conservancy, Mountain Chapter, USA;

James Thorsell, Commission on National Parks and Protected Areas, World Conservation Union (IUCN), Switzerland;

Lori Ann Thrupp, Director, Sustainable Agriculture, World Resources Institute, USA;

Tilemann, Dept. of Foreign Affairs, Australia

Justino Tillmann, Deputy Secretary, Secretariat for the Environment, Interior and Justice, Boa Vista, Brazil;

A. Timoshenko, Officer in Charge, ELIU, UNEP, Nairobi, Kenya;

Jon Tinker, The Panos Institute, United Kingdom;

Timothy Titus, Director, Science, Economics and, Statistics Division, U.S. Environmental Protection Agency, USA;

Reza Tjayhadi, Pesticide Action Network (PAN), Indonesia;

Amado Tolentino, Pollution Administration Board, the Philippines;

Hernán Torres, IUCN, Chile;

Michel Trommetter, National Institute of Agronomic Research (INRA), France;

Marcelo Ribeiro Tunes, Sub-Secretary, Amazonas Secretariat of the Environment, Science and Technology, Brazil;

Schwann Tunhlkorn, Chief of Technical Section, Wildlife Conservation Division, Royal Forest Department, Thailand;

Dan Tunstall, Senior Associate, World Resources Institute, USA;

Robert Turner, Regional V. President, National Audubon Soc., USA;

Alan Tye, East Africa Regional Office, World Conservation Union (IUCN), Kenya;

Alvaro Ugalde, Director, National Parks Service, Costa Rica;

Alvaro Umaña, Center for Environmental Studies, Costa Rica;

Jean Untermaier, France Nature Environment, France;

F. Urban, Ministry of Environment, Czechoslovakia;

M.B. Usher, Chief Scientific Adviser, Nature Conservancy Council for Scotland, United Kingdom;

Rauno Vaisanen, Water & Environmental Research Institute, Finland;

Elier Valdivieso, Prof. Biology & Natural Sciences, Chief, Chinchilla Project, National Forestry Corporation (CONAF), Chile;

Cleidemar Valerio, Senior Technician, ELETRONORTE, Brazil;

Ignacio Valero, Assist. Mgr./Adminstration, National Institute for Renewable Resources and the Environment (INDERENA), Colombia;

Celio Carvalho Valle, President, Biodiversitas Foundation, Brazil;

Joaquin Vallejo, Board of Directors, Foundation for Higher Education, Colombia;

Luiz van Beethoven Abreu, Director of UPIS and Consultant, FUNATURA, Brazil;

Peter J.H. van Bree, Netherlands Foundation for International Nature Protection, The Netherlands;

Cornelius van Tuyll, German Society for Technical Cooperation (GTZ), Germany;

Jeroean van Wylx, University of Amsterdam, The Netherlands;

John Vanderwalker, Executive Director, Whooping Crane Habitat Maintenance Trust, USA;

R.I. Vane-Wright, Natural History Museum, United Kingdom;

Vera Varela, General Director, Neotropical Foundation, Costa Rica;

Michael Vecchione, Acting Director, National Systematics Laboratory, National Marine Fisheries Service, USA;

Wouter Veening, Coordinator, Netherlands Committee for IUCN, The Netherlands;

José Vicente Rodriguez, Director of Animal Wildlife, National Institute for Renewable Resources and the Environment (INDERENA), Colombia;

Marco Vinicio Cerezo, Director General, Foundation for Eco-Development and Conservation, Guatemala;

R. Voles, United Kingdom;

Miguel Von Behr, Mgr., APA of Guaraquecaba, Brasilian Institute for the Environment & Renewable Natural Resources (IBAMA),Brazil;

Bernd von Droste, Director, Ecological Sciences Division, UNESCO, France;

Andrew P. Vovides, Botanical Gardens, Ecology Institute, Mexico;

Kimani Waithaka, University of Nairobi, Kenya;

M. Walkery, Durell Institute of Conservation and Ecology, University of Kent, United Kingdom;

Cliff Wallis, Vice President, Alberta Wilderness Association, Canada;

Wang Xianpu, Chairman, Institute of Botany, Academy of Science, China;

V. Watkins, Regional Director, World Society for the Protection of Animals, United Kingdom;

R. Wayne, Zoological Society of London, United Kingdom;

Ji Weizhi, Kunming Institute of Zoology, China;

Magaly V.S. Wetzel, Brazilian Corporation for Farm and Agriculture Research (EMBRAPA), Brazil;

R.J. Wheater, The Royal Zoological Society of Scotland, U.K.;

S. Whitehead, ICI Seeds, United Kingdom;

John Whiting, Senior Advisor, International Affairs, Canadian Wildlife Service, Canada;

A. Wijkman, Conservation Officer, Swedish Society for Nature Conservation, Sweden;

Keith Williams, Mgr., Wildlife Research Unit, Australian Capital Territory (ACT) Parks and Conservation Service, Australia;

Paul Williams, Natural History Museum, United Kingdom

Trevor Williams, Director, Tropical Trees Crops Program, International Fund for Agricultural Research, USA;

Jim Williamson, Forest Biometrician, Tennessee Valley Authority, USA;

N. Winser, Assistant Director, Royal Geographical Society, U.K.

Donna Wise, Director, Policy Affairs, World Resources Institute, USA;

Sonia Witte, Friedrich Naumann Foundation (FNS), Indonesia;

Ted Wolf, Conservation International, USA;

D. Wood, International Germplasm, United Kingdom;

C.S. Woods, SKS Information, England;

George Woodwell, Director, The Woods Hole Research Center, USA;

Philip Woollaston, UNEP, Nairobi, Kenya;

Melaku Worede, Director, Plant Genetic Resources Centre, Ethiopia;

Michael Wright, Vice President, World Wildlife Fund, USA;

Bounthong Xaisida, Head, Wildlife and Fishery Conservation Division, Ministry of Agriculture and Forestry, Laos;

Alexey Yablokov, Deputy Chairman, Committee of Ecology USSR Supreme Soviet, USSR;

Fernando Yaluk, Technical Manager, Moises Bertoni Foundation, Paraguay;

S.K. Yap, Seed Technologist, Forest Research Institute of Malaysia, Malaysia;

Masaaki Yoneda, Research Associate, Japan Wildlife Research Center, Japan;

Abdulqawi Yusuf, Officer-in-Charge, Legal Policies, Technology Programme, United Nations Conference on Trade and Development (UNCTAD), Switzerland;

Hemdallah Zedan, Officer in Charge, Biodiversity, UNEP, Kenya;

Newton Jordao Zerbini, Forestry Engineer, ELETRONORTE, Brazil;

Charles Zerner, Woodrow Wilson Ctr for International Scholars, USA;

Max Zieren, Conservation Officer, Asian Wetlands Bureau, Indonesia;

M.S. Zulkarnanen, Director Executive, WALHI, Indonesia.

Glossary

Accession. A sample of a crop variety collected at a specific location and time; may be of any size.

Alien species. A species occurring in an area outside of its historically known natural range as a result of intentional or accidental dispersal by human activities. (Also known as an exotic or introduced species.)

Assemblage. *See* "Community."

Biodiversity. The totality of genes, species, and ecosystems in a region or the world.

Biogeography. The scientific study of the geographic distribution of organisms.

Biological Resources. Those components of biodiversity of direct, indirect, or potential use to humanity. *(Used interchangeably with "Biotic Resources")*

Biome. A major portion of the living environment of a particular region (such as a fir forest or grassland), characterized by its distinctive vegetation and maintained by local climatic conditions.

Bioregion [bioregional planning]. A territory defined by a combination of biological, social, and geographic criteria, rather than geopolitical considerations; generally, a system of related, interconnected ecosystems.

Biota. All of the organisms, including animals, plants, fungi, and microorganisms, found in a given area.

Biotechnology. Any technology that is applied to living organisms to make them more valuable to people.

Biotic. Pertaining to any aspect of life, especially to characteristics of entire populations or ecosystems.

Buffer zone. The region near the border of a protected area; a transition zone between areas managed for different objectives.

Carrying Capacity. The maximum number of people, or individuals of a particular species, that a given part of the environment can maintain indefinitely.

Climax Community. The end of a successional sequence; a community that has reached stability under a particular set of environmental conditions.

Co-management. The sharing of authority, responsibility, and benefits between government and local communities in the management of natural resources.

Common Property Resource Management. The management of a specific resource (such as a forest or pasture) by a well-defined group of resource users with the authority to regulate its use by members and outsiders.

Community. An integrated group of species inhabiting a given area; the organisms within a community influence one another's distribution, abundance, and evolution. (A Human Community is a social group of any size whose members reside in a specific locality.)

Comparative Advantage. Relative superiority with which a region or state may produce a good or service.

Conservation. The management of human use of the biosphere so that it may yield the greatest sustainable benefit to current generations while maintaining its potential to meet the needs and aspirations of future generations: Thus conservation is positive, embracing preservation, maintenance, sustainable utilization, restoration, *and* enhancement of the natural environment.

Conservation of Biodiversity. The management of human interactions with genes, species, and ecosystems so as to provide the maximum benefit to the present generation while maintaining their potential to meet the needs and aspirations of future generations; encompasses elements of saving, studying, and using biodiversity.

Cultivar. A cultivated variety (genetic strain) of a domesticated crop plant.

Cultural diversity. Variety or multiformity of human social structures, belief systems, and strategies for adapting to situations in different parts of the world.

Ecosystem. A dynamic complex of plant, animal, fungal, and microorganism communities and their associated non-living environment interacting as an ecological unit.

Ecotourism. Travel undertaken to witness sites or regions of unique natural or ecologic quality, or the provision of services to facilitate such travel.

Endemic. Restricted to a specified region or locality.

Ex situ Conservation. Keeping components of biodiversity alive outside of their original habitat or natural environment.

Fauna. All of the animals found in a given area.

Flora. All of the plants found in a given area.

Gene. The functional unit of heredity; the part of the DNA molecule that encodes a single enzyme or structural protein unit.

Gene Bank. A facility established for the *ex situ* conservation of individuals (seeds), tissues, or reproductive cells of plants or animals.

Genetic diversity. Variation in the genetic composition of individuals within or among species; the heritable genetic variation within and among populations.

Germplasm. The genetic material, especially its specific molecular and chemical constitution, that comprises the physical basis of the inherited qualities of an organism.

Grassroots [organizations or movements]. People or society at a local level, rather than at the center of major political activity.

Habitat. The environment in which an organism lives. Habitat can also refer to the organisms and physical environment in a particular place.

Hybridization. Crossing of individuals from genetically different strains, populations, or species.

In situ Conservation. The conservation of biodiversity within the evolutionary dynamic ecosystems of the original habitat or natural environment.

Indicator Species. A species whose status provides information on the overall condition of the ecosystem and of other species in that ecosystem.

Indigenous Peoples. People whose ancestors inhabited a place or country when persons from another culture or ethnic background arrived on the scene and dominated them through conquest, settlement, or other means and who today live more in conformity with their own social, economic, and cultural customs and traditions than with those of the country of which they now form a part. (also: "native peoples" or "tribal peoples")

Intellectual Property Right. A right enabling an inventor to exclude imitators from the market for a limited time.

Introduced Species. *See* alien species.

Keystone Species. A species whose loss from an ecosystem would cause a greater than average change in other species populations or ecosystem processes.

Landraces. A crop cultivar or animal breed that evolved with and has been genetically improved by traditional agriculturalists, but has not been influenced by modern breeding practices.

Minimum Viable Population. The smallest isolated population having a good chance of surviving for a given number of years despite the foreseeable effects of demographic, environmental, and genetic events and natural catastrophes. (The probability of persistence and the time of persistence are often taken to be 99 percent and 1000 years, respectively.)

Mycorrhizal Fungi. A fungus living in a mutualistic association with plants and facilitating nutrient and water uptake.

National Income Accounts. System of record by which the vigor of a nation's economy is measured. (Results are often listed as Gross National Product, or Gross Domestic Product.)

Native Species. Plants, animals, fungi, and microorganisms that occur naturally in a given area or region.

Nitrogen Fixation. A process whereby *nitrogen fixing bacteria* living in mutualistic associations with plants convert atmospheric nitrogen to nitrogen compounds that plants can utilize directly.

Non-governmental Organization (NGO). A nonprofit group or association organized outside of institutionalized political structures to realize particular social objectives (such as environmental protection) or serve particular constituencies (such as indigenous peoples). NGO activities range from research, information distribution, training, local organization, and community service to legal advocacy, lobbying for legislative change, and civil disobedience. NGOs range in size from small groups within a particular community to huge membership groups with a national or international scope.

Parataxonomists. Field-trained biodiversity collection and inventory specialists recruited from local areas.

Patent. A government grant of temporary monopoly rights on innovative processes or products.

Pathogen. A disease-causing microorganism; a bacterium or virus.

Phylogenetic. Pertaining to the evolutionary history of a particular group of organisms.

Phylum. In taxonomy, a high-level category just beneath the kingdom and above the class; a group of related, similar classes.

Population. A group of individuals with common ancestry that are much more likely to mate with one another than with individuals from another such group.

Primary [or natural] forest. A forest largely undisturbed by human activities.

Primary Productivity. The transformation of chemical or solar energy to biomass. Most primary production occurs through photosynthesis, whereby green plants convert solar energy, carbon dioxide, and water to glucose and eventually to plant tissue. In addition, some bacteria in the deep sea can convert chemical energy to biomass through chemosynthesis.

Protected Area. A legally established land or water area under either public or private ownership that is regulated and managed to achieve specific conservation objectives.

Recalcitrant Seed. Seed that does not survive drying and freezing.

Rehabilitation. The recovery of specific ecosystem services in a degraded ecosystem or habitat.

Restoration. The return of an ecosystem or habitat to its original community structure, natural complement of species, and natural functions.

Seedbank. A facility designed for the *ex situ* conservation of individual plant varieties through seed preservation and storage.

Selection. Natural selection is the differential contribution of offspring to the next generation by various genetic types belonging to the same populations. Artificial selection is the intentional manipulation by man of the fitness of individuals in a population to produce a desired evolutionary response.

Species. A group of organisms capable of interbreeding freely with each other but not with members of other species.

Species Richness. The number of species within a region. (A term commonly used as a measure of species diversity, but technically only one aspect of diversity.)

Subspecies. A subdivision of a species; a population or series of populations occupying a discrete range and differing genetically from other subspecies of the same species.

Succession. The more or less predictable changes in the composition of communities following a natural or human disturbance.

Sustainable development. Development that meets the needs and aspirations of the current generation without compromising the ability to meet those of future generations.

Systematics. The study of the historical evolutionary and genetic relationships among organisms and of their phenotypic similarities and differences.

Taxon (pl. taxa). The named classification unit (e.g. *Homo sapiens*, Hominidae, or Mammalia) to which individuals, or sets of species, are assigned. *Higher taxa* are those above the species level.

Taxonomy. The naming and assignment of organisms to taxa.

Trophic Level. Position in the food chain, determined by the number of energy-transfer steps to that level.

Variety. *See* Cultivar.

List of Acronyms

BGCI	Botanic Gardens Conservation International
BGCS	Botanic Gardens Conservation Secretariat of IUCN
BIC	Bank Information Center
CCAMLR	Convention on the Conservation of Antarctic Marine Living Resources
CDC	Conservation Data Center
CITES	Convention on International Trade in Endangered Species of Wild Flora and Fauna
CNPPA	Commission on National Parks and Protected Areas of IUCN
CPC	Center for Plant Conservation
ECG	Ecosystems Conservation Group
ELCI	Environmental Liaison Center/International
FAO	Food and Agriculture Organization of the United Nations
GATT	General Agreement on Tariffs and Trade
GEF	Global Environment Facility
GEF/STAP	Global Environment Facility/Science and Technology Advisory Panel
GEMS	Global Environment Monitoring System of UNEP
GNP	Gross National Product
IARC	International Agricultural Research Center
IBPGR	International Board for Plant Genetic Resources
ICBP	International Council for Bird Preservation
ICDP	Integrated Conservation/ Development Project
IMF	International Monetary Fund
IPBC	International Panel on Biodiversity Conservation
IPR	Intellectual Property Right
ISIS	International Species Inventory System
ITTA	International Tropical Timber Agreement
ITTO	International Tropical Timber Organization
IUBS	International Union of Biological Sciences
IUCN	International Union for Conservation of Nature and Natural Resources, also known as World Conservation Union
MCDP	Marine Conservation and Development Program

MIRCEN Microbiological Resources Center

NGO Non-governmental Organization

PVP Plant Variety Protection

SCOPE Scientific Committee on Problems of the Environment

SNA System of National Accounts of the United Nations

SSC Species Survival Commission of IUCN

TFAP Tropical Forestry Action Plan

TNC Transnational corporation

TRAFFIC Trade Record Analysis of Flora and Fauna in Commerce

TRIPS Trade-Related Aspects of Intellectual Property Rights negotiating group of GATT

UN United Nations

UNCED United Nations Conference on Environment and Development, also known as the "Earth Summit"

UNDP United Nations Development Programme

UNEP United Nations Environment Programme

UNESCO United Nations Education, Scientific, and Cultural Organization

UPOV International Union for the Protection of New Varieties of Plants

USAID United States Agency for International Development

USDA United States Department of Agriculture

WCMC World Conservation Monitoring Centre

WHSRN Western Hemisphere Shorebird Reserve Network

WIPO World Intellectual Property Organization

WRI World Resources Institute

WWF World Wide Fund for Nature (previously World Wildlife Fund and still World Wildlife Fund in the USA)

Index

Acid rain, 14

Action alerts, 33

Africa
  family planning services, 50-51
  native grazing animals, 107
  protected areas management, 120
  role of women, 70-71
  species-specific conservation, 134-135
  traditional medicines, 93

African Centre for Technology Studies, 59

African cichlid fish, 45-46, 146

Agriculture
  conserving biodiversity, 109-115
  cropland areas, 49-50
  decline of species numbers, 15-16
  economic value, 2-4
  "Green Revolution" varieties, 9
  introduced species, 46
  land restoration, 114-115
  loss of biodiversity, 15
  loss of genetic diversity, 9, 11
  plant breeding, 5
  policies for biodiversity conservation, 41-43
  value of diversity, 4-5

Agrochemical, 114

AIDESEP, 114-115

Alaska, 48, 146

Alien species, 14, 40
  and decline of freshwater ecosystems, 10, 11
  guidelines for translocations, 45

Alkaline-tolerant species, 111-112

Amazon
  Brazil nuts, 88, 91
  cattle ranches, 112
  indigenous approaches to restoration, 113, 114-115
  indigenous peoples, 84

Amazon Treaty, 125

Amboseli Park (Kenya), 132

American Minor Breeds Conservancy, 139

Amerindians, 102

Antarctica, 120

Antelopes
  conservation action plans, 134
  migratory, 63

Aquaria, 25
  role in conservation of biodiversity, 145-146

Arboreta, 137, 143-144, 146

Arizona, 131

Asia
  family planning services, 50-51
  protected areas management, 120
  role of women, 70-71
  See also Southeast Asia

Association of Forest Service Employees for Environmental Ethics (AFSEE), 85

Auk, Great, 12, 14
Australia, 128-129
 and biodiversity conservation plan, 34
 botanic garden networks, 144
 loss of diversity, 8
 protected areas management, 120
 zoo breeding programs, 144
Azores, 8

Bangladesh, 120
Bank Information Center (BIC), 158
Basic Law on Conservation of Living Resources and
 their Ecosystems, 100
Bats, 8, 108
Bear, Asiatic black, 93
Bering Sea, 12
Bhutan Trust Fund, 76
Biodiversity
 building a sustainable society, 21
 categories, 2-3
 components, 1, 2-4
 definition, 2
 developing national policies, 34
 Early Warning Network, 33
 economic considerations, 16-17
 freshwater ecosystems, 10-11
 fundamental causes of problem, 12, 15-18
 increasing awareness of importance, 148-150
 international information network, 157
 losses of, 7-11
 in marine ecosystems, 12-13
 mechanisms for loss of, 14-15
 species numbers, 9
 value of, 4-5
Biodiversity conservation, 5
 availability of institutional information, 150-157
 basic and applied research, 158-161
 contribution of protected areas, 121, 125-132
 development assistance process, 67-71
 expanding human capacity, 147-166
 funding, 71-77
 goals, 19-20, 22-23
 human resources development, 162-165
 integrated approach, 133, 135
 integration into international economic policy, 56-61

 local incentives, 79-95
 management of biological resources, 107-115
 non-governmental organizations, 165-167
 objectives, 22-25
 off-site facilities, 137-146
 principles and guidelines, 23, 35-36
 private sector initiatives, 105-107
 protected areas, 117-131
 public policies, 38-49
 reducing demand for resources, 49-54
 restoring degraded lands, 110-115
 role of women, 70-71
 strategy, 26-28
 technologies for, 58-59
Biodiversity Conservation Trusts, 106-107
Biodiversity Country Reports, 72
Biodiversity Information and Monitoring Centers,
 151-155
Biological and Conservation Data System, 154
Biological diversity, international legal framework,
 62-66
Biological Diversity and Genetic Resources Project,
 162
Biological inventories, 153-155
Biological resources, 107-115
Biopolicy Institute, 59
Bioregion
 definition, 97
 elements and dynamics, 98-99
Bioregional approach, 24
Bioregional management, 97-115
 information centers, 105
 institutional conditions for conservation and
 development, 101-105
 meaning of, 97, 100
Biosphere reserve concept, 100
Biota, 4
Biotechnology, 43
 genetic resources and, 22-23
 preventing negative impact, 47
Biotechnology Trusts, 59
Birds
 fruit-eating, 108
 migratory, 63
 protected area assessments, 121, 124

Bolivia, 91
Bonn, 63
Boston, 146
Botanic gardens, 24, 25, 137
    conserving wild plant resources, 143-144
    network, 144
Botanic Gardens Conservation International (BGCI),
    134, 143
Botswana, 120
Brachiaria bryzantha (forage species), 112
Brazil
    cattle ranches, 112
    genetic resource conservation, 91
    harvesting non-timber forest products, 85-86
    national protected area system plans, 120
    off-site conservation facilities, 137
    restoring degraded watersheds, 112, 113
    soybeans, 52, 53
Brazil nuts, 88, 91
Breeders' rights, 93
Bribi (Amerindians), 102
Buffer Overlay Zone, 131
Buffer zones, 100, 111, 128-131
By-catch, 40

Cabecar (Amerindians), 102
Cacti, 133, 143
California
    loss of diversity, 8
    timber production, 52, 54
Cambridge Botanic Garden, 137
Canada
    botanic gardens, 143
    co-management of caribou, 86
    conservation data center network, 154
    land trusts, 107
    national protected area system plans, 120
    protected areas, 130
Canary Islands
    botanic garden, 137
    extinction of plant species, 8
Captive Breeding Specialist Group (CBSG), 145
Caribbean
    conservation data center network, 154
    monk seal, 12

    protected areas assessment, 123
    traditional medicines, 92
Caribou, 86
Carrying capacity, 21
Cattle ranches, 112
Center for Plant Conservation (CPC), 144, 146
Central America, 120, 130
Cerradao, 143
Chemical fertilizers, 42
Chile
    loss of diversity, 8
    national protected area system plans, 120
China
    botanic garden networks, 144
    cultivated medicinal plants, 142
Citrus canker, 9, 11
Climate changes
    international agreements, 65
    and loss of biodiversity, 14-15
Climate Convention, 65
Co-management of resources, 84-86
    marine, 87
Coastal areas, 86
Coastal waters, 39-41
Coelacanth fish, 12
Colombia, 105
Commission on National Parks and Protected Areas
    (CNPPA), 121, 162
Commission on Plant Genetic Resources, 47, 64,
    93, 157
Commonwealth Science Council, 162
Communities
    See Local communities
Condor, California, 146
Conference of Parties, 63
Conservataire et Jardin Botanique du Mascarin,
    143-144
Conservation, 5
    building a sustainable society, 21
    catalytic actions, 26-28
    developing national policies, 34
    goals, 19-20, 22-23
    legal and institutional constraints, 18
    marine, 13
    principles and guidelines, 23, 35-36

reducing resource consumption, 51-52
species, population, and genetic diversity, 133-146
strategic objectives, 22-25
Conservation Data Centers (CDCs), 154
Conservation easements, 106
Conservation International, 102
Convention Concerning the Protection of the World Cultural and Natural Heritage, 63
Convention on the Conservation of Migratory Species of Wild Animals, 63
Convention on Biological Diversity, 26, 27, 29
essential elements, 30
funding mechanism, 72-73
international framework, 62-66
Convention on International Trade in Endangered Species (CITES), 62, 63, 93, 136
Convention on the Conservation of Antarctic Marine Living Resources (CCAMLR), 64
Convention on Wetlands of International Importance Especially as Waterfowl Habitat, 63
Coordinating Body for the Indigenous Peoples' Organizations of the Amazon Basin (COICA), 84
Coral reefs, 12, 13, 40, 145
Corals, exploitation, 40
Core area, 100
Corridors of habitat, 130
Costa Rica, 44, 59
biodiversity information institute, 152, 153
biosphere reserve concept, 100, 102-103
co-management of protected areas, 86
land restoration, 112
national protected area system plans, 120
species inventory, 156
Crayfish, 14
Critical and Sensitive Biological Communities, 131
Crop breeding, 109-110
Crops
conservation of local and regional species, 142-143
diversity, 4, 11, 90-92, 109
genetic resources royalties, 45
herbicide-resistant, 109
traditional varieties, 43
uniformity of varieties, 42
Cultural diversity, 3
indigenous peoples, 83

link with biodiversity, 5, 11
Dams, 113
Data bases, 153, 154-155
Debt-for-nature swaps, 74-75
Decade of Action, 26
Deforestation, 38-39
funding protection from, 73
Guatemala, 82
rates, 7
Developing countries, 25
assistance projects, 67-71
biodiversity conservation and, 29
debt, 57
funding biodiversity conservation, 72-73
maintaining ecological security, 56
non-governmental organizations, 165-167
role of women, 70-71
training biodiversity professionals, 162-165
transferring technology for biodiversity conservation, 58-59
Development assistance process, 67-71
Diversification
See Biodiversity
Dolphins, 57
Drugs. See Medicines; Traditional medicines

Early Warning Network, 26, 28, 30, 33, 157
Earth Summit conference, 167
Earthwatch System, 26
East Asia, 93
Ecological carrying capacity, 15
Ecological literacy, 148
Economic policies
development assistance, 67-71
international, 56-61
Ecosystem diversity, 2
value of, 4-5
Ecosystems Conservation Group, 32
Ecotourism, 89
Education
biodiversity awareness, 148-150
Elephants, 4
Endangered Species Reserves, 126
Endowments, 75-76
Environmental Impact Assessments, 68, 69, 161

Environmental Resource Zone, 131
Estuarine ecosystems, 5, 13
Ethics Working Group, 161
Ethiopia, 111
Eucalyptus, 142
Europe
    botanic gardens, 143
    loss of diversity, 7
    protected areas management, 120
Ex situ conservation
    facilities, 137
    microorganism culture collections, 140-141
    plant genetic resources, 141-143
    wild plant resources, 143-144
Exclusive Economic Zones, 13, 40
Extinction
    documentation, 8
    fungal species, 7
    plant and animal species, 8-11
Extractivism, 85-86, 90-91
    protected areas, 120
Exxon Valdez oil spill, 48, 146

Family planning services, 50-51
Farmers' rights, 64, 93
Ferret, black-footed, 146
Figs, 108
Fisheries
    community-based, 40
    decline of species numbers, 15-16
    destruction of estuarine ecosystems, 5
    interbreeding, 46
    loss of biodiversity, 40
    sustainable yields, 40
    value, 2
Fishes
    African cichlid, 45-46, 146
    coelacanth, 12
    extinction, 10
    number of species, 10
    surface-dwellers, 13
    totoaba, 13
Flagship species, 133, 136
Flora of North America Project, 156
Florida, 112

Food and Agriculture Organization (FAO), 47, 64, 157
Food price controls, 42
Forestry
    co-management, 85-86
    conserving biodiversity, 108
    decline of species numbers, 15-16
    international agreements, 65-66
    non-timber products, 85-86, 88, 90-91
    policies for biodiversity conservation, 38-39
    recycling and conservation, 51-52
    resource consumption, 52, 54
    restoration, 114-115
    schools, 162, 164
    See also Trees; Tropical forests
Freshwater aquaria, 145-146
Freshwater ecosystems
    biodiversity, 8, 10-11
    policies for conservation, 41
Fund for Plant Genetic Resources, 72-73
Fundación Reservas para Colombia, 106
Funding
    biodiversity conservation, 71-77
Fungal species diversity, 7

Galápagos Islands, 8
Gatun Lake (Panama), 45
Gene banks, 11, 44, 111, 140
General Agreement on Tariffs and Trade (GATT), 34, 56-57, 61, 66
General Use zones, 128
Genetic diversity, 2
    checks, 109-110
    conservation, 133-146
    loss of, 9, 11
    value, 4-5
Genetic engineering, 4
Genetic resources
    conservation, 91-92
    crops and livestock, 138-140
    equity in distribution of benefits, 93-95
    plants, 141-143
    policies for biodiversity conservation, 43-45
Genetic uniformity, 109
Genetically modified organisms, 47
Geographic Information Systems, 153

Germplasm, 43, 44
  banks, 11
  conservation centers, 138-140
  conservation training, 164
  microbial, 141
Global alliance, 21
  forests, 66
  See also International policies
Global Biodiversity Status Report, 157
Global Biodiversity Strategy, 23, 26-28
Global Environment Facility (GEF), 29, 72, 73
Global Heritage Species Program, 136
Global Initiative for the Security and Sustainable Use
  of Plant Genetic Resources, 139
Government, resource management, 80-86
Government agencies, bioregional planning, 104-105
Grassroots organizations, 165-167
  funding, 76-77
Great Barrier Reef Marine Park (Australia), 128-129
  aquarium, 145
Green Market, 91
Green Revolution varieties, 9, 49, 138-139
Greenhouse gases, 14-15
Gross Domestic Product, 2-3
Gross National Product (GNP), 48
Groundwater extraction, 41
Guanacaste Conservation Area (Costa Rica), 86, 112
Guardians of the Sea, 87
Guatemala, 81-82

Habitats
  coastal and marine, 39-40
  freshwater, 11, 41
  islands, 10
  loss of, 8, 9, 14
  management areas, 120
  migratory species, 63
  protection, 134-136
  saving, 19
  waterfowl, 63
Herbicide-resistant crops, 109
HIFCO project, 113, 114-115
Honduras, 146
Hopi Blue Corn, 95
Human resources, 162-165

Hydroelectric plants, 113
Hydrothermal vents, 9, 12-13

Ibero-Macronesian Association, 144
India
  cultivated medicinal plants, 142
  disease susceptible wheat, 109
  minor forest products, 86, 88
  reforesting state lands, 85
  restoring degraded land, 111-112
Indian Ocean islands, 143
Indicator species, 25
Indigenous peoples, 83, 84
  restoration of ecosystems, 113, 114-115
Indo-Malaya, 120
Indonesia
  and biodiversity conservation plan, 34
  biosphere reserve concept, 100
  cultivated medicinal plants, 142
  genetic resources conservation, 92
  national protected area system plans, 120
  non-timber forest products, 86, 88
  reforesting state lands, 85
Industry
  opportunities for, 39
Input subsidies, 42
Instituto Nacional de Biodiversidad (INBio)
  (Costa Rica), 152
Intellectual property rights (IPR), 44, 47
  countries' rights to adopt policies, 60-61
  as incentive for commercial innovation, 93-95
Interim Multilateral Fund for the Montreal Protocol,
  29, 73-74
International Agricultural Research Centers (IARCs),
  58, 138, 167
International assessments, protected areas, 121, 123,
  125
International Biodiversity Decade, 26, 30
International Board for Plant Genetic Resources
  (IBPGR), 138, 157, 164
International Code of Conduct for Plant Germplasm
  Collecting and Transfer, 47
International Conservation Financing Project, 72
International conventions, 62-66

International cooperation
    protected area management, 125
    shorebird conservation, 127
International Council for Bird Preservation
    (ICBP), 125
International Debt Management Authority, 57
International Forum for Biodiversity Data, 157
International Monetary Fund (IMF), 69
International Panel on Biodiversity Conservation
    (IPBC), 26, 30-32, 68, 157
International policies
    for biodiversity conservation, 55-77
    development assistance, 67-71
    economic, 56-61
    legal framework, 62-66
International Species Inventory System (ISIS),
    145, 157
International Tropical Timber Organization (ITTO),
    34, 74, 167
International Undertaking on Plant Genetic
    Resources, 64, 73
International Union for the Protection of New Vari-
    eties of Plants (UPOV), 48
International Union of Biological Sciences
    (IUBS), 159
International Zoo Yearbook, 145
Introduced species. See Alien species
Inventory and assessment. See Biological inventories

Japan, 144
Jardin Botánico de Brasilia, 143
Java, 110

Kelp beds, 12
Kenya
    nature tourism, 119
    protected areas, 132
Keystone International Dialogue Series on Plant
    Genetic Resources, 73, 138-139, 167
Keystone species, 25, 133
    in forests, 108
Kissimmee River (Florida), 112

La Amistad Biosphere Reserve (Costa Rica),
    100, 102-103
Lakes
    freshwater, 10
Lancetilla Botanic Garden and Experimental Station
    (Honduras), 146
Land ownership, 81-82
Land rights, 83
Land-tenure systems, 24
Landraces, 9
    conservation, 111
Lands
    degraded, 110-113
    private, 105-107
    public, 84-86
    restoration within protected areas, 132
Latin America
    botanic gardens, 143
    conservation data center network, 154
    family planning, 51
    hardwood exports, 53
    protected areas assessment, 123
    role of women, 70
Latin American-Caribbean Association, 144
Legal framework
    international policies, 62-66
Libya, 46
Local communities
    benefits from genetic resources use, 93-95
    benefits of protected areas, 131-132
    freedom of information, 157-158
    resource management partnerships with
        government, 80-86
    role in information gathering, 153-155
    use of products from the wild, 86-93
Logging, 108

Madagascar
    national protected area system plans, 120
    role of women, 71
Malaysia
    hardwood exports, 53
    oil-palm cultivation, 53
    palm oil exports, 52
    rattan, 88

Man and the Biosphere Program, 100

Mangrove forests, 12, 13, 14, 40

Mapimí Biosphere Reserve (Mexico), 100

Mariculture, 40

Marine Conservation and Development Program (MCDP), 87

Marine ecosystems
    biodiversity, 8, 12-13
    co-management, 86
    policies for biodiversity conservation, 39-41

Marine National Park zones, 128

Marine resources
    co-management, 87
    convention, 64
    management, 40-41

Medicines
    from marine species, 12
    plant and animal sources, 43, 142
    See also Traditional medicines

Merck Pharmaceutical, 152

Mexico
    biosphere reserve concept, 100
    botanic garden networks, 144
    species-specific conservation, 135

Microbial Information Network Europe, 141

Microbial Strain Data Network, 141

Microbiological Resources Centers (MIRCENs), 140

Microorganisms
    culture collections, 140-141

Migratory species, 63

Mindanao (Philippines), 92

Mining, 52

Ministry of National Planning and Economic Policy, 102

Mollusks, 40

Monkeys, tamarin, 137

Monofilament drift nets, 40

Monterey Bay Aquarium, 146

Montreal Protocol Fund, 73-74

Moorea (South Pacific island), 46

National assessments, protected areas, 119-121

National Biodiversity Action Plan, 34

National Biodiversity Data Base, 152

National Biodiversity Institute (INBio), 25, 44, 59, 152, 153

National Conservation Strategy, 68

National ecological security policy, 56

National Management Authorities, 63

National parks, 120

National policies
    for biodiversity conservation, 37-54
    funding for biodiversity conservation, 71-77
    integrating biodiversity conservation, 34

Native species, 113

Natural Heritage Programs, 154

Natural monuments, 120

Natural resources
    consumption, 15
    goal of national policies, 38

Natural sciences research, 160

Nature Conservancy (United States), 106, 123, 154

Nature reserves, 120

Nature tourism, 119

Nature Trust of British Columbia, 107

Nematodes, 165

Nepal, 126

Net-afforestation strategies, 65

Netherlands, 59
    resource use, 52-53

Netherlands Committee of the World Conservation Union, 52

Network on Conservation and Religion, 161

New Guinea, 60

New Zealand
    nature tourism, 119
    zoo breeding programs, 144

Niger, 53

Non-governmental organizations (NGOs), 165-167

Non-native species. See Alien species

North America
    off-site conservation, 146
    protected areas management, 120
    zoo breeding programs, 144-145

Oceania, 120
Oceanic islands, 8
Oceans, biodiversity, 12-13
Off-site conservation facilities, 137-146
Open access, 82
Organization of American States, 102
Ornamental species, 143
Otters, 8
Over-exploitation, 13, 14
   and freshwater ecosystems, 11
Owl, barn, 14

Pakistan, 109
Palcazu (Peru), 108
Panama, 45
   biodiversity research, 158
   biosphere reserve concept, 102
Panda, giant, 133
Parataxonomists, 152, 165
Paris, 63
   Convention on Intellectual Property, 61
Parks in Peril program, 123
Patent standards, 61
Peru
   forest management, 108
   genetic resource conservation, 91
   indigenous approaches to restoration, 113, 114-115
   national protected area system plans, 120
   non-timber forest products, 86, 88
Pesticides, 42
Pharmaceuticals, 4
   patents, 61
Philippine Development Forum (PDF), 165, 166
Philippines
   co-management of coastal and marine areas, 86, 87
   genetic resource conservation, 92
   reforesting state lands, 85
Philippines Fisheries Code, 87
Physical property rights, 44-45
Planktonic larvae, 13
Plant breeding, 47-48

Plant genetic resources, 141-143
   conservation and use, 111
   funding, 72-73
   international agreement, 64
Plant Genetic Resources Center/Ethiopia (PGRC/E), 111
Plant variety protection (PVP), 110
Plants
   medicinal, 4, 93, 142
   species extinction, 8
Policy. See Economic policy; National policy
Pollution
   and freshwater ecosystems, 8, 11, 41
   and loss of biodiversity, 14-15
   marine ecosystems, 13, 40
Population growth, 12, 15, 49-50
Populations, conservation, 133-146
Potatoes, 4, 11
Precautionary principle, 40
Preservation zones, 128
Preserve Appalachian Wilderness, 130
Preventive restoration, 112-113
Primates, 134
Protected areas, 117-131
   130, 129
   contribution to biodiversity conservation, 121
   management categories, 120
   manager training, 162
   national and international priorities, 119-125
   preparing a system plan, 122
   private, 125
   species, populations, and genetic resources
      conservation, 134-135
   sustainability, 125-132
Protected Areas Network, 123
Protected landscapes, 120
Pucalpa (Peru), 114-115
Punjab (Pakistan/India), 109

Rattan, 88
Recreation
   biotic resources and, 4
Recycling, 51-52
Red Data Lists, 135, 157
Redwoods, 133

Regional Seas Programme, 40
Research activities, 158-161
Resource consumption, 49-50
    audits, 52-54
    recycling and conservation, 51-52
Resource management
    partnerships between government and local
        communities, 80-86
    training, 162, 164-165
Resources, non-renewable, 21
Rhinoceros, 14, 93
Rice, 5, 9, 11
Rincon Institute, 131
Rio de Janeiro Botanic Garden (Brazil), 137
Rivers
    biodiversity, 11
Rodents, 134
Rome, 64
Royal Botanic Garden Peradeniya (Sri Lanka), 146
Royal Chitwan National Park (Nepal), 126
Royalties
    genetic resources, 45, 94-95

Sabah (Southeast Asia), 88
Saguaro National Monument (Arizona), 131
Salinization, 14
São Paulo Electric Company (Brazil), 112, 113
Sarawak (Southeast Asia), 88
Saudi Arabia, 55
Schools, biodiversity awareness, 148-150
Science Society of Thailand, 159
Scientific Committee on Problems of the Environ-
    ment (SCOPE), 159
Scientific Research zones, 128
Screwworm, 46
Sea otters, 4, 146
Sea urchins, 4
Sea World/Hubbs Research Institute, 146
Secretariats, 32, 33, 63, 64
Seed Savers Exchange, 92
Seedbanks, 11, 24, 25, 115
Shorebirds, 127
Sierra de Manantlán Biosphere Reserve
    (Mexico), 135
Sierra Leone, 120

Sierra Nevada de Santa Marta (Colombia), 105
Snails, 10, 46
Social forestry, 85
Social science research, 159-161
South Africa
    hardwood exports, 53
    loss of diversity, 8
South America
    protected areas management, 120
    soil degradation, 110
South Pacific, 120
Southeast Asia
    and deforestation, 39
    non-timber forest products, 88
    species-specific conservation, 135
    traditional medicine, 93
    See also Asia
Soviet Union, 120
Species
    conservation, 133-146
    coordinating collections, 151, 153
Species diversity, 2-3
    estimates of global diversity, 9
    extinctions, 7-8
Species Survival Commission (SSC), 134, 136, 145
Spices, 114
Sri Lanka
    cultivated medicinal plants, 142
    reforestation, 146
Steller's sea cow, 12
Stewardship, 80, 82
Sub-Saharan Africa, 120
Sustainability in protected areas, 125-132
Sustainable living, 21
Swift fox, 146
System of National Accounts (SNA), 49

Tasmania, 64
Tax incentives, 106
    for private protected areas, 125
Taxonomy
    diversity, 2-3
Technology for Rural and Ecological Enrichment
    (TREE), 92
Temperate rain forests, 7

Thailand
  biodiversity research, 159
  cassava production, 52
  genetic resources conservation, 92
  logging ban, 54
  non-timber forest products, 86, 88
  reforesting state lands, 85
  tapioca exports, 52
Third World. See Developing countries
Timber plantations, 38-39
Tourism, 89
  economic value, 4
  nature, 119
Trade policies, 56
Trade-Related Aspects of Intellectual Property Rights
  (TRIPS), 61
Trade Specialist Group, 136
Traditional medicines, 4
  intellectual property rights, 94
  role of, 92-93
  See also Medicines
TRAFFIC offices, 136
Training
  biodiversity professionals, 162-165
TRAMIL (Caribbean traditional medicine
  program), 92
Transboundary protected areas, 125
Transition areas, 100, 128, 130
Transnational corporations (TNCs), 59-60
Tree gap dynamics, 108
Trees
  genebank conservation, 142
  See also Forestry, Tropical forests
Tropical Forestry Action Plan (TFAP), 74, 167
Tropical forests
  deforestation, 7
  dry, 14
  funding protection, 73
  keystone species, 108
  species extinction rates, 7
Tropical pines, 142
Trust funds, 75-76

Turtles
  migratory, 63
  sea, 13
Turtles,green (Chelonia mydas), 125

Uniform patent standards, 61
United Kingdom, 144
United Nations Convention on the Law of the Sea,
  13, 40
United Nations Development Programme (UNDP),
  72, 76
United Nations Education, Scientific, and Cultural
  Organization (UNESCO), 63, 100, 140, 159
United Nations Environment Programme (UNEP),
  29, 40, 63, 153
United Nations General Assembly, 26, 30
United States
  botanic gardens, 143, 144
  buffer zones, 131
  conservation data center network, 154
  genetic resource conservation, 91-92
  land trusts, 106
  marketing local genetic resources, 95
  non-governmental organizations, 165
  protected areas, 130
  zoological parks, 137
U.S. Agency for International Development, 59, 159
U.S. Fish and Wildlife Service, 135
U.S. National Research Council, 165

Varietal diversity, 90-92, 109
Visayas Islands (Philippines), 87

Washington, 63
Water rights, 41
Watersheds, 113
Western Hemisphere Shorebird Reserve Network
  (WHSRN), 125,
    127
Wetland Conservation Fund, 63
Whales
  blue, 13
  great, 133
  migratory, 63

Wheat, 11, 109

Whooping crane, 146

Wild animal species, 145

Wild plant resources, 143-144

Wild products, 86-93

Wildlife management areas, 120

Wildlife Trade Monitoring Unit, 136

Women
    biodiversity conservation research, 159
    management of biological resources, 70-71

Working Party on Trade and the Environment, 57

World Bank, 67, 69, 73, 76, 167

World Commission on Environment and
    Development, 20

World Congress on National Parks and Protected
    Areas, 123

World Conservation Monitoring Centre (WCMC),
    123, 136, 144, 153, 157

World Conservation Union (IUCN), 63, 123, 134, 136
    botanic gardens conservation role, 143
    training protected area managers, 162
    zoo staff network, 145

World Data Center, 141

World Federation of Culture Collections, 141

World Health Organization, 4

World Heritage Sites, 63, 68, 123

World Intellectual Property Organization (WIPO), 61

World Resources Institute (WRI), 72

World Wildlife Fund (WWF), 76

Zea diploperennis (maize), 135

Zebra mussels, 46

Zoning, 128-132

Zoological parks, 24, 25, 137, 138
    conservation role, 144-145
    information networks, 145